AF732003

"It may be an understatement of the century that the past few years have stressed individuals and organizations in unprecedented ways. Consequently the need for human centered holistic person approaches to navigating these challenging times to support individual wellbeing and organizational resilience has never been more important. This book is an indispensable guide for decision-makers trying to create a better path forward."

Scott Behson, *Professor of Management, Fairleigh Dickinson University, USA, Author,* The Whole-Person Workplace: Building Better Workplaces through Work-Life, Wellness and Employee Support

"When crises happen unexpectedly and more often, then Human Centered Management offers a clear path and guidance to navigate today's challenges. This book is a must-read for managers, entrepreneurs and academics. It offers specific problem-solving strategies applicable in the domains of higher education, health care and entrepreneurship."

Andrea Caputo, *Associate Professor, University of Trento, Italy; University of Lincoln, United Kingdom*

"The book pertinently covers challenges management is going through during disruptive times drawing readers' attention to key elements of wellbeing such as family, socio-emotional risks, resilience, health, quality of working life and work performance. The book includes comprehensive revision of ongoing changes in organizations."

Sigmar Malvezzi, *Professor of Organizational Behavior, Department of Social and Work Psychology, Instituto de Psicologia, Universidade de São Paulo, Brazil*

"Work-related sciences need new frameworks that inspire appropriate approaches to face threats and opportunities posed by the contemporary social and labor change. We welcome this book of the Human Centered Management Series that significantly enriches these perspectives."

Julio Cesar Neffa, *CONICET Senior Researcher, Professor, La Plata, Nordeste and Moreno Universities, Argentina*

Human Centered Management and Crisis

Human Centered Management and Crisis: Disruptions, Resilience, Wellbeing and Sustainability is the newly edited book of the Human Centered Management (HCM) Series developed to respond to surmounting concerns of global audiences and human centered scholars, practitioners and students searching for answers to better and objectively understand the effects of unprecedented Covid-19 pandemic disruptions and ongoing crises, affecting the wellbeing of people and workplaces since 2019. The effects linger and solutions are pressing. This new HCM volume presents analytical expertise and practical experiences of a team of international HCM scholars and practitioners targeting objective assessment of causes and effects of disruptions and offering coherent solutions applying HCM principles and practices. The book chapters include topics dealing with specific problem-solving strategies in numerous industries, among them, higher education, health care and entrepreneurship. The book will help readers worldwide to understand the challenges people and organizations are facing in the present global VUCA (volatile, uncertain, complex, ambiguous) environment. The audience will benefit from the book and its purpose to deliver enduring HCM solutions anchored in the wellbeing of people as a precondition for organizations to secure high performance, quality standards and long-term sustainability.

Peter Essens is the Director of the Center of Expertise in the Department of Human Resource Management and Organisational Behavior at the University of Groningen, The Netherlands, and Editor of the Human Centered Management Book Series.

Maria-Teresa Lepeley is the President and CEO of the Global Institute for Quality Education, USA, and Founder and Principal Editor of the Human Centered Management Book Series.

Nicholas J. Beutell is a Professor of Management in the LaPenta School of Business at Iona University, USA, and the Editor of the Human Centered Management Book Series.

Linda Ronnie is a Professor and Senior Research Scholar at the School of Management Studies at the University of Cape Town, South Africa.

Anielson Barbosa da Silva is a Professor in the Management Department at Federal University of Paraíba – UFPB, Brazil.

Human Centered Management Series

The purpose of the book series is to re-position people to be at the center of organizations, the economy and society. Using management as the common denominator, the ultimate goal is to perform a paradigm shift from the entrenched approaches of the industrial past to a human centered methodology which is convergent with the needs of people and organizations in the constantly changing interconnected world that frames the new Knowledge Society.

The challenges that management is facing when dealing with human development, active participation, responsible leadership, financial accountability and social responsibility issues can only be understood and solved through the cross-fertilization of ideas from different disciplines. Better integration between management, psychology, neuroscience, economics, education, business and others needs to happen to accrue the benefits. The reason is simple. Global conditions create increasingly complex problems that can be highly disruptive. Solutions require approaches that build resilience through embedding multidisciplinary models that are effective in building productive organizations, transparent markets, sustainable economies and inclusive societies.

Maria-Teresa Lepeley, Peter Essens, Nicholas J. Beutell, Book Series Editors

Other books in the Human Centered Management Series

Human Centered Management
5 Pillars of Organizational Quality and Global Sustainability
Maria-Teresa Lepeley

Wellbeing for Sustainability in the Global Workplace
Edited by Paola Ochoa, Maria-Teresa Lepeley and Peter Essens

The Wellbeing of Women in Entrepreneurship
A Global Perspective
Edited by Maria-Teresa Lepeley, Katherina Kuschel, Nicholas Beutell, Nicky Pouw and Emiel L. Eijdenberg

Human Centered Organizational Culture
Global Dimensions
Edited by Maria-Teresa Lepeley, Oswaldo Morales, Peter Essens, Nicholas J. Beutell, Nicolas Majluf

For more information about this series, please visit: www.routledge.com/Human-Centered-Management/book-series/HUMCM

Human Centered Management and Crisis

Disruptions, Resilience, Wellbeing and Sustainability

Edited by Peter Essens, Maria-Teresa Lepeley, Nicholas J. Beutell, Linda Ronnie and Anielson Barbosa da Silva

Routledge
Taylor & Francis Group
NEW YORK AND LONDON

First published 2023
by Routledge
605 Third Avenue, New York, NY 10158

and by Routledge
4 Park Square, Milton Park, Abingdon, Oxon, OX14 4RN

Routledge is an imprint of the Taylor & Francis Group, an informa business

Library of Congress Cataloguing-in-Publication Data
Names: Essens, Peter, editor. | Lepeley, María Teresa, editor. | Beutell, Nicholas J., editor.
Title: Human centered management and crisis : disruptions, resilience, wellbeing and sustainability / edited by Peter Essens, Maria-Teresa Lepeley, Nicholas J. Beutell, Linda Ronnie and Anielson Barbosa da Silva.
Description: 1 Edition. | New York : Routledge, 2023. | Series: Human centered management | Includes bibliographical references and index.
Identifiers: LCCN 2022057010 | ISBN 9781032360423 (hardback) | ISBN 9781032360478 (paperback) | ISBN 9781003330011 (ebook)
Subjects: LCSH: Management--Social aspects--Study and teaching. | Executives--Education. | Humanism.
Classification: LCC HD30.4 .H85 2023 | DDC 658.4/07124--dc23.eng/20230210
LC record available at https://lccn.loc.gov/2022057010

ISBN: 978-1-032-36042-3 (hbk)
ISBN: 978-1-032-36047-8 (pbk)
ISBN: 978-1-003-33001-1 (ebk)

DOI: 10.4324/9781003330011

Typeset in Bembo
by MPS Limited, Dehradun

Contents

Figures

Tables

Foreword

I would like to congratulate the Editors and contributing scholars on bringing this next volume in the Routledge Human Centered Management Series to publication. Given the very turbulent times in which we are living, this book will make a significant contribution to the literature, providing an important support for both the academic and the practitioner. Organizations consist of people working together to achieve a common goal.

Resilient organizations are those capable of thriving in this turbulent and uncertain world, as well as surviving the range of crises thrown at them. They do this by caring for their people, building trust that leads to effective collaboration and cutting-edge innovation. This is a key to human flourishing and the ability to create a sustainable future for all of us, our children and generations not yet born.

A hearty thanks is due to all who have invested their time and talent, expertise and wisdom in bringing this book to fruition. I pray that its pages will offer readers the knowledge, insight and skills to successfully surf the tsunami of change we are facing. And may it do so in such a way that we grow workplace and community cultures that cause us to look after the most vulnerable and grow the prosperity and wisdom to heal our environment and create a thriving future for all.

Dr. John Vargo
Resilient Organizations Ltd.
Christchurch, New Zealand

Foreword by the Editors of the Human Centered Management Book Series

Routledge's HCM Book Series was launched in 2017 as a compendium of decades of experience validating conditions that determine long-term sustainability of organizations across industries and sectors in the global VUCA (volatile, uncertain, complex, ambiguous) environment. The Lepeley book, *Human Centered Management: The 5 Pillars of Organization Quality and Global Sustainability* (2017), that started the HCM Series, supports organizations worldwide in achieving standards of quality and excellence necessary to remain competitive in performance and productivity, where systemic and systematic improvement is only reachable when the people working IN and FOR these organizations are empowered to attain high levels of engagement with their work in organizations that foster their wellbeing.

Maria-Teresa Lepeley founded the Human Centered Management Book Series based on her experience as a Quality Management professor, researcher and practitioner with a unique opportunity as examiner of the United States Baldrige National Quality Award and adviser to NQAs Programs in Chile, Brazil, Peru, Colombia and Ecuador and related NQAs Programs in Europe. Lepeley's background in economics, management, education and entrepreneurship expedite design of multidisciplinary solutions for a broad range of disruptions challenging organizations in the 21st century. Her management solutions are aligned with pioneering human centered management scholars and authors of 15 of the 25 most influential management books of the 20th century recorded by the Academy of Management, like Edwards Deming, Douglas McGregor, Abraham Maslow, Chris Argyris and Elton Mayo.

Lepeley advanced the development of the Human Centered Management Book Series by addressing complex human centered challenges that organizations face, with Peter Essens, with his long-standing experience in applied scientific research, currently Director of the Center of Expertise of HRM and Organisational Behavior at the Faculty of Economics and Business of the University of Groningen and a PhD in social sciences, with extensive research how people work, organize and collaborate to solve complex problems in organizations across industries and sectors, including the military. Nicholas J. Beutell has made a significant contribution to the Series as a professor of management, business administration, health care management and a former Dean of the Hagan/LaPenta School of Business at Iona University. His research areas include the Life–Work Continuum and family issues affecting small business and entrepreneurship, entrepreneurial intentions and people's wellbeing, supported by extensive research contributions in national and international publications. He also has a background in Quality Management and developed the quality teams at Iona University leading to the AACSB accreditation.

Coming from different academic and international backgrounds, Lepeley, Essens and Beutell provide a uniquely strong common ground for supporting high performing organizations in the global VUCA environment always positioning humans at the center – people are the engine. Under their human centered editorial guidance, the Routledge *Human Centered Management* Book Series has experienced exponential growth steering the attention of human centered scholars and organizations around the world.

PE MTL NJB

Book Editors' Preface

Since the publication of *Human Centered Management: The 5 Pillars of Organizational Quality and Global Sustainability* in 2017, that launched Routledge's Human Centered Management (HCM) Series, the number of HCM volumes has grown rapidly, driven by increasing interest of scholars, practitioners, management students and general audiences from countries around the world.

This new book, *Human Centered Management and Crisis: Disruptions, Resilience, Wellbeing and Sustainability*, was conceived by the book editors driven by experience and concerns about the detrimental effects of unprecedented disruptions unleashed by the Covid-19 pandemic since 2020 and exacerbated by ongoing global crises. Previous HCM volumes have provided innovative realistic human centered strategies to help organizations face and solve challenges in the global VUCA (volatile, uncertain, complex and ambiguous) environment across industries and countries worldwide. In this volume, the editors and contributors were challenged to advance in-depth proposals based on lived experiences during the turmoil to counterbalance the negative consequences and elicit positive outcomes for people and organizations under exceptionally volatile local and global conditions.

The 16 chapters bring into focus the 5 HCM Pillars as a capacity building Model to identify and anticipate disruptions using resilience to offset negative effects and agility to innovate and move forward, closely alignment with structures and strategies strengthened by human capital, talent and quality standards. Organizations seeking sustainability deploy HCM principles to optimize benefits while minimizing the costs of disruptions in normal times but particularly in times of crises.

This book discusses critical current disruptions in management and organizations. It addresses vulnerabilities that most generations currently in the workplace and marketplace have not experienced in their lifetimes. The chapters cover HCM principles and practices from theoretical perspectives to practical applications in higher education, healthcare and entrepreneurship. This international team of editors and contributing scholars created a comprehensive HCM treatise exploring complex issues affecting people's wellbeing and organizational sustainability delivered in fascinating and provocative chapters.

The editors commend the efforts and audacity of the chapter authors for pioneering new ideas and ideals aimed at enhancing human wellbeing.

We hope that you, our readers, find pertinent answers that inspire the creation of new ideas leading to a deeper understanding of the turmoil we are facing, so that we can all benefit from this human centered journey embedded in continuous improvement of people and organizations.

We appreciate the support of our families, colleagues and friends around the world who inspired and challenged us to write this new volume that is adding significant value to Routledge's Human Centered Management Book Series.

We appreciate the support of our families, colleagues and friends around the world who inspired and challenged us to write this new volume that is adding significant value to Routledge's Human Centered Management Book Series.

PE MTL NJB LR ABS

About the Editors

Peter Essens
University of Groningen
Faculty of Economics and Business
The Netherlands

Peter Essens is the Director Center of Expertise of HRM and Organisational Behavior at the Faculty of Economics and Business of the University of Groningen. He received his PhD in Social Sciences from the Radboud University of Nijmegen, The Netherlands and worked until 2013 at the Netherlands Applied Scientific Research Organization TNO, innovating knowledge to serve the common good. His current research focus is on how people and organizations work, organize and collaborate to master complex problems in settings with multiple actors. He has over 25 years of experience in the functioning of people and organizations in diverse domains, including the military. Peter has been leading key investigations in effectiveness within and between teams and organizations interaction processes, published as *The human in command: Peace support operations*; *Military command team effectiveness: Model and instrument for assessment and improvement*; *Team effectiveness in complex settings*; *Multiteam systems in the public sector*; *Managing risk and resilience*. His recent work has been published in leading journals including the *Journal of Occupational and Organizational Psychology*, *Journal of Management Studies*, *Journal of Organizational Behavior* and *Academy of Management Journal*. He is the editor of Routledge Book Series Human Centered Management and co-editor of the books *Wellbeing for Sustainability in the Global Workplace* and *"Human Centered Organizational Culture: Global Dimensions"*.

Maria-Teresa Lepeley
Global Institute for Quality Education
United States

Maria-Teresa Lepeley is the Founder and Principal Editor of Routledge's *Human Centered Management* Book Series. She is the President of *Global Institute for Quality Education*, United States, Former Examiner of United States Baldrige National Quality Award and Adviser to NQAs Programs in Chile, Brazil, Colombia, Peru, Ecuador. She holds MS in Economics (economic development), and MA in Education (Higher Education Management and Leadership), both from the University of Miami, United States and BS in Education and English from University of Santiago, Chile. Her academic experience includes being the Director and Professor of Executive Management Programs, University of Connecticut, United States; the Director and Professor, Division of Executive Programs, Department of Economics, School of Business and Economics, University of Chile; the President, Entrepreneurial College, Santiago, Chile and academic experience. She is Founder and Principal Editor of the Book Series Human Centered Management Series with Routledge and the Series *Innovation* in *Human Centered Sustainability with* Information Age Publishing. Her books include *Human Centered Management: 5 Pillars of Organizational Quality and Global Sustainability, EDUCONOMY. Unleashing Wellbeing and Human Centered Sustainability, EDUQUALITY. Human Centered Quality Management in Education. A Model for Deployment, Assessment and Sustainability, Management and Quality in Education. A Model for Assessment.* She is editor of the Routledge books *Wellbeing for Sustainability in the Workplace. A Global View, The Wellbeing of Women in Entrepreneurship, Soft Skills for Human Centered Management and Global Sustainability, Human Centered Organizational Culture: Global Dimensions and Human Centered Management in Executive Education* by Palgrave Macmillan.

Nicholas J. Beutell
Professor of Management
LaPenta School of Business
Iona University, New Rochelle, NY, USA

Nicholas J. Beutell is a Professor of Management, Business Administration and Health Care Management at Iona University. For a decade, he was Dean of the Hagan/LaPenta School of Business at Iona University. Previously, he served as the Acting Dean at Stillman School of Business at Seton Hall University. He developed a quality management team at Iona leading to the AACSB accreditation. He has been a consultant for Equitable Life Assurance Society, Public Service Electric and Gas and AT&T. His main areas of research include work–family issues affecting small business and entrepreneurship, entrepreneurial intentions and wellbeing. He is an active member of a research group on work–life issues among entrepreneurs. He is the co-editor of a special issue on work–family issues in South Asia for the *South Asian Journal of Business Studies*. He is the author of the book *Evaluating Scholarship and Research Impact* (Emerald) and the co-editor of Routledge HCM Books *"The Wellbeing of Women in Entrepreneurship"*, *"Soft Skills for Human Centered Management and Global Sustainability"*, *"Human Centered Organizational Culture: Global Dimensions"*. His research is widely cited in publications including the *Academy of Management Review*, *Journal of Vocational Behavior*, *Journal of Small Business and Entrepreneurship*, *Journal of Managerial Psychology*, among many others. He is a member of the Academy of Management, Eastern Academy of Management and Work–Family Researchers Network.

Linda Ronnie
University of Cape Town
Faculty of Commerce
South Africa

Linda Ronnie is a Professor of Organizational Behavior and People Management, School of Management Studies, University of Cape Town, South Africa. She was a Former Dean of the Faculty of Commerce, UCT. She has completed her MS in Education and Psychology and PhD in Education. She has published extensively on diversity, psychological contract, employer–employee relationship in health, agricultural, engineering, financial services and education sectors. She is the recipient of UCT Distinguished Teacher Award. She is the winner of the inaugural Emerald Case Writing Competition and runner-up in the 2021 Ceeman's Case Writing Competition. Prior to her academic career, Linda worked in the manufacturing sector in management. She is a consultant for organizations in the private and public sectors on managing change, employee–employer relationships effectiveness and improvement.

Anielson Barbosa da Silva
Federal University of Paraíba, Northeastern Brazil
Department of Management

Anielson Barbosa da Silva is a Professor of Management, Federal University of Paraíba (UFPB), Brazil. He teaches People Management in the Management Department and in the Graduate School of Management. He is the Principal Researcher in the Center for Studies in Learning and Knowledge registered with the Brazilian research agency (CNPq). He participated in the National Association of Postgraduate and Research in Administration (ANPAD), in the Division of Teaching and Research in Management and Accounting – EPQ (2009–2014) as Graduate Teaching Director (2018–2020). He holds an MS in Management and PhD in Production Engineering. He has published books, book chapters, papers in national and international journals. Anielson has received 17 recognition awards in the fields of management and organizational learning, management education, competence management, active learning methodologies and socio-emotional learning.

Contributors

Josep M. Blanch, PhD in Psychology, Diploma in Social Sciences, retired Full Professor of Applied Social Psychology, Professor Emeritus at Autonomous University of Barcelona (UAB), Full Professor at San Buenaventura University (USB) in Cali, Colombia, where he is director of the program Doctorate in Psychology. Researcher Emeritus (IE) Minciencias (Colombia) and member of some scientific societies. He has coordinated international teams and has been a consultant to public organizations in Spain, Europe and Latin America. Has taught courses, seminars and has been a speaker in conferences in universities in the Iber-American sphere. He studies and publishes about work and the relationship in organizations and management, psychosocial risks, occupational health, job wellbeing and working quality of life.

Stacy Brecht, Assistant Professor of Marketing and Entrepreneurship at Azusa Pacific University in the United States, pursuing PhD in Business Administration from Grenoble Ecole de Management, France. Her research focuses on entrepreneurship with an emphasis on women entrepreneurship. She owns and operates a public relations company in the Los Angeles area.

David Coello-Montecel, Researcher at ESPAE Graduate School of Management, Escuela Superior Politécnica del Litoral (ESPOL), Ecuador. He has an MA in Economics, minor in Business Management from ESPOL. His research fields include behavioral labor economics, wellbeing, working conditions, digital transformation, applied microeconomics, competition and market regulation. Conducts research with Mexico and Spain.

Marieta du Plessis, Professor at the Department of Industrial Psychology at the University of the Western Cape, South Africa. She is a Registered Industrial Psychologist dedicated to creating healthy human centered management and positive leadership practices in organizatios, whether through consulting, research or teaching, and an avid researcher in positive organizational practices and leadership, specifically within the Higher Education industry. She is working in an emerging research niche area on academic leadership focused on producing high-quality interdisciplinary research outputs and capacity building of students and emerging academics.

Katherina Kuschel, Lecturer and Researcher, CENTRUM Graduate Business School and Catholic University of Peru. She is a Researcher at DAAD and KIT, International Excellence Fellowship in entrepreneurship fields: soft-landing and 'expat-preneurs' in technology ventures. Her research areas in entrepreneurship are development of entrepreneurial ecosystems for women, fundraising and internationalization of start-up business, entrepreneurial education, performance evaluation. She leads research groups in Life–Work sustainability in entrepreneurship. She is the book editor and author in Routledge Human Centered Management Series, co-editor of *Wellbeing of Women in Entrepreneurship. A Global Perspective*. She has published extensively in Entrepreneurship, including book chapters and journals including *International Journal of Entrepreneurship and Small Business, Cross Cultural & Strategic Management*, *Latin American Management Journal*. She is a guest editor of the International Entrepreneurship and *Management Journal on Women Entrepreneurship* in STEM fields.

Séverine Le Loarne-Lemaire, Full Professor, Grenoble Ecole de Management, France. Chairperson, FERE Research (Female Entrepreneurship for a Renewed Economy). MS in Management from EM Lyon. She has completed her PhD with honors from Lyon and Ecole Polytechnique Paris, France. Her research focus includes women in entrepreneurship, spousal support to women entrepreneurship in practice. She has published articles in peer-reviewed journals, books and articles in her fields. She is a Lecturer and Sponsor of professional networks of women entrepreneurs.

José Wilker Macêdo, Researcher at the Center for Studies in Learning and Knowledge with Brazilian research agency (CNPq) at Federal University of Paraiba, Brazil. He has completed his PhD in Business Administration, specializing in innovation and knowledge. His research fields include behavioral development in organizations.

Fernando Merino, Full Professor in Applied Economics, University of Murcia, Spain. He is a Former Consultant for World Bank. He teaches at ESAN University, Lima, Peru. His research fields include firm behavior, family business. entrepreneurship. He has published in international journals, including *Strategic Management Journal, Global Strategy Journal, European Journal of International Management*, among others. He is a contributor in the Routledge Human Centered Management Series.

Oswaldo Morales, Associate Professor of Management and Vice President for Research, ESAN University, Peru; PhD in International Studies, University of Waseda, Japan. He holds an MBA, ESAN, Peru, an MA in economics and Public Service, University of Barcelona, Spain and Master in business law, University of Lima, Peru. His research interests include organization management, intercultural management, strategic analysis.

Sergio Morales, Research Assistant, ESAN University, Peru; Master in Epistemology; Bachelor, Anthropology, San Marcos National University, Lima, Peru. He has published articles in journals in Peru, Argentina, Spain, Colombia and UK. His areas of specialization include cultural evolution, anthropological theory, methodology and epistemology of anthropology and organizational behavior.

Paola Ochoa, Associate Professor and Associate Dean of Research at ESPAE Graduate School of Management at Escuela Superior Politécnica del Litoral (ESPOL), Ecuador; PhD in Social Psychology, graduated cum laude from Autonomous University of Barcelona. Previously worked in business, leading HR projects in a petroleum company in Venezuela; pursued academic career in Ecuador and Spain; consultant in organizational development; co-editor with Maria-Teresa Lepeley and Peter Essens of the book *Wellbeing for Sustainability in the Global Workplace* in Routledge Human Centered Management Series. Her research fields include psychological-social issues, work risks and wellbeing.

Maureen O'Callaghan, PhD student, Department of Psychology, University of Lincoln, United Kingdom and researcher in prosocial behavior in entrepreneurs. She has an MS in Mindfulness-Based Approaches, Bangor University. She is retired and pursuing research in these fields with 30 years of work experience. She works in team building and change initiatives locally, nationally and internationally.

Gareth H. Rees, Assistant Professor of Management, School of Economics and Management Sciences, ESAN University, Lima. Peru; teaches undergraduate and graduate courses; completed PhD and MBA from the University of Otago, New Zealand. His research areas include entrepreneurship, supply chains, organizational performance in healthcare. He has co-authored a chapter in the book *Human Centered Organizational Culture: Global Dimensions*, of Routledge Human Centered Management Series. He is a consultant for the World Health Organization in health in workforce development and planning issues.

Rosa Ulloa, Full Professor at Virtual University, Guadalajara University, México. BS in Education; MS in Educational Policies and Management; PhD in Information Technologies; and is a visiting student at the University of Montreal, Canada. Her research interests include computer sciences and education. She is a Journal reviewer and author in her fields in a special issue for the anniversary of the *Genetic Programming and Evolvable Machines Journal*. She is author of a chapter in *Soft Skills for Human Centered Management and Global Sustainability* in Routledge Human Centered Management Series.

Cyrill Walters, Research Fellow in higher education studies at Stellenbosch University, South Africa and teaches the MBA and PGDip Business Administration programs at the University's Business School. She is currently working on projects examining the decolonization of knowledge in South African universities, the impact of Covid-19 on the academic work of women scholars and the application of complexity theory in decision-making and higher education leadership.

Part 1

Human Centered Management and Crisis Fundamentals

1 Resilience as an Outcome of Human Centered Empowerment

Peter Essens

Introduction

In this chapter, I propose that resilience, essential for coping with adversity, finds a solid basis in the principle of empowerment. The principle is that people are best served by creating conditions that enable and support them to achieve their goals and determine their development. Empowered people develop a stronger sense of control and use of strategic resources, such as competences, capabilities and social networks, to influence their environment bending circumstances to their needs. The important role of resources for people's wellbeing is captured by the conservation of resources (COR) theory, which is based on "the assumption that people strive to conserve, protect and build resources and that what is threatening to them is the potential or actual loss of valued resources" (Hobfoll, 1989). According to the COR theory, the more resources a person has available and can use, the more resilient the person is and the better that person can respond to adverse events.

Resilience is important for individuals and organizations given recurrent threats and changing environmental conditions, such as Covid-19. But even in quasi-normal circumstances burnout and stress are unprecedentedly high and threaten the wellbeing of professionals and the functioning of organizations (e.g., Abramson, 2022). So, the discussion unfolds exploring what organizations can do to provide the resources necessary to deal with stress and adverse conditions affecting people's wellbeing and sustainability of the workplace. The discussion starts focusing on empowerment and resilience and the concept of resources that links them. Practical examples from the healthcare sector provide evidence of their complementarity. The chapter closes with an assessment of the results.

Empowerment

Psychological empowerment

The concept of empowerment has a long history with extensive use in social services, public health, community development, politics and business. It

DOI: 10.4324/9781003330011-2

relates to ideas of positive orientation to change, active engagement, supported by capacity building operating in a social context. While definitions may differ related to the context, a basic principle is that individuals and groups should be enabled to determine their own development and conditions for wellbeing. Instead of offering solutions or development paths, people are best served by conditions that facilitate achievement of their goals. Directive guidance creates dependence, often unconsciously, which commonly leads to developing passive followers (Zimmerman, 1995).

Empowerment concepts developed from two perspectives: the individual-level perspective as psychological empowerment focusing on work-related motivation factors; and the organizational-level perspective as structural empowerment relating to the structures, policies and practices in the organization that make empowerment possible.

Psychological empowerment is defined and measured by four factors that give strong intrinsic task motivation: namely, meaning, autonomy or self-determination, competence and impact (Spreitzer, 1995). Meaning represents how meaningful and important the work is for a person, self-determination represents perceptions of autonomy and freedom to determine how to go about doing the work, competence represents how confident and self-assured the person is of personal abilities and capacity to perform the work; impact represents the degree of influence or control a person has on what happens at the higher (department) level (Spreitzer, 1995, pp. 1464–1465).

Psychological empowerment has shown to have positive effect on important work-related outcomes, such as increasing job satisfaction, organizational commitment and decreased strain and turnover intentions (Seibert, Wang, & Courtright, 2011).

Promoting psychological empowerment means enabling employees to do complete and varied work that is challenging but feasible, is significant, contributes to a larger purpose and matches with personal values and interests:

- providing opportunities to grow, supporting the development competences and skills that match current and possibly future work and providing constructive feedback with learning challenges
- supporting control over task execution providing clear specification of *what* needs to be done but leave the *how* to do the job to the choice of the person
- stimulating employees to influence strategic choices concerning development and content of their work.

Structural empowerment

Structural empowerment refers to the idea that giving employees access to information, support, resources and opportunities enables psychological empowerment to develop and use. This condition is strongly linked to the principle that delegating power and authority to people in lower levels increases participating in decision-making processes. From our perspective, structural empowerment is more than delegating power, it is about creating structural conditions necessary for people to work, grow and develop as professionals, enabling to focus on the content and quality of their work and assuming more responsibility in the direction and outcomes of the organization. When employees have access to resources, information, support and opportunities relevant to facilitate their work, they feel able to mobilize resources, affect decision making and achieve goals and consequently more likely to feel empowered.

Promoting structural empowerment means:

- establishing policies to decentralize decision-making to allow employees to shape their work and take appropriate actions in response to emerging developments in their work environment without consulting higher management levels
- developing social structures in the organization influencing decision making and providing access to resources
- consolidating feedback and help from colleagues and management
- providing opportunities for learning and developing professional skills in courses and managing challenging and situational complexity of work
- broadening professional skills working in different jobs in the organization and learning from more experienced colleagues
- engaging employees in developing organizational goals and strategies.

Team as empowerment structure

The team (work unit, department) is the lowest structural entity in the organization. The team leader plays an important role in creating and maintaining psychological and structural empowerment conditions. Beyond its function as a management unit organizing the work and dealing with personnel aspects, teams provide the social structure for interaction and mutual support and a platform for team members to influence the direction of the team and presenting the interests of the team in the organization. Teams provide a strong identity for the employees in the organization.

Professionals in the team with expertise and experience to lead in the execution of work (principle of autonomy), team leaders, have roles to improve safe and effective functioning of a team (Yukl, 2012):

- a task-oriented role: supporting planning and organizing work, granting autonomy, coordinating professionals when needed, ensuring sufficient resources, listening and problem solving, synchronizing team tasks with strategic and operational goals (team meaningfulness)
- a relation-oriented role: empowering team members recognizing and valuing their contributions and achievements, promoting development and career advancement, building cohesion in the team, guarding psychological safety to speak up and influence decision making

- a change-oriented role: learning from experience, reflecting on results and development, using organizational and outside information to identify when change or innovation is necessary considering potential threats from other parties or societal developments
- a boundary-spanning role: representing the team in the organization and beyond (team impact), being informed of external events and communicating in the team, coordinating with other parties, advocating for resources and assistance.

Team members develop a shared perception of empowerment promoted in the organization (empowerment climate) aligned with perceptions team members have about individual psychological empowerment. Empowerment climate has shown to be positively related to work-unit performance outcomes (Seibert, Silver & Randolph, 2004).

Empowered teams

The concept of empowerment is also applied to the team level, called "self-managing" teams. These teams have autonomy and responsibility to make decisions managing operational and tactical challenges at their level, before going up in the hierarchy. Self-managing teams are usually assumed to have no formal leader in a directing and controlling role. In such teams, the outcome of team efforts is a collective responsibility. Team members work interdependently on tasks and self-regulate methods, schedules and actions. Team members decide how to carry out tasks at hand with a member acting as an informal leader if the situation requires.

Team members need to have a variety of skills to perform in a diversity of tasks as well as managing the roles a team leader usually has. The success of teams depends to a large extent on the knowledge and skills of members in self-management, switching roles and ability to back up each other accepting responsibilities for the collective (Magpili & Pazos, 2018).

The same team-empowerment strategies work as empowerment of individuals (Seibert, Wang, & Courtright, 2011). However, there are a number of conflicts between individual and team empowerment. For instance, individual autonomy, an essential value for empowered employees, may work against team-level autonomy. Team members need to put the team results first, even at the cost of their autonomy (Magpili & Pazos, 2018).

The idea behind self-managing teams is that it would lead to a flatter organization, with less or no mid-level management and less bureaucracy making the organization more agile and responsive to demands and dynamics in the environment. Crucial to success of self-managing teams is a flat organizational structure with no hierarchy, in a shared culture of empowerment, with clarity of organizational goals and constructive performance feedback (Magpili & Pazos, 2018).

Leadership in empowered teams

There is continuous debate whether self-managing teams are better off without a leader (Cohen, Ledfort, Spreitzer, 1996). Consider that the removal of a formal leader from a team does not immediately create a self-managing team. Tasks that were previously covered by the leader still need to be organized. Social processes like psychological safety (feeling safe within the team) and cohesion (feeling part of the whole) and talent management may be distributed among team members introducing new management roles in the team. Allocation of the leadership role to an external leader or supervisor can sometimes be a solution to assume responsibility for administrative and personnel issues and coordination across teams and relations with upper management. This creates new interdependencies with external power, which are not a problem if the external leader grants autonomy to the team (Magpili & Pazos, 2018).

Another issue with self-managing teams without a formal leader is that informal hierarchies may dominate decision processes of the team. This may be accepted by the group when based on expertise and competence ("seniors") and the results will be positive. But when based on dominance, conflicts may arise. Empowered teams with less optimal internal processes and being under pressures to achieve effective work outcomes, may develop stricter management rules. Research shows that because of high-complexity tasks and overlap of roles with risk of role conflict, the need for leadership is strongest (Oedzes et al., 2019). Failure to coordinate within the team and between teams about the use of resources may create extra production costs and loss of quality standards.

Having a formal leader in a team does not necessarily reduce autonomy of team members. On the contrary, the leader can further empowering conditions facilitating, supporting, connecting, developing team climate and representing the team in the organization (boundary spanning). The changing role of the leader from directing to enabling is not an easy change – being responsible to control and correct without using formal authority requires special skills and natural orientation to people. At higher levels it requires a clear empowerment orientation to the leaders in the organization. When upper management sees productivity as a most important key performance indicator (a short-term measurement) for the team, the leader and team members may feel less empowered in their work.

Empowerment outcomes

The promise of empowerment is that structural and psychological empowerments have positive effects on a broader range of personal and organizational outcomes. Research has shown that psychological empowerment is the mechanism through which structural empowerment affects employees work attitudes and behaviors that foster job satisfaction and identification with the organization (e.g., Laschinger et al., 2004).

As mentioned above, leaders at all levels must be empowered with decision-making power and the means to respond appropriately to diverse needs of the people under their responsibility. People differ in maturity, skills, knowledge, attitudes, personality. Thus, while strategic empowerment should be a clear, stable and transparent organizational strategy to promote psychological empowerment, the leader or seniors in the team must consider level of maturity and readiness of team members to balance autonomy and freedom to best arrange their work and the guidance needed.

There is substantive evidence that both psychological and strategic empowerments are effective approaches in organizations for improving employee wellbeing and team effectiveness (Seibert, Wang, & Courtright, 2011). The motivation of organizations to adopt an empowerment approach may be driven by economic arguments based on apparent effects of improved employee engagement and increased productivity. However, while market-driven arguments may be first in mind, this does not reduce the relevance and value of empowerment of employees, if implemented effectively. Putting employees' wellbeing as a central orientation in the organization of work makes organizations' sustainability stronger (Lepeley, 2017).

The central role of resources

Great importance is attached to resources as an essential means of achieving and maintaining wellbeing, but what works for people as a resource? A valuable resource in work context is something that helps the individual achieve their goals or meet their needs (Halbesleben et al., 2014). Anything that an individual perceives useful to achieve a goal is considered a resource, independent of what the goal is (Although resources may also support goals that may be negative in moral sense, we think here of positive and morally just goals). Loss of resources can lead to feelings of stress and burnout and people will try to avoid loss or invest to protect against resource loss.

What is valued as a resource may vary between individuals, situations, time and cultures. Some resources have a fundamental role as a motivating factor, such as self-determination or autonomy, competences, social support or relatedness, already mentioned above in the context of empowerment. And these have a greater role in building and protecting other resources affecting wellbeing. Indeed, studies and practice show that having autonomy and control over personal work is an important motivating factor for people. However, the importance given to such resources may vary between people and cultures, some individuals prefer clear directions from a supervisor while others prefer to organize work themselves. And regarding social support, some cultures are more individualistic while others are more collectivistic with stronger group orientation.

Investing in competences is a clear example how building on such resources can determine investment decisions allocating time, effort and money. Access to money (e.g., via family, loans) is a supportive resource which can help achieve goals that require these competences. Having a collection of complementary, reinforcing resources (a resources caravan, in COR terms) provides a broader and stronger foundation for gaining resources and protecting against the loss of resources. For instance, leading a successful project with an influential and satisfied external party may help to influence a supportive manager when the project leader claims a promotion. The personal ability to effectively utilize those resources is as such a personal resource.

Resources developed and linked together play an important role-building resilience and using it in the face of threats and adversity. Empowerment provides a set of resources that may be used in resilient responses to persevere and recover from shocks, which is discussed in detail next.

Empowerment in practice

Empowerment was enthusiastically adopted as a management technique in the early nineties to promote employee motivation, to gain benefits of increased performance and reduce operational costs. Empowerment initiatives are estimated to be implemented in over 70 per cent of the organizations (Seibert, Wang, & Courtright, 2011). Some critics have compared empowerment as a management trick to cover up shortcomings. Others point to it as a hype, which will disappear as soon as the problem fades away. Indeed, optimal empowerment assumes achievement in multiple dimensions, including self-determination or autonomy, competence, impact and supporting structural conditions. Moreover, empowerment is a process in continuous development, adapting to and growing with changing environmental conditions and job requirements.

Empowerment is not a "laissez-faire" unplanned process, but it takes into account the diversity of experiences and task maturity and preparedness of employees. This diversity requires close monitoring to maintain roles of guidance and critical facilitation by senior employees or team leaders. Empowerment needs to account for the type of jobs. For instance, in a laboratory setting where high routing performance is crucial then autonomy is not what operators are looking for. In this case clear tasking, team spirit and close monitoring prevail. In other settings, such as First Responders with high external dynamics, autonomy is imperative to adapt to emergency settings and making decisions to deal with issues and coordinating with others if necessary.

Effective team performance builds on psychological empowerment by actively sharing knowledge and insights within the team. In team work, the level of autonomy of each member depends on the interdependencies of tasks distributed among team members. Stronger interdependencies require higher levels of coordination, which is implicit when routines and rules are in place. But in more complex conditions involving multiple options and time pressures, overarching coordination is needed with a central person making final decisions. This role can be undertaken by formal leadership (with formal authority) or informal leadership (the most competent for the case in the team decides).

From our discussions with a number of organizations where we study the development of employees and organizations (i.e., multi-year studies with five organizations from different sectors), we learn that empowerment to a large degree is embedded in their strategy of working as professionals with clients. In one healthcare organization an explicit strategy of empowerment of employees (and their clients) has been implemented. In the other organizations a variation of empowerment strategies was followed from self-managing teams that deliver integrated care to a focus on professional autonomy where employees work in multiple teams contributing with their specific expertise. Empowerment in these organizations to a large extent was a mix of operational needs combined with ideas how professionals prefer work.

An example of an empowerment strategy is from one mental healthcare organization. The organization formulated a "strength-based" empowerment approach as a basic attitude in professionals–client relationships as well as between professionals and leadership. Strength was based in the collection of talent, competences, skills and knowledge a person has, displays and deploys. The exchange of professionals and employees is to encourage each other in the deployment and further development of these strengths. The organization's leadership strategy is also based on the same empowerment principles. Starting from the premise that employees have personal capacity to grow, they receive autonomy in the execution of their work, perform the work outcome-oriented, in a socially supporting resourceful collegial environment, with the leadership supporting this, taking into account the level of task maturity of the employees. The delegation of power to the team (self-management) was not included in the strategy and all focus was on individual psychological empowerment with a clear role of the team leaders in guiding and realizing the empowerment process.

In data of successive surveys, we analyzed the relationship of the empowerment factors, *meaning*, *autonomy*, *competence* and *impact* (Spreitzer, 1995). Interesting findings showed that meaning was consistently the most important factor to improve job satisfaction and reduce job burnout, followed by autonomy and impact; competence was only related to burnout in the sense that employees with less experience (competence) in the job are more susceptible to burnout complaints. Adding social context (psychological safety and team identification) showed that this has a strong positive relationship with satisfaction and reduces burnout complaints. Negative organizational factors such as administrative hassles and bureaucracy did not change the role of meaning, which remained as a central factor. The basic proposition is that when individuals view their work environment as empowering, they also feel personally (psychologically) empowered.

In the example above, representing the development of an empowerment strategy, we observed that all four empowerment concepts contribute to the functioning of the teams, but with different strength most likely related to the phase of development of empowerment in this organization.

In the next part we focus on the resilience strategies of an organization, first we explore organizational resilience, then provide an example of resilience in practice – the impact of Covid-19 on a healthcare organization. Finally, we discuss the strong connection between resilience and empowerment.

Resilience

Organizational resilience

Resilience is defined as a positive, systemic response to adversity. It is a response resisting change, aiming to get back to stable conditions and learning from the situation to prevent being disrupted again.

Individual resilience emerges when a person confronts unexpected and potentially threatening situations. It can be a sudden incident or an adversity that slowly develops until it comes to the surface. Individual resilience evolves from nature and nurture, as a natural disposition to recover from adversity, augmented with skills learned through exposure and training. Family resilience is a crucial source for individuals to develop resilience, learning about the ways the family – as social unit – can mobilize resources between each other and in their social environment to deal with setbacks and crises (see Chapter 4, this book).

Working in a team – as social unit – resilience is defined as the capacity of team members in a collective to resist, bounce back and recover from adversity (Chapman et al., 2020). However, resilient team members do not necessarily add up to a resilient team. A resilient team needs to develop as a cohesive collective, providing mutual support and, most importantly, develop a shared belief that the team is able to achieve results needed for the (task) challenges at hand. Team resilience is a process emerging from dynamic interactions of individual members learning from each other and from setbacks and adversity situations. Exposure to adversity seems to be essential for learning about how the team works under stress. Organizational resilience, in turn, builds on individual and team resilience. But, similar to team resilience, there is an organizational-level component needed for building a resilient organization.

Organizational resilience is built on a sense of collectivity, connected with a shared mission and sharing similar values, a common understanding of the challenges and what each person and team can contribute. Essential component of organizational resilience is a developed social network of individual members and between teams (Van de Vegt et al., 2015), which allows activation of latent resources sharing knowledge and capacities. For organizational resilience to develop organizations need to make sense of their experiences – how setbacks and adversity situations are overcome and what positive impact these experiences have to strengthen the collective.

High reliability organizations empower their employees to speak up to report errors or conditions with potential to foster errors and continuously strive to strengthen resources to cope with diverse stressors.

Resilience in the HCM model, in addition to Human Capital, Talent Management, Agility and Quality Management, is seen as a structural element for organizations to anticipate and deal with disruptions, but also taking resilience's positive energy to transform setbacks into opportunities to learn, improve and innovate (Lepeley, 2017).

Resilience preparation

Evaluations of post-crisis resilience responses abound, reviewing what was successful and what needs improvement with the idea to learn from crisis situations allows to develop stronger responses to disruptions in the future. Preparation focusing on assessment of potential risk factors may protect from adverse events developing routines. Unfortunately, there is not one resilience cure for all situations. Moreover, we hardly can imagine the conditions of more complex threat situations, limiting effective preparation from future threats. While resilience responses are context dependent and can demonstrate effectiveness in one situation, this does not guarantee effective response in another. Only experience and preparation increase the likelihood of effective responses in the organization.

Empowerment and resilience are related concepts of strength and empowerment providing important psychological and structural conditions for resilience to develop. While empowerment at work is a process showing continuity in the way employees do their work and influence functioning of their team and the organization, resilience emerges at moments of distress, as a response related to disruptive contexts. Both concepts refer to processes of control and setting goals, discovering opportunities in interaction with other people and with the structural environment. The next section discusses how empowerment and resilience work out in practice.

Resilience in practice

In the early phase of the Covid-19 in the Netherlands, we conducted a study (mid-2020) in a hospital that was hit by the early wave of Covid-19 with a huge number of Covid-19 patients. Within 10 days (March 2020) it went from handling one Covid-19 patient to a complete stop of regular healthcare and only focus on Covid-19 patients. As a result, a large number of medics without intensive care training were almost suddenly without a job. Doctors and nurses from all departments were asked to voluntarily assist in the Covid-19-related sections. Despite this massive organizational change, a positive attitude emerged to cope with the situation implying significant additional working hours for all relevant actors, including support staff, such as the cleaners of contaminated patient rooms.

During this first period, we found that frequency of taking care of Covid-19 patients (daily, a few times a week, once a week) had low direct negative impact on their wellbeing. To the contrary, data showed that Covid-19 conditions were strongly related to a positive perception of the meaningfulness of their work and a high identification with their job. Also, organized structural support by the so-called peer-support groups, additional services like "anytime food" and web-based resilience/recovery advice showed to significantly contribute to the positive mood in the hospital. Obviously, these high stress conditions had high costs in energy, with daily fears and concerns about own and partners' safety and health, but during the ongoing crisis motivation seemed to buffer direct threat effects, suppressing (overt) negative feelings from the change, triggering extra-role behaviors when needed, in this way resulting in an overall resilient response to the crisis situation.

There was one measure in our assessment that showed to be dominant in predicting outcomes which was appreciation ("I experience appreciation for my effort" 7-point scale from Not at all to Very much). Also, on the open answer question "How could employees be supported even more?" 430 out of 1000 responses responded with appreciation, recognition, attention and similar terms.

One may expect that with longer lasting setback conditions when the adrenaline from the first encounter with the threat is over, the call for normal conditions will become stronger (e.g., picking up regular care again) and negative feelings looking backward may arise. To get better insight in this, we asked employees in the same hospital in March 2022 still working with Covid-19 patients (more recent patient peaks were in November 2021 and March 2022) to reflect on the impact of Covid-19 on themselves.

Often positive and negative feelings are reported in the same response, e.g., *"It was an intensive period in which in the emergency IC I saw a relatively large number of patients die, often without family being able to be there. That did have an impact on me privately (…). On the other hand, it also created solidarity within the organization. People became more flexible and put their shoulders to the wheel together and I got to know many new colleagues. You really made history together … unfortunately …"*

Reflecting on organizational performance, employees were largely positive. About 60 percent of the 1830 responses related to adequate organization and clear communication (comment e.g., *"Suddenly things were possible while normally a lot of bureaucracy is involved to get things done"*). Ten percent had clear negative reflections, in terms of insufficient, unclear, too much focus on integrated care neglecting others, e.g., *"The hospital was totally unprepared for this crisis. Personnel were simply deployed to other departments such as the IC. Teams were taken apart during the first wave, so you also miss each other to share experiences and to be able to rely on each other during your work. But management learned quickly and improved the approach".*

In the process of recovering from the initial blow back to providing regular care, still Covid-19 patients came in big numbers. This created an unbalance in how the crisis was perceived by the employees, which was well formulated by this nurse in her answer to the question on the way the organization performed: *"The first wave happened to everyone. (…) However, with the second very intense wave the whole hospital was running normal again with everyone back in their own place, but we had to work as a* [Covid-19] *cohort again, as if this was the most normal thing. Where you felt the appreciation and solidarity in the first wave, this was absolutely not the case in the second wave".*

Also, in the 2022 assessment frequency of taking care of Covid-19 patients was positively related with meaningfulness. But other were dominant in predicting wellbeing, in particular personal growth (with questions such as "my work challenges me to achieve my personal goals" and "my tasks help me to grow personally") was the most dominant factor in predicting job satisfaction.

What can we conclude about the relationship between empowerment and resilience in the context of the Covid-19 crisis? The most important link between empowerment and resilience seems to be meaningfulness linked to a solid professional perspective. The example illustrates that in conditions of immediate threat a collective resilience response (putting the shoulders to the wheel) can be triggered with the leadership using clear communications of strategic choices and with highly engaged professionals.

Resilience is linked to meaningful work of professionals feeling responsible for what is at the heart of their profession. Autonomy as second empowerment dimension scored high in both assessments. Apparently, the centralized strategic decisions taken from the start of the crisis to break up teams and scale down regular care did not affect the appreciation at operational level. Autonomy was firmly grounded in the professional position of providing care. Breaking up teams brings the risk of losing direct social support which is known to buffer high workload and emotional threats. The organization responded to this by organizing a peer-support system, a "Full Resilience" support program and other practical support actions, such as meals any time of the day – functional but effective.

Feeling competent was challenged in this crisis situation. The number of intensive care nurses was not enough to handle the influx of patients; volunteers stepped in with even less experience and needed a lot of guidance. To address this issue, almost immediately a new training program was set up to learn how to deal with Covid-19 and how to work on the Covid-19 units which steeped the influx of competent personnel. Interestingly several employees explicitly mentioned that they learned a lot during the first Covid-19 phase because of the unknown challenging situation. Mastering professional skills should include how to professionally operate in extraordinary situations with general broad skills and a proactive attitude. Thus, existing competences may not match the crisis requirements and need a quick response to build those.

During crisis, organizations usually centralize decision making, often supported by a crisis management team with representation from the organization, introducing directive leadership. The argument is that this is needed to survive or overcome the setback caused by the disruption by creatively organize people and resources. The ad hoc formation of a Covid-19 treatment section breaking up the regular teams is an example in case. In this sense having impact on strategic decision making may be limited during a crisis. However, building on experiences during normal times the newness of the situation at operational level proactively influencing operational outcomes with creativity is highly needed.

Resilience, empowerment and Human Centered Management

Our claim is that empowerment of employees forms a solid basis for resilience in organizations. We presented an example of implementing empowerment and one concerning resilience and empowerment in a concrete crisis situation. The example of the Covid-19 situation shows that resilience strongly relied on the professional engagement and the perceived high meaningfulness of their work and their job. In fact, empowerment is closely linked to how professionals see their work, doing meaningful tasks, operate with autonomy to decide themselves on how to do their work and influence the decisions that impact their work, growing personally and developing their competencies. With this as a basis, the organization can count on these professionals in crisis situations. While disruptive, top-down decisions may be accepted as an immediate response to disruptive conditions, with adequate communication and sense making supporting that such conditions should have a short life. When a crisis continues for a longer time and new, quasi-normal conditions are established, professionals need to be empowered as before, which may help to maintain a stable and sustainable condition for the organization to survive.

Our examples come from healthcare settings. We posit that similar drivers work in other sectors where professionalism, craftsmanship and meaningfulness of work are important values. Empowerment embedded in organizational values and structures forms the basis for enabling and developing empowerment at individual level. From a strategic empowerment perspective, furthering professionalism with opportunities to learn and grow is investing in the resilience capacity of the organization. Leadership needs to ensure that the best conditions are in place enabling employees to access relevant information, receiving support and encouragement for ongoing opportunities for professional development.

HCM operationalizes the fundamental principles of valuing and treating employees as humans, rather than resources, enabling employees to further their wellbeing in the work as an integral part of their life. Empowerment is a human centered strategy for implementing HCM contributing to effective resilience at personal and organizational levels. To realize this, it is essential that empowerment is not just an organizational strategy, but a lived strategy based on these fundamental principles.

References

Abramson, A. (2022, January 1). Burnout and stress are everywhere. *Monitor on Psychology*, 53(1). https://www.apa.org/monitor/2022/01/special-burnout-stress

Bowers, C., Kreutzer, C., Cannon-Bowers, J., & Lamb, J. (2017). Team resilience as a second-order emergent state: A theoretical model and research directions. *Frontiers in psychology*, 8, 1360. 10.3389/fpsyg.2017.01360

Chapman, M. T., Lines, R. L. J., Crane, M., Ducker, K. J., Ntoumanis, N., Peeling, P., Parker, S. K., Quested, E., Temby, P., Thøgersen-Ntoumani, C., & Gucciardi, D. F. (2020). Team resilience: A scoping review of conceptual and empirical work. *Work & Stress*, 34(1), 57–81. 10.1080/02678373.2018.1529064

Cohen, S. G., Ledford, G. E., & Spreitzer, G. M. (1996). A predictive model of self-managing work team effectiveness. *Human Relations*, 49(5), 643–676. 10.1177/001872679604900506

Halbesleben, J. R. B., Neveu, J.-P., Paustian-Underdahl, S. C., & Westman, M. (2014). Getting to the "COR": Understanding the role of resources in conservation of resources theory. *Journal of Management*, 40(5), 1334–1364. 10.1177/0149206314527130

Hobfoll, S. E. (1989). Conservation of resources: a new attempt at conceptualizing stress. *American psychologist*, 44(3), 513. 10.1037/0003-066X.44.3.513

Larkin, M., Cierpial, C., Stack, J., Morrison, V., & Griffith, C. (2008). Empowerment theory in action: The wisdom of collaborative governance. OJIN: *Online Journal of Issues in Nursing*, 13(2). 10.3912/ojin.vol13no02ppt03

Laschinger, H. K. S., Finegan, J. E., Shamian, J., & Wilk, P. (2004). A longitudinal analysis of the impact of workplace empowerment on work satisfaction. *Journal of Organizational Behavior*, 25(4), 527–545. 10.1002/job.256

Lepeley, M. T. (2017). *Human centered management: Five pillars of organization quality and global sustainability*. Routledge.

Magpili, N. C., & Pazos, P. (2018). Self-managing team performance: A systematic review of multilevel input factors. *Small Group Research*, 49(1), 3–33. 10.1177/1046496417710500

Oedzes, J. J., Van der Vegt, G. S., Rink, F. A., & Walter, F. (2019). On the origins of informal hierarchy: The interactive role of formal leadership and task complexity. *Journal of Organizational Behavior*, 40(3), 311–324. 10.1002/job.2330

Raub, S., & Robert, C. (2010). Differential effects of empowering leadership on in-role and extra-role employee behaviors: Exploring the role of psychological empowerment and power values. *Human Relations*, 63(11), 1743–1770. 10.1177/0018726710365092

Ryan, R. M., & Deci, E. L. (2000). Self-determination theory and the facilitation of intrinsic motivation, social development, and well-being. *American psychologist*, 55(1), 68–78. 10.1037/0003-066x.55.1.68

Seibert, S. E., Wang, G., & Courtright, S. H. (2011). Antecedents and consequences of psychological and team empowerment in organizations: A meta-analytic review. *Journal of Applied Psychology*, 96(5), 981–1003. 10.1037/a0022676

Seibert, S. E., Silver, S. R., & Randolph, W. A. (2004). Taking empowerment to the next level: A multiple-level model of empowerment, performance, and satisfaction *Academy of Management Journal*, 47, 332–349. 10.2307/20159585.

Spreitzer, G. M. (1995). Psychological empowerment in the workplace: Dimensions, measurement, and validation. *The Academy of Management Journal*, 38(5), 1442–1465. 10.5465/256865

Van der Vegt, G. S., Essens, P., Wahlström, M., & George, G. (2015). From the editors—Managing risk and resilience [Editorial]. *Academy of Management Journal*, 58(4), 971–980. 10.5465/amj.2015.4004

Yukl, G. (2012). Effective leadership behavior: What we know and what questions need more attention. *Academy of Management perspectives*, 26(4), 66–85. 10.5465/amp.2012.0088

Zimmerman, M. A. (1995). Psychological empowerment: Issues and illustrations. *American Journal of Community Psychology*, 23(5), 581–599. 10.1007/bf02506983

2 The Multiplier Effect of HCM

Maria-Teresa Lepeley

A different kind of global disruptions requiring human centered solutions

In the past, I started numerous Human Centered Management (HCM) publications with the following quote from Albert Einstein: *Things do not change if we keep doing the same thing. A crisis is a real blessing for any person or nation. For all crises bring change and progress.* This quote is well aligned with HCM principles and synthesizes how disruptions and crises affecting people can lead to positive outcomes bringing change, improvement, progress and prosperity. Based on my experience, I add to this quote that positive change after a crisis is possible only and "IF" - in capitals – people want to change, have the courage, will, enthusiasm and feel empowered to make decisions and follow actions required to transform bad experiences into a bunch of benefits.

These human centered principles that are at the core of the mission and vision of HCM organizations facilitate comparison with other management approaches that have remained from the industrial past, such as resource-focused trends that exist today. Considering that one of the main differences with HCM is that traditional management in organizations is limited to an inward-looking focus that contrasts significantly with the inward-outward multidimensional view of HCM. While the inward-looking focus is limited to the boundaries of an organization, HCM integrates the organizations with external constituencies of customers and users that come from the community and represent society.

Besides, it is a detrimental management approach to consider people as an organizational resource, because regardless of the quantity of resources, it is the Quality of products and services the organization produces that takes precedent and sustainability. And this is only possible when people who work in the organization assume responsibility for Quality results with their work and efforts accomplish transformation from mediocrity to excellence. This is the central discussion in this chapter that gives origin to the Multiplier Effects of HCM. Arguments are aligned with the principles that the wellbeing of people is a necessary condition for long-term organizational sustainability in prosperous times but especially in times of crises, this book is addressing.

DOI: 10.4324/9781003330011-3

The next sections discuss the transition from resources to people at the center in management and organizations. Records show that although the importance to put people at the center is not new, it is not easy to achieve. The discussion is critical to address unprecedented disruptions affecting people in the workplace and the marketplace and communities not seen since the end of WWII that are exposing regressive conditions in human wellbeing.

The discussion calls attention to the importance of continuous training to develop the capacity of people to identify causes and effects of disruptions to support organizations understand and optimize the transformation from resource focus to people at the center of management.

Calls for human centered solutions: Views from global development organizations

In 2016 the United Nations published its first report on *Happiness, Wellbeing and Human Development.* The purpose was to explore correlation between economic progress and social development introducing psychological measures of wellbeing. The report called for solutions to improve human development, highlighting wellbeing assessments of life satisfaction. This was a driving principle of the Human Development Index and UN's 17 Sustainable Development Goals program intended to end global poverty by 2030. Based on reasons, I discuss in this and other chapters I have reasons to doubt the target will be achieved.

The Organization for Economic Cooperation and Development (OECD), a forum represented by the governments of 37 democracies with market-based economies that collaborate to develop policy standards to promote sustainable economic growth, in 2020 launched the Better Life Initiative to measure wellbeing and progress aiming to a better understanding of people's wellbeing to guide OECD to improve metrics to bridge gaps between metrics and policy intervention[1]. In my view, to the largest extent OECD success promoting people's wellbeing will depend on 1) emphasizing Quality education and 2) OECD provision of reliable data to facilitate decision making in affiliate countries instead of interventions in national policies.

The World Bank 2022 Conference titled *Human Capital at the Crossroad: Reversing Losses, Reclaiming our Future* focused on people's wellbeing. WB studies confirmed that the Covid pandemic induced major setbacks in human capital progress[2]. A poll conducted to identify the most pressing priorities to help people achieve their potential, showed Quality education as the most pressing need.

I discuss an important point here about education quality because this is a reiterative concern among all international development organizations. Two decades ago, in 2002, the WB invited me to present the Quality Management Education Model I developed and had published in book with McGraw-Hill (Lepeley, 2001). This book was based on my experiences in Quality Management including supporting development of National Quality Awards (details are discussed in my chapter *Managing the Quality Crisis: Restoring People's Wellbeing* in this book). My presentation was the keynote speech at the event to inaugurate WB new Global Network. The online conference was forecasted from WB headquarters in Washington DC to terminals in university campuses across countries in Latin America[3]. Two decades later the urgency to provide quality education to all students is pending (Lepeley, 2001, 2019a, b). Management geared at continuous improvement to attain quality standards is required to optimize efforts. After the pandemic this is a paramount global imperative.

David Malpass, president of the World Bank, in a 2022 conference, stated that the world may face a *human catastrophe* from a food crisis arising from Russia's invasion of Ukraine. He emphasized that record inflation in food prices has potential to put hundreds of millions of people into poverty if the Russia–Ukraine crisis continues. WB calculates a potential 37 percent jump in food prices that would hit low-income people and low-income nations hardest given their traditional constraints to afford food and schooling expenses[4]. Furthermore, from the low energy prices in April 2020 to the high in March 2022, the world is paying the largest increase in energy since 1973 oil price hike as tensions in the Middle East sent prices soaring[5].

A poll conducted at the WB 2022 conference confirmed another critical priority: the wellbeing of "*women and girls is at the heart of the solutions*", as much as quality education for women. This global priority was covered by HCM Series in the 2020 book *The Wellbeing of Women in Entrepreneurship. A Global Perspective* (Lepeley, 2020a). In this book I wrote a chapter on "*The Multiplier Effect of Women Entrepreneurs*".

I have numerous publications in terms of disruptions affecting economic and social development in general and in particular education quality that remains the most formidable obstacles for growth and sustainable inclusive development. My concerns are covered in the books *EDUCONOMY: Unleashing Wellbeing and Human Centered Sustainable Development* and *EDUQUALITY: Human Centered Quality Management in Education. A Model for Development, Assessment and Sustainability*.

Global vision that directly or indirectly influences national policies and studies needs to be analyzed closely to ensure it offers effective human centered solutions beyond empty slogans.

Calls for human centered solutions: Views from the workplace

Surmounting amount of literature is addressing causes and effects of ongoing disruptions in the workplace. This section discusses some of them and other chapters in this book address them in deeper detail. The discussion is necessary because it reinforces the need for change highlighting benefits associated to the Multiplier Effects of HCM, as an approach offering human centered solutions to most pressing challenges.

Harvard professors point to *The Great Resignation* (HBR Sep 15, 2021) and McKinsey global management consultants reports on *The Great Attrition and the Great Attraction* effects of the Covid pandemic in the workforce (September 2021 McKinsey)[6]. The Washington DC Pew Research Center reports that the *Great Resignation* started in 2021 as a wave of workers were unsatisfied and quitting their jobs, with a majority citing low pay, no opportunities for advancement, feeling disrespected at work as major sources of dissatisfaction with their working conditions[7]. McKinsey expanded the discussion referring to workers considering or leaving their jobs seeking better work in organizations offering conditions that closely satisfy their personal needs and provide optimal condition for "*Life Work Continuum*" LWC (Beutell, Kuschel, & Lepeley, 2021). But in reality, many workers who left their jobs, later realized that *the great attraction* to fulfill wellbeing in new jobs was not met and large numbers tried to go back to previous jobs[8].

In September 2021, over 19 million U.S. workers had quit their jobs based on dissatisfaction with working condition. The literature confirms that the problem is also affecting other countries. In United States, the high level of attrition has been a major shock for employers struggling to understand reasons for employees' departure. Yet many problems associated with pandemic effects overlook internal organizational cultures and conditions that preceded the pandemic. Studies report that organizations even implementing well-intentioned, but traditional, quick fixes, like increasing pay, financial perks and bonuses, overlooked and failed to monitor internal problems and conflicts affecting the wellbeing of people.

Among the shortcoming to understand the situation, there is evidence of failure to effectively assess the capacity of human capital (HCM Pillar 1) in organizations and optimize Soft Skills including communication effectiveness among workers, between colleagues and with employers. Research findings show that employees consider that traditional compensatory arrangements overlook important need for attention to improve *human* aspects of work, work satisfaction and engagement that support a common organizational identity critical to optimize talent management (HCM Pillar 3). Authors highlight that employees do seek higher pay, benefits and perks, but pandemic disruptions exposed that what they want most is to feel valued by co-workers, managers and the organizations (Parker & Horowitz, 2022).

Moreover, for most workers the return to the office is causing increasing in expenses and higher budgets than before the pandemic (Epstein, 2022) which is negatively affecting their wellbeing. Employees who, during the pandemic, had decreased expenses in transportation, train tickets and office clothes, discovered significant increases in expenses associated with work at the office compared with savings working remotely from home. Inflation is hurting across generations but particularly cohorts of seniors living on fixed retirement incomes and workers close to retirement forcing them to remain in the workforce beyond plans and expectations (Torrit, 2022).

By the end of 2022, cost of living increases unleashed after the pandemic and the ongoing energy crisis are leading unparalleled levels of inflation with increased potential to intensify a global economic recession reversing record gains in standards of living since WW II and resulting in substantial increases in poverty rates.

Human at the center is not new, but recent crisis exposes need for review

The following section addresses challenges organizations are facing to advance the transition from resource focused to human at the center management.

The human at the center of management paradigm has long data. In 2001 the Academy of Management conducted a survey among prominent management scholars to identify the 25 most influential management books of the 20th century (Bedeian &Wren, 2001). Fifteen among the 25 books identified were related to the importance of human beings in organizations. This result seems paradoxical compared with still extensive use the resource-focused organizations embedded in HRM that started a century ago with Frederick Taylor's *Scientific Management* book (1911) in the United States and in Europe with Max Weber's *The Theory of Social and Economic Organizations* (1922) as initial studies on bureaucracy.

In my view the most outstanding human at the center management theoretical approaches and efforts, that I used to develop HCM, are the following, all are included in the Academy of Management list of most influential management books of the 20th century: Elton Mayo (1933), Abraham Maslow (1943), Peter Drucker (1954), Douglas McGregor (1960) Edwards Deming (1982) 092). Deming is known as the Father of Quality for his Total Quality Management (TQM), model that served as a framework for the creation of National Quality Awards in countries around the world and I include it as Pillar 5 in my HCM book (2017) and discuss it in my chapter *Managing the Quality Crisis* of this book.

Maslow's *Theory of Human Needs* (1954) was pivotal to develop my HCM model, as was McGregor's *The Human Side of the Enterprise* (1960). But Deming's principles and practices are explicitly part of HCM expressed in Pillar 5 *Sustainable Quality Management.*

Understanding the nature of resource in management

The resource-focused management, embedded in HR and HRM that have prevailed for over a century and are still taught, is part of the management analysis. The subject merits attention to recognize differences with HRM and HCM.

Resources, represented by capital, building, infrastructure, among many others, are necessary for organizations to conduct operations. Resources are always limited and finite. This is the economic principle that justifies why organizations must be always compelled to optimize the use of resources. Resources are necessary for organizations to survive. But there are some critical dimensions HRM overlooks. First people are not an organizational resource, this is extremely important because it is the leading cause of ongoing management and organizational shortcomings. This is the explanation why people should not be considered an organizational resource. Resources are inert. Only people can optimize the use of resources for organizations to thrive and become sustainable. This is a fundamental HCM principle.

What cannot be objectively measured, cannot be actually improved

When I started to think in HCM decades ago, to frame an analytical model, I realized that traditional management features aiming to secure outputs with minimum inputs and efforts, utilizing humans, material and financial resources were limited and missed critical components to assess outcome including wellbeing of people. Under a basic consideration that happy and autonomous people are able to assume responsibility to optimize efforts leading to optimal results, I considered wellbeing an essential component of management to secure sustainability. This was a major challenge to create a Human Centered Management in order to differentiate from traditional approaches that could objectively measure outcome and achievements. So, I built the HCM framework on five pillars that included dimensions of people wellbeing embedded on Pillar 1: Human Capital and Pillar 3: Talent Management, supported by two critical components Pillar 2: Disruptions Resilience and Pillar 4: Agility, and tied the four pillars around Pillar 5: Sustainable Quality Management that provided necessary instruments to evaluate outcome and results leading to continuous improvement and Quality standards. In terms of differences with resource – focus management and organization approached that deal with talent, resilience and agility, none of them was integrated with Quality Management standards to demonstrate how the wellbeing of people in organizations leads to high performance, productivity and sustainability.

A nontraditional multiplier effect in management

A multiplier effect occurs when one of more inputs, that may be small in magnitude, can set in motion a chain of reactions amplifying results significantly increasing gains and benefits. The Multiplier Effect ME is an economic concept I apply to management to illustrate effects of HCM based on people's wellbeing and contrasting with resource-focused approaches. The next section discusses details of HCM's five Pillars to understand the implications of each pillar in relation to the contributions to the ME, including how people and organizations, exposed to the disruptions and ongoing global crises, can strengthen structure and strategies to attain sustainability in VUCA environment.

Pillar 1: Human capital

Human capital is an economic concept developed by Gary Backer, a Nobel Laureate in Economics (1992). Becker described Human Capital (HC) as intangible assets that cannot be detached from the person who owns them. The term needs a management interpretation because many people associate capital with the value of money, a bank account, investments, corporate stock. Another important difference is that while physical capital can increase or decline; human capital is constantly updated and improved throughout a person's lifetime mainly with education.

In HCM, human capital refers to the value each person provides to an organization offering their knowledge, skills, including hard and overall Soft Skills (Lepeley et al., 2021) making significant contributions that shape organizational culture and outcomes that determine level performance in the workplace. In spite of the great importance few organizations use optimal methods to count and keep manageable records of their human capital. This is an important concern because HC deeply impacts Talent Management (Pillar 3) principles, practices and outcome. It is necessary to recall that Quality education is one of the most critical determinants of HC.

Pillar 2: Disruption resilience

Disruptions affecting people and organizations are discussed extensively in my book *Human Centered Management* (2017). The argument is that people and organizations able to recognize incoming disruptions and potential threats, can gain advantages to secure solutions. People and organizations unable to recognize or anticipate the effects of disruptions pay higher tolls, face increasing risks and accrue more costs than benefits from disruptions. Developing resilience capacity is crucial to optimize benefits and minimize costs of disruptions and crises affecting people and organizations (Lepeley, 2021a,b,c). Resilience is covered in other chapters of the book.

Pillar 3: Talent management

People's talent is a unique and valuable human asset that people and organizations use and get benefits from. In HCM, talent refers to the creativity, ingenuity, drive and courage people have to advance and improve, beyond the capacity to identify and anticipate disruptions and crisis but to strive to make the difference between good and excellent performance. It is not surprising that companies and countries compete for people's talent. It is important to recall the impact of Quality education on talent development. As much as the shortcomings, gaps and human losses are created by lack of education quality. Talent surges when people have access to information, opportunity for discussion and trust in themselves and others. All people have talent, the key is to discover it and put it to the best possible use. Optimal use of talent management plays a crucial role in positive effects to the HCM multiplier. Furthermore, in the Knowledge Economy, also occasionally called the Talent Economy, talent is at the core of human capital.

Talent management is related to the capacity of organizations to identify the talent of people to focus training programs targeting highest possible synchrony between people's talents with organizational tasks, aiming to help people improve themselves first and in turn optimize their contribution to improve performance and productivity required for long-term organizational sustainability. The effectiveness of talent management has significant effects on the HCM Multiplier.

It is important to highlight that effects of disruptions caused by the Covid pandemic and ongoing crises are impacting talent management and increasing the capacity to monitor and evaluate outcome.

Pillar 4: Agility

In times of high volatility and uncertainty, agility is an attribute people and organizations seek to attain sustainability. In the chapter *Master Soft Skills: The Resilience – Agility Umbrella* (Lepeley, 2021c), I discuss the interactions between resilience and agility and the need to integrate them to foster human capital and optimize talent management. Agility is an operational dimension organizations are placing increasing attention to overcome the negative effects of disruptions and crises. Agility has major implications in the effects of the HCM Multiplier.

Change commonly has a negative impact on people, performance and productivity when it is not properly managed. Today the speed of change is an unprecedented experience, so many organizations lack resilient capacity to adapt fast to threats paying high human and monetary costs.

In the same venue as resilience, agility has personal and organizational dimensions. Personal agility refers to the ability to react fast and move quickly and easily confronting new situations and challenges. Organizational agility refers to the capacity to change and advance efficiently integrating people and processes aiming to optimize operations maintaining equilibrium and the drive to move forward.

In order to be agile, organizations need to have or develop structures and strategies that accept change and stimulate innovation. To achieve this objective, organizations need to be closely connected to their external environments – customers, markets, the community – as necessary condition to strengthen agility in the internal environment and the workplace enhancing employees' trust and autonomy necessary to stimulate experimentation, new practices, use of new technologies and discipline for continuous improvement impacting HCM and the multiplier.

HCM emphasizes that agile humans produce agile organizations. It is shortsighted for organizations to try to advance agile capacity ignoring and overlooking this HC principle.

Pillar 5: Sustainable Quality Management and need for objective assessment

What cannot be measured cannot be improved. This is a core HCM axiom and a sine qua non condition to measure effects of the Multiplier, the previous four pillars provide a strong framework for deployment of HCM in organizations, but only organizations able to effectively implement Pillar 5: Sustainable Quality Management (SQM) can demonstrate capacity to assess improvement of the wellbeing of people synchronized with organizational performance and sustainability. SQM is a critical HCM endorsing the Multiplier Effect. This is also the main difference between HCM and HRM approaches.

Details of Pillar 5 SQM are discussed extensively in my chapter *Managing the Quality Crisis* in this book. Figure 2.1 shows the seven Management Areas and the integration of internal organizational dimensions with external dimensions that are represented by customers, markets, community and vertical and horizontal integration (1 and 7) required to assess

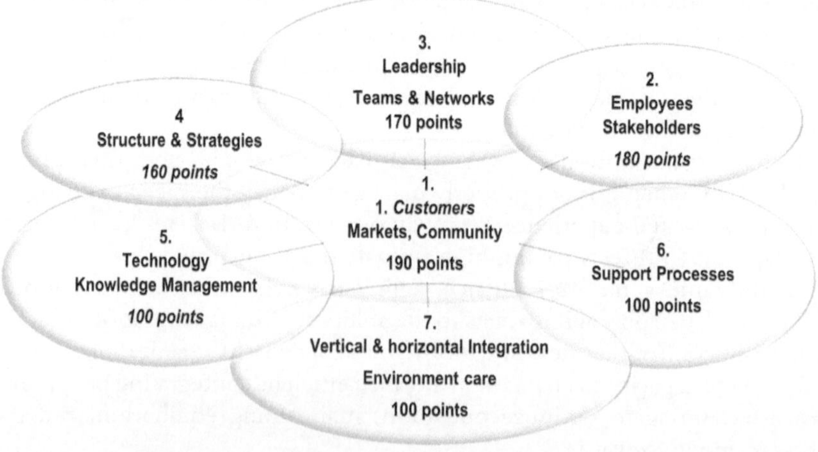

Figure 2.1 Sustainable Quality Management – Seven Management Areas with integration of internal and external organizational dimensions.

Note: Adapted from Lepeley (2017).

continuous improvement and demonstrate attainment of Quality standards to show the positive cumulative effects of the Multiplier.

The variables used to measure systematic performance improvement included in the 35 Elements of Assessment (EAs) are monitors with the measuring instrument called *IPIEM Cycle*. IPIEM consists of five progressive stages to assess progress which are discussed in Chapter 3.

Concluding discussion

Surmounting number of publications are addressing causes and effects of ongoing disruptions in the workplace in response to urgency for solutions. All sources coincide that traditional management approaches utilize humans, material and financial resources in the best combination, but are no longer effective to solve ongoing problems in the 21st century. Pending solutions require to put people at center or management and organizations. Yet, HCM is different because it puts human at the center adding the condition that objective assessment of people's wellbeing must be at the core. In this respect, HCM offers unique solutions that I have discussed in this chapter for the first time. The benefits management and organizations accrue from HCM deployment results in a unique Multiplier Effect (ME). The ME integrates wellbeing in the workplace, the marketplace and communities.

The solutions organizations seek to face unprecedented global disruptions and sustainability threats require to focus first on the wellbeing of people to secure high performance and Quality standards. The global VUCA environment positions HCM and its ME as a realistic option for people and organizations to overcome surmounting disruptions. Recalling Einstein quote: *Things do not change if people and organizations keep doing the same thing*. Yet I add, disruptions and crises can become blessing when people are encouraged, empowered and are trusted to be creative and responsible for continuous improvement. It is an option management and organizations can no longer overlook or delay.

Notes

1 https://www.oecd.org/wise/better-life-initiative.htm
2 Conference of David Malpass, President of the World Bank in Conference at Warsaw School of Economics (April 12, 2022). Addressing Challenges to Growth, Security, and Stability. https://live.worldbank.org/sm22/speech?cid=ecr_e_wblconnect_en_post&deliveryName=DM140275
3 Until now my 2002 Quality Education book is extensively used in the Region and in Spanish-speaking countries.
4 Faisal, I. BBC economics editor (2022). *Interview with David Malpass. Ukraine war: World Bank warns of 'human catastrophe' food crisis*. April 21. https://www.bbc.com/news/business-61171529
5 Josephs, J. (2022). *Ukraine war to cause biggest price shock in 50 years - World Bank*. April 27. https://www.bbc.com/news/business-61235528

6 https://www.mckinsey.com/business-functions/people-and-organizational-performance/our-insights/great-attrition-or-great-attraction-the-choice-is-yours
7 https://www.pewresearch.org/fact-tank/2022/03/09/majority-of-workers-who-quit-a-job-in-2021-cite-low-pay-no-opportunities-for-advancement-feeling-disrespected/
8 https://www.bbc.com/worklife/article/20220428-quitters-remorse-the-workers-who-regret-resigning

References

Argyris, C. (1957). *Personality and organization. The conflict between the system and the individual.*Harpers.

Bam, A., & Ronnie, L. (2021). Virtuous human centered organizational culture: The case of people with disabilities. In Lepeley, M. T., Morales, O., Essens, P., & Beutell, N., Majluf (Eds.). *Human centered organizational culture: Global dimensions.* Routledge, UK.

Beutell, N., Kuschel, K., & Lepeley, M. T. (2021). Life–work continuum: The new organizational culture. In Lepeley, M. T., Morales, O., Essens, P., Beutell, N., & Majluf, N. (Eds.). *Human centered organizational culture: Global dimensions.* Routledge, UK.

Beutell, N., Kuschel, K., & Lepeley, M. T. (2021). Learning from failure: Soft skills for sustainability in the VUCA environment. In Lepeley, M. T., Beutell, N., Abarca, N., & Majful, N. (Eds.) (2021). *Soft Skills for human centered management and global sustainability.* Routledge, UK.

Beutell, N., & O'Hare, M. (2020). Wellbeing, family support, and health among married women entrepreneurs in the United States. In Lepeley, M. T., Kuschel, K., Beutell, N., Pouw, N., & Eijdenberg, E. (Eds.). *The wellbeing of women in entrepreneurship: A global perspective.* Routledge, UK.

Bedeian, A., & Wren, D. (2001). Most influential management books of the 20th century. *Organizational Dynamics*, 29(3), 223–225.

Drucker, P. (1954). *The Practice of Management.* Harvard Business Press.

Epstein, S. (2022). *The sky-high cost of returning to the office.* BBC.com. April 20. https://www.bbc.com/worklife/article/20220420-the-sky-high-cost-of-returning-to-the-office

Essens, P., Wermser, F., & Täuber, S., (2021). Cultural interoperability in interorganizational collaborations. In Lepeley, M. T., Morales, O., Essens, P., Beutell, N., & Majluf, N. (Eds.). *Human centered organizational culture: Global dimensions.* Routledge, UK.

Essens, P., & Lepeley, M. T. (2018). Wellbeing@work: Is buffering stress enough? In Ochoa, P., Lepeley, M. T., & Essens, P. (Eds.). *Wellbeing for sustainability in the workplace.* Routledge, UK.

Greenhaus, J., & Beutell, N., (1985). Source of conflict between work and family roles. *Academy of Management Review*, 10(1), 76–88.

Lepeley, M. T., Morales, O., Essens, P., Beutell, N., & Majluf, N. (Eds.). (2021). *Human centered organizational culture: Global dimensions.* Routledge, UK.

Lepeley, M. T. (2021a). The human centered sustainable culture in organizations. In Lepeley, M. T., Morales, O. , Essens, P., Beutell, N. , & Majluf, N . *Human centered organizational culture: Global dimensions.* Routledge, UK.

Lepeley, M. T., Beutell, N., Abarca, N., & Majluf, N. (Eds.). (2021b). *Soft skills for human centered management and global sustainability.* Routledge, UK.

Lepeley, M. T. (2021c). Master soft skills. The resilience – agility umbrella. In Lepeley, M. T., Beutell, N., Abarca, N., & Majluf, N. (Eds.). Soft skills for human centered management and global sustainability. Routledge, UK.

Lepeley, M. T., (2021b). Soft skills. The Lingua Franca of human centered management in the global VUCA environment. In Lepeley, M. T., Beutell, N., Abarca, N., & Majluf, N. (Eds.). *Soft skills for human centered management and global sustainability*. Routledge, UK.

Lepeley, M. T., Kuschel, K., Beutell, N., Pouw, N., & Eijdenberg, E. (2020a). *The wellbeing of women in entrepreneurship: A global perspective*. Routledge, UK.

Lepeley, M. T. (2020b). The multiplier effect of wellbeing of women entrepreneurs. In Lepeley, M. T., Kuschel, K., Beutell, N., Pouw, N., & Eijdenberg, E. (Eds.). *The wellbeing of women in entrepreneurship: A global perspective*. Routledge, UK.

Lepeley, M. T. (2019). Balanced sustainable development ESTE (economic, social, technical, environment). Part II in Lepeley, M. T. (Ed.) (2019). *EDUCONOMY. Unleashing wellbeing and human centered sustainable development*. Information Age Publishing, Charlotte, NC.

Lepeley, M. T. (2019a). *EDUCONOMY. Unleashing wellbeing and human centered sustainable development*. Information Age Publishing, Charlotte, NC.

Lepeley, M. T. (2019b). *EDUQUALITY. Human centered quality management in education. A model for deployment, assessment and sustainability*. Information Age Publishing, Charlotte, NC.

Lepeley, M. T. (2017a). *Human centered management: The 5 pillars of organizational quality and global sustainability*. Routledge, UK.

Lepeley, M. T. (2001). *Quality and management in education. A model for assessment*. (Original title: *Gestion y Calidad en Educacion. Un Modelo de Evaluacion*). McGraw-Hill.

Majluf, N., & Abarca, N. (2021). *Sensible leadership. Human centered, insightful and prudent*. Routledge, UK.

Maslow, A. (1954). *Motivation and personality*. Harpers.

Maslow, A. (1943). A theory of human motivation. *Psychological Review*, 50(4), 370–396.

Mayo, E. (1933). *The Human Problems pf an Industrial Civilization*. Routledge.

McGregor, D. (1960). *The human side of the enterprise*. McGraw-Hill.

Ochoa, P., Lepeley, M. T., & Essens, P. (Eds.) (2019). *Wellbeing for sustainability in the global workforce*. Routledge, UK.

Parker, K., & Horowitz, J. (2022). *Majority of workers who quit a job in 2021 cite low pay, no opportunities for advancement, feeling disrespected. PEW Research Center. March 9*. https://www.pewresearch.org/fact-tank/2022/03/09/majority-of-workers-who-quit-a-job-in-2021-cite-low-pay-no-opportunities-for-advancement-feeling-disrespected/

Ronnie, L. (2019). Wellbeing challenges of millennials. South Africa "born free" generation. In Ochoa, P., Lepeley, M. T., & Essens, P. (Eds.). *Wellbeing for sustainability in the global workforce*. Routledge, UK.

Silva, A. B., Canos, L., De Araujo, A., & Perello, M. R., (2019). Comparison of learning styles and strategies of students of management in Spain and Brazil. *Journal of Management and Education*, 2(3), 192–214. 10.35564/jmbe.2019.0014

Smith, A. (1759). *The theory of moral sentiments*. London: Printed for A. Millar, and A. Kincaid and J. Bell, in Edinburgh.

Torrit, A. (2022). *How inflation is causing Americans to "unretire"*. Wall Street Journal. April 2. https://www.wsj.com/podcasts/the-journal/how-inflation-is-causing-americans-to-unretire/6f972656-d706-4dff-9ef0-af2aab86ed4e

Van der Vegt, G., Essens, P., Wahlstrom, M., & George, G. (2015). Managing risk and resilience. From the Editors. *Academy of Management Journal*, 58(4), 971–980.

3 Managing the Quality Crisis

Restoring Human Wellbeing

Maria-Teresa Lepeley

Introduction

Since World War II global landmarks in human development, industrial progress and international trade have led to unpatrolled performance of the labor force and national productivity resulting in continuous increases in standards of living of the population in countries worldwide. Abundant evidence and studies show that the creativity, ingenuity and innovation of people are the main engines of progress. This evidence is aligned with studies I connected for four decades about implications of education on development and sustainability. Human talent is the leading factor in sustainable development, or what I have defined as ***ESTE*** sustainable development (economic, social, technology and environmental) (Lepeley, 2019a). In reality every human being adds more value to the economy and society than each person consumes. This shows an important positive relationship between population growth and sustainable development. My studies point out to the importance of Quality (Q); and specifically of Quality education on development. I highlight that to attain sustainable development anchored in people's wellbeing, education with Quality standards for ALL is the key for inclusive development. I develop these arguments in my books *EDUCONOMY* and *EDUQUALITY* (Lepeley, 2019a, b).

In reference to the title of this book on Human Centered Management (HCM) and crisis, the 2020' decade started with Covid-19 pandemic – one of the worst disruptions most people have seen in their lifetime, with deep and relentless negative effects on human wellbeing. By the end of 2022, the pandemic is barely subsiding. On the contrary, disruptions are exacerbated by new crises, a war in Europe, unprecedented increases in energy prices, economic, political and social turmoil with high potential to pull the world into a recession. Challenges are surmounting and in this environment Quality standards are also a victim and a hostage.

The creativity, energy and drive of people that have ignited progress before and even when it seemed almost possible coincide with the history of Quality and positive effects of Quality Management (QM) discussed in this chapter. Shared principles are empowering trust in Quality rebuilding in times of crises.

DOI: 10.4324/9781003330011-4

The next sections describe paramount events that launched the global Quality Movement and QM, and identify the obstacles impacting Quality standards during the last decade. The chapter closes by presenting solutions to rebuild Quality embedded in HCM's Pillar 5 *Sustainable Quality Management* (SQM) (Lepeley, 2017a).

The QM boom

By the turn of the 21st century the world population had attained the highest levels of prosperity and wellbeing since WWII. Since 1980 progress and human prosperity increased at a faster pace propelled by effects of the Quality Movement embedded in QM. QM surged as a discipline designed to spur performance and productivity centered on people's creativity and work ingenuity fostering continuous improvement. QM started in industrial organizations and Q principles and practices were soon adopted by organizations in all sectors and countries around the world. From industry to business, from education and health care, in the private and public sectors, all embraced QM to trigger high performance and long-term sustainability.

QM is the human centered operational methodology that led the paradigm shift in management from resources-fixed organizations to people's wellbeing in the workplace. Details are explained in the section presenting HCM Pillar 5 *Sustainable Quality Management* (SQM).

Consistent results of QM resulting in remarkable increases in performance and productivity induced countries worldwide to establish national Quality programs and policies to support organizations advance people-based Q-based development. QM transformed the traditional inward-looking-mediocre-resource focus adding the outward-looking scope putting people at the center of Quality standards and targeting needs in the community and society. These principles and practices are core to HCM and pivotal to Pillar # 5 Sustainable Quality Management (SQM).

The people's nebulous and ill-defined role in management that had persisted since the first industrial revolution and was harming more than helping people as a major obstacle for progress was a crucial incentive driving me to create the HCM Model (Lepeley, 2017) and the HCM Series.

TQM: Genesis of organization sustainability and people's wellbeing

The QM revolution started with Edwards Deming's visionary TQM Model. Deming was an American statistician recognized as The Father of Quality who worked as a consultant in Japan after WWII. TQM reinvented Japanese management and rebuilt industry devastated during WWII. His model was so powerful to increase performance and productivity that Japan was the first country that established a National Quality Award (NQA) program and called it The Deming Award.[1] TQM spread across nations and industries in all sectors and nations seeking to model effective increases in performance and productivity after decades of sluggish growth. The Academy of Management includes Deming's book "*Quality, Productivity and Competitiveness Position*" (1982) among the 25 most influential Management Books of the 20th century.

The Quality Movement grew exponentially with the creation of NQA Programs around the world. The United States Baldrige National Quality Award was created in 1987[2] and was most influential in global Q advances. The European Quality Award EFQM was founded in 1990.[3] Over 70 countries and regions have established Quality Awards.

I was member of the Board of Examiners of the United States Baldrige National Quality Award and adviser to National Quality Award Program in Chile, Brazil, Colombia, Peru and Ecuador. To the largest extent this experience added to previous background in Q, required to become Baldrige examiner, drove my efforts to develop the HCM Model. All my work pursuits are based on the same QM principles.

TQM was the missing link necessary to replace obsolete inward-looking organizations framed by strategies of the industrial past with TQM's inward–outward multidimensional vision. TQM significantly improved the structure of hierarchical and bureaucratic shortcomings of organizations that were established successfully by Frederick Taylor and Max Weber at the beginning of 20th century. Resource-based management models were highly effective then, when the workforce had very low levels of education. But HRM approaches are obsolete to meet demands of the 21st century and a highly educated labor force.

During the boom of the QM movement in late 1980s, the United States, followed by Europe, Latin America and countries around the world, experienced unprecedented increases in performance, productivity and prosperity in economic growth and social development resulting in significant decreases in poverty rates (Lepeley, 2017b, 2019a, b, c, 2020, 2021a, b, c). Progress was the result of human creativity and QM innovation in small- and medium-sized businesses, large corporations and organizations in all sectors and industries, discovering the benefits and adopting the transformation to increase productivity leading to sustainability.

Expanding prestige of QM led to fast growth in demand for consulting services and expertise across industries and organizations in the private and government sectors, increasingly aware of the benefits but overall about the surmounting costs accrued from lack of Q standards resulting in deteriorating competitiveness. High imperativeness to achieve Q standards resulted in fast increase of a large diversity of QM derivative approaches. In United States, there was a blast of consulting firms specialized in Six Sigma, Lean 6 Sigma and similar. Europe focused on ISO Norms, specialized by industries, including the general ISO Norm 9000 with versions for medical ISO 13485, food ISO 22000, services ISO 2000000, IT ISO 27001, aerospace AS 9100D and Automotive IATF 16949 among others.

QM and HCM shared fundamentals

The following arguments underline fundamental Q principles and practices aligned with HCM axioms that are underlined throughout the chapter. They are important to understand the basics of QM embedded in people's wellbeing.

1 Organizations exist because there are customers – clients, users – who have needs and to fulfill their needs they buy or receive (in the case of public agencies administered by government agencies financed by tax collection) products and/or services the organization produces.

  a Organizations exist because there are people who require their products and services; otherwise, they do not have reason to exist.
  b HCM organizations play an important contribution when they provide Quality standards and continuous improvement in the distribution of products and services required to enhance wellbeing in the workplace, the marketplace and society at large.

2 Organizations cannot meet the needs of external customers unless they first meet the needs and provide workplace wellbeing to the people who work in the organization.

QM, national productivity and people's wellbeing

Up to this point the benefits of Q and QM have focused at the organizational or micro level. But Quality does not work in a vacuum. On the contrary, Q initiatives have major impact on national economic growth and inclusive social development. Because Q standards increase labor force participation, stimulate work engagement and high performance in the workplace, it results in increasing national productivity and consequently higher income for workers and standard of living of the population (Lepeley, 2019a, b, c, 2017b).

The effect of NQA programs and other Q initiatives are shown in United States statistics. Data reveal significant differences in periods that national administrations emphasized Q with policies promoting labor force productivity resulting in higher standards of living. Results show decreases in productivity and the wellbeing of working people during administrations following other priorities. The comparison is based on longitudinal data of labor productivity reported by the United States Bureau of Labor Statistics, comparing periods of Q booms and declines. Labor productivity increased on an average of 1.2 percent between 1973 and 1979, before the emergence of the Q Movement. It increased on an average of 2.2 percent between 1990 and 2000 when QM was booming across industries led by the influence of the Baldrige National Quality Award Program launched in 1987. Productivity decreased on an average of 1.4 percent between 2007 and 2019 when national policies followed other priorities deterring labor force participation and decreasing productivity. Productivity increased by 2.2 percent between 2019 and 2021 coinciding with national policies stimulating participation and productivity. In the second quarter of 2022, nonfarm business sector labor productivity decreased by 4.1 percent. This is the largest decline in the series, which began in the first quarter of 1948,[4] forecasting recession in the US economy. In terms of standards of living related to productivity, the US Census Bureau data per capital income PCI show a direct correlation between labor force productivity and higher standards of living increases proxy by per capita income. Between 1990 and 2007 per capita income increased from $US 27,000 to $34,000. In the next eight years there was a small increase to $US 36,000 showing effects of decreases in labor force productivity and productivity. In the next two years, 2018–2020, increases in labor productivity resulted in average PCI increase reaching $US 39,000.

Declining labor productivity is concerning because it negatively impacts the wellbeing of people in the workplace, the marketplace and society. Negative effects are greater in cohorts with low formal education, low income and restricted participation in the workforce.

In May 2022, *The Wall Street Journal* reported about constraint and hardships US organizations in all sectors are facing to hire workers. To large extent because of extended unemployment compensation and welfare programs that disincentivized people to seek paid jobs.

Labor shortages present significant obstacles to advance Q and productivity. To such extent, that it can be said that Q is also a victim of the crisis exacerbated by prolonged Covid-19 pandemic lockdowns and ongoing disruptions that are affecting organizational sustainability and hindering the wellbeing of people worldwide.

The quality crisis

Q standards become a competitive edge securing benefits for organizations delivering Q products and services to customers and users. QM was backed up by organizations' increasing interest for the wellbeing of workers as a precondition for high performance. For the first time, QM integrated satisfaction of needs and expectations and wellbeing of customers (external view) in parallel with workers (internal view).

The search for solutions to the Quality crisis requires clear understanding of causes and effects of the global overreach of the ongoing disruptions hindering QM, and consequently HCM based on continuous improvement of people and organizations. A critical point leading Q standards is a systemic organizational approach aligned with systematic monitoring of results to secure continuous improvement and Q standards that required specific knowledge. From the Talent Management perspective, HCM Pillar 3, it is important for people in organizations to develop QM knowledge supported with hard and particularly Soft Skills to (1) deploy QM principles and practices across the organizations. And critically important (2) to recognize crucial differences between Q standards – or the real "Q" – from commonly used "quality" and specially "high quality" which are nothing more than adjectives qualifying any noun. Consequently, it is essential to know that the real "Quality concept sells well". So it is not surprising that there are abundant misuses, abuses and rude imitations and fake quality slogans. The problem of counterfeit quality is of such magnitude that authentic Q initiatives, including NQAs, are dropping the word quality and substituting for Performance Excellence, High Performance, High Productivity.

Fake quality in advertisement damages trust, trustworthiness, engagement, legitimate workmanship and organizational sustainability. But, again, fake quality can be easily recognized when people – customers and workers – have access to information necessary to recognize "q" tricks. The same occurs in organizations where employees who work to attain Quality standards are distracted by organizational intents resulting in fake quality attempts. Organizations that try to change customers' perceptions often overlook evidence that Quality prestige is built on persistent longitudinal efforts. Q is not attained overnight. On the contrary, it takes time to reach continuous efforts of people, time and resources to develop organizational structures and strategies strong enough to build *the Quality culture*. Promotional tactics alone backfire for savvy and well-informed customers and employees. When quality promises fail people increasingly perceive them as gimmicks and bad tricks, enhancing needs to be able to differentiate between real Quality (with capital Q) from fake quality (with small q). In the present environment, costs and complaints associated with Quality gaps are growing exponentially. So customers, workers and organizations need to be aware of surrounding threats and circumstances to avoid further deception of fake quality.

In terms of competitive advantages where Q is a major component, until a decade ago Q standards and programs worldwide worked as intended by Deming. That is to say Q was a world-recognized instrument promoting ***constructive competition.*** But later good Q intentions to pursue constructive competition started to deteriorate. Among other causes of the Q decay, illegitimate quality pushed limits to the other extreme of unfair ***destructive competition***. Differences between both constructive and destructive competitions need to be recognized and acknowledged because destructive competition leads to detrimental harm to the wellbeing in the workplace, the marketplace and the standard of living of people.

Unfair practices of destructive competition are easily hidden behind surmounting disruptions and abuses occurring during economic turmoil, the pandemic, long-lasting war in Europe between Russia and Ukraine, the energy crisis leading to escalating inflation with increasing potential to lead the world into a global recession. The erosion of living standards harming the wellbeing of people is unprecedented for many generations. In terms of global consequences, the ongoing disruptions are increasing poverty levels, blocking and reversing the goals set by international development organizations intending to end poverty by 2030.

QM needed to restore wellbeing and productivity

In spite of all, Q remains the most realistic alternative and a priority across sectors and industries seeking high performance and productivity that determine sustainability in VUCA environments. Education around the world is claiming immediate restoration of Q standards for ALL (Lepeley, 2019a, b) to compensate for dramatic deterioration during the pandemic lockdowns that affected all students and at all levels, but mostly students in vulnerable cohorts that benefit most from Q education.

Overall, emerging claims to restore Q highlight that organizations that lack systematic integration of QM principles in their structure and strategies to secure operations and performance during and after crises are suffering the highest damages (Reeves et al., 2022). Gianluca Pescaroli, Lecturer in Business Continuity and Organizational Resilience at University College London's Institute for Risk and Disaster Reduction in the School of Math and Physical Sciences and adviser to UN, argues that in an interconnected world organizations impacted by effects of the Covid pandemic, the Ukraine–Russia war and the ongoing energy crisis are deeply affected and one of the most critical concerns in risk management is the human dimension.

HCM, QM and wellbeing

This section discusses principles and practices of Sustainable Quality Management (SQM) or Pillar 5 in HCM (Lepeley, 2017). SQM is a principal methodology in the HCM model synchronizing and stimulating cohesiveness and synergy between the other four Pillars: Human Capital, Talent Management, Disruption Resilience and Agility. SQM is an adaptation of Deming's TQM and the foundations of NQA Programs previously discussed. The importance of SQM is that, as Q centered model, monitors continuous improvement of organizational structure, strategies and processes in parallel with the wellbeing of people in the workplace and the marketplace, community and society.

SQM has a multidimensional inward–outward-looking focus synchronizing external demands, created by customers, with internal demands for high performance and productivity aligned with the wellbeing of people. Where wellbeing in the HCM context follows Lepeley Model 7 *Complementary Interactive Life Dimensions* (2021a, page 15).

The seven life dimensions of wellbeing are the following:

- Life Purpose
- Freedom and Autonomy
- Love, Affection and Meaningful Relations

- Physical Fitness and Good Health
- Financial Security and Income
- Intellectual/Spiritual Growth
- Contribution to Improve Society.

Description and deployment of HCM's SQM

To facilitate deployment and expedite application in organizations, in all sectors and industries worldwide, the SQM Model is divided in seven Management Areas (MA). Its purpose is to facilitate systematic monitoring and assessment of continuous improvement, supervised by Q teams, reporting areas of improvement as well as areas of areas that need improvement in order to advance performance required to demonstrate achievement of Q standards (Lepeley, 2017). Each MA is subdivided in *Elements of Assessment* EA including variable the organization selects to assess improvement meeting SQM guidelines for reporting (Lepeley, 2017, pp. 144–145).

MAs 1,2,3 are people focused and receive the highest scores in the SQM Model. MAs 4,5,6,7 monitor operations supporting people in the Q Teams leading and guiding everybody in the organization to optimize work and efforts leading to Q standards and performance excellence.

The seven MAs of the SQM Model are in order of scores:

- MA1. ***Consumers' wellbeing***: Satisfaction of needs and expectations of customers and users, including knowledge of the market and community where customers come from (includes society focus, corporate/organizational social responsibility).
- MA2. ***Wellbeing of people who work in the organization***: Satisfaction of needs, human capital and talent development, work engagement, merit recognition, workplace wellbeing.
- MA3. ***Human centered leadership***: Human centered, resilient, agile securing wellbeing as precondition for high performance, productivity, constructive competition and long-term organizational sustainability.
- MA4. ***Planning***: Synchronization of long-term structural planning with short-term strategic planning anchored on Quality standards.
- MA5. ***Knowledge management and optimal use of technology***.
- MA6. ***Quality standards of supporting organizational processes***: Ensuring that all organizational divisions including finances, accounting, people management, physical facilities maintenance and others follow the same Quality seeking standards.
- MA7. ***Horizontal and vertical integration and environment care***: Monitors continuous improvement in horizontal integration (benchmarking, constructive competition and deterring destructive competition), aiming to strengthen the community. Vertical integration (supply chains). Constant monitoring and improvement of the environment inside and outside the organization.

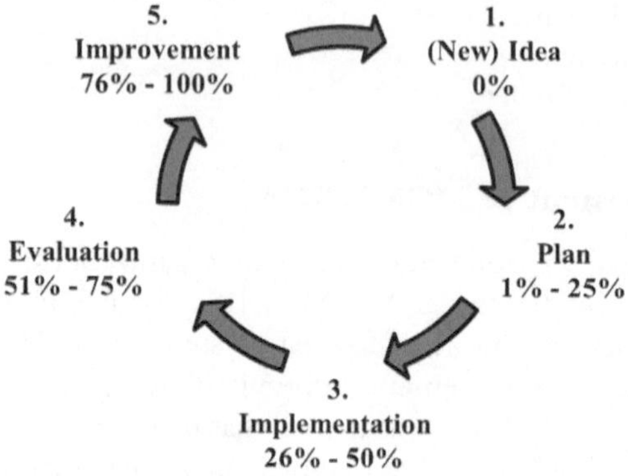

Figure 3.1 IPIEM Cycle of Continuous Improvement.

Each one of the variables included in the 35 Elements of Assessment is evaluated to secure continuous improvement using the IPIEM Cycle of Continuous improvement using five stages of progress ranging from the creation of an idea to concrete data of continuous improvement, required across the organization to certify Q standards.

Stages of the IPIEM Cycle of Continuous Improvement include (1) Idea generation, (2) Planning, (3) Implementation, (4) Evaluation, (5) Improvement as shown in Figure 3.1.

Assessment with IPIEM provides objective score of progress and advances towards continuous improvement required to certify levels of performance. Objectively organizations need to achieve scores over 800 points to show Quality standards. Scores below 800 points show different levels of performance.

SQM makes a difference between levels of performance and Q standards. Levels of performance can be high or low. But Q exists or not. Q standards are supported with evidence of 800 or higher score. Lower scores show levels of performance, not Q standard. Consequently, references to quality as high or low are invalid, it is a clear indication of ignorance of real Q standards.

Concluding comments

Human creativity, ingenuity, work ethics and persistent efforts that resulted in the highest levels of progress, prosperity and highest standards of living since WWII were extensively propelled by the global QM and Quality Management standard. Q standards provided organizations with unprecedented methodology to work and produce efficiently optimizing efforts and outcomes. Q achievements were successful and subdued resource-based approaches that persisted from the industrial past, because QM is centered on people. On the importance of the wellbeing of workers in the workplace as a necessary condition to attain high performance and productivity required to secure sustainability. QM is unique because for the first time it integrated the traditional inward-looking organizational vision, adding an outward-looking vision that allowed organizations to focus also on the needs of external clients, the communities and society, as a necessary condition to respond and integrate external demands in production processes of products and services to fulfill their Q mission.

Human centered Q standards expanded rapidly across industries, from industrial to business, from education to health care, and across countries and candidates.

The focus on the wellbeing of people in all dimensions of work and life, in the workplace, the marketplace, community and society, was the genesis to launch the HCM Book Series using QM as one of the components – Pillar 5 – to secure long-term organizational sustainability anchored in the wellbeing of people.

Thriving deployment of QM and Q standards leading to the highest levels of productivity, prosperity required to attain people's wellbeing is reported across industries and countries worldwide. Today people in general and customers in particular know what Quality is, and can recognize legitimate Quality from fake quality slogans. Consequently, people are increasingly demanding Quality standards that faded in the last decade pressed by trends going-back-to-industrial-past prioritizing again resource-driven causes at the expense of the continuous improvement of people's wellbeing. Obstacles to Q advances hindering the wellbeing of people were exacerbated by the pandemic, one of the worst wars with global outreach in the 21st century, escalating inflation and spiraling crises with no end in sight.

But in this global VUCA environment, there is an increasing volume of evidence that people all over are seeking peace and prosperity with increased awareness that Quality and QM are at the center of solutions and critical to HCM. Surmounting evidence we receive confirms the value of the HCM efforts and the amazing creativity and ingenuity of people will move Q standards forward as soon as these crises subside.

Notes

1 Deming Award https://www.juse.or.jp/deming_en/award/
2 The Baldrige Foundation https://baldrigefoundation.org/who-we-are/history.html?gclid=EAIaIQobChMIpvPr987L9wIVD2pvBB18Rgj-EAAYASAAEgJ2uPD_BwE
3 EFQM Model https://efqm.org/efqm-model/
4 US Bureau of Labor Statistics (5/2022) https://www.bls.gov/news.release/prod2.nr0.htm

References

Bedeian, A., & Wren, D. (2001). Most influential management books of the 20th century. *Organizational Dynamics*, 29(3), 223–225.

Bloom, J. (2022, March 10). *The risk management experts now in high demand*. BBC Business. https://www.bbc.com/news/business-60660760

Deming, W. E. (1994). *The new economics for industry, government and education.* MIT Press.

Deming, W. E. (1982). *Out of the crisis.* MIT Press.

Deming, W. E. (1982). *Quality, Productivity and Competitive Position.* MIT Press.

Epstein, S. (2022, April 20). *The sky-high cost of returning to the office.* BBC.com. https://www.bbc.com/worklife/article/20220420-the-sky-high-cost-of-returning-to-the-office

Essens, P., & Lepeley, M. T. (2018). Wellbeing@work: Is buffering stress enough? In Ochoa, P., Lepeley, M. T., & Essens, P. (Eds.). *Wellbeing for sustainability in the workplace.* (pp. 76–84). Routledge, UK.

Lepeley, M. T. (2021a). The human centered sustainable culture in organizations. In Lepeley, M. T., Morales, O., Essens, P., Beutell, N., & Majluf (Eds). *Human centered organizational culture: Global dimensions* (pp. 3–22). Routledge.

Lepeley, M. T., (2021b). Soft skills: The lingua franca of human centered management in the global VUCA environment. In Lepeley, M. T., Beutell, N. J., Abarca, N., & Majluf, N. (Eds.). *Soft skills for human centered management and global sustainability* (pp. 3–22). Routledge.

Lepeley, M. T. (2021c). Master soft skills: The resilience – agility umbrella. In Lepeley, M. T., Beutell, N. J., Abarca, N., & Majluf, N. (Eds.). *Soft skills for human centered management and global sustainability* (pp. 23–37). Routledge.

Lepeley, M. T., Beutell, N. J., Abarca, N., & Majluf, N. (Eds.). (2021). *Soft skills for human centered management and global sustainability.* Routledge.

Lepeley, M. T., Morales, O., Essens, P., Beutell, N., & Majluf (Eds). (2021). *Human centered organizational culture: Global dimensions.* Routledge, UK.

Lepeley, M. T. (2020). The multiplier effect of wellbeing of women entrepreneurs. In Lepeley, M. T., Kuschel, K., Beutell, N., Pouw, N., & Eijdenberg, E. (Eds.). *The wellbeing of women in entrepreneurship: A global perspective* (pp. 3–22). Routledge.

Lepeley, M. T. (2019a). *EDUCONOMY: Unleashing wellbeing and human centered sustainable development.* Information Age Publishing.

Lepeley, M. T. (2019b). *EDUQUALITY: Human centered quality management in education: A model for deployment, assessment and sustainability.* Information Age Publishing.

Lepeley, M. T. (2019c). Balanced sustainable development ESTE (economic, social, technical, environment). Part II in Lepeley, M. T. (Ed.) (2019). *EDUCONOMY: Unleashing wellbeing and human centered sustainable development.* Information Age Publishing.

Lepeley, M. T. (2017a). *Human centered management: 5 pillars of organizational quality and global sustainability.* Routledge.

Lepeley, M. T. (2017b). Bhutan's gross national happiness: An approach to human centered sustainable development. *South Asian Journal of Human Resource Management,* 4 (2), 174 – 184. 10.1177/2322093717731634

Lepeley, M. T. (2001). *Quality and management in education: a model for assessment.* (Original title: *Gestion y calidad en educación: Un modelo de evaluación*). McGraw-Hill.

Majluf, N., & Abarca, N. (2021). *Sensible leadership: Human centered, insightful and prudent.* Routledge.

McGregor, D. (1960). *The human side of the enterprise.* McGraw-Hill.

Ochoa, P., Lepeley, M. T., & Essens, P. (Eds.). (2019). *Wellbeing for sustainability in the global workforce.* Routledge.

Parker, K., & Horowitz, J. (2022, March 9). Majority of workers who quit a job in 2021 cite low pay, no opportunities for advancement, feeling disrespected. *PEW Research Center.* https://www.pewresearch.org/fact-tank/2022/03/09/majority-of-workers-who-quit-a-job-in-2021-cite-low-pay-no-opportunities-for-advancement-feeling-disrespected/

Reeves, M., O'Dea, A., & Carlsson-Szlezak, P. (2022, March 25). Make resilience your company's strategic advantage. *Harvard Business Review*. https://hbr.org/2022/03/make-resilience-your-companys-strategic-advantage

Ronnie, L. (2019). Wellbeing challenges of millennials: South Africa "born free" generation. In Ochoa, P., Lepeley, M. T., & Essens, P. (Eds.). *Wellbeing for sustainability in the global workforce* (pp. 117–132). Routledge.

Takeuchi, H., & Quelch, T. (1983, July). Quality is more than making a good product. *Harvard Business Review*. https://hbr.org/1983/07/quality-is-more-than-making-a-good-product

Torrit, A. (2022, May 2). How inflation is causing Americans to "unretire". *Wall Street Journal*. https://www.wsj.com/podcasts/the-journal/how-inflation-is-causing-americans-to-unretire/6f972656-d706-4dff-9ef0-af2aab86ed4e

Van der Vegt, G., Essens, P., Wahlstrom, M., & George, G. (2015). From the editors: Managing risk and resilience [Editorial]. *Academy of Management Journal*, 58(4), 971–980. 10.5465/amj.2015.4004

4 Life-Work Continuum in Times of Crisis

A Family Perspective

Nicholas J. Beutell

Introduction

The Covid-19 pandemic and other ongoing crises have induced unmatched disruptions in families, affecting individual and collective wellbeing in extreme disruptions not seen in many decades and unknown to younger generations. Despite the critical importance of the Life-Work Continuum (LWC), emerging but fully revealed by the pandemic, research and analysis on this "whole person approach" (Behson, 2021) are still scarce and inadequate. This chapter examines the most critical issues and challenges that emerged from the effects of the pandemic while exploring solutions that create opportunities for families to develop resilience capacity to lessen the negative outcomes during crises. It addresses how the family contributes to individual and collective efforts for achieving and preserving wellbeing necessary for the enjoyment of life but also for stimulating performance and productivity at work by contributing to long-term organizational sustainability.

Although the global Covid-19 pandemic is a most recent example, disruptions are continuously affecting families, including local and global crises, brought about by natural disasters, migrations, economic recessions, wars and many other causes. Families facing disruptions can have far-reaching consequences on wellbeing, work performance, organizational productivity, the economy and society at large. These are some of the multiple dimensions that need attention for understanding and minimizing the detrimental effects of disruptions and crises by developing resilience at all levels.

Family disruptions in the 21st century

There are multiple features that define a family. Despite broad variations in family size, kinship recognition and expectations of family groupings, historically the family represents the oldest and the most common human and social structures. Some authors consider the family "the most important and enduring of all human social groupings" (Smith et al., 2009). Family

DOI: 10.4324/9781003330011-5

remains among the oldest human organizations because it is the foundation for social structure and plays a critical role in socialization processes.

A family is commonly defined as a group of people living together and supporting each other. The concept of a family has changed overtime. However, the essential role of family remains intact. Today the family may not include the traditional grouping of a mother and a father living with their biological children, because there are many variations in family structure and form. The Pew Research Center (2010), using a randomly chosen sample of adults, reports seven emerging family trends in the United States:

unmarried couples raising children
gay and lesbian couples raising children together
single women having children without male partner to support raise them
people living together without getting married
mothers of young children working outside home
interracial marriages
women without children

These trends show the diversity of family groupings that increase the complexity of assessing pandemic effects and the pervasive healthcare crisis affecting families. Pandemic disruptions have imposed extreme changes in family routines, social behavior, remote working, schooling, financial resources, mental and physical health, while heightening the impact of the digital divide (i.e., unequal access to technology), taking a toll on daily life of families. But the pandemic is one among many constant disruptions testing and threatening the resilience of families. Furthermore, research highlights the importance of children's socialization for developing resilience skills and capacity directly affecting human wellbeing in adulthood. In fact, the detrimental impact of the pandemic on children's socialization will likely be one of the most enduring consequences of the pandemic lockdowns for generations to come.

The need to face disruptions has significantly increased the demands for resilience in the face of diminishing access to resources, creating new challenges for parental systems because of the considerable and unpredictable influences of crises on children. Family disruptions affect the world of work because children and families are major stakeholders of organizations making the family an essential issue for Human Centered Management (HCM), organizational effectiveness and sustainability.

The discussion suggests how family exposure to disruptive environments requires Soft Skills to enhance and strengthen resilience (Lepeley, 2021b) that significantly affect the LWC by integrating life responsibilities. In this context, family stress theory (FST) helps to explain how families are affected by crises. This theory is foundational in family resilience models and helps in understanding child development, including skills that foster resilience in children. Family resilience is examined from a process perspective that transforms family resilience into "resilience spirals", resulting in increasing individual and dyadic resilience of family members and family system with projections in organizations performance, communities and society. The chapter closes by addressing resilience dimensions moving beyond a crisis and emerging stronger by restoring and increasing the wellbeing of people.

Life-Work Continuum and disruptions

Organizations overlook, or fail to understand, the complex and close connection between family life and work life because their focus is on work and the workplace. This creates a closed system with strict boundaries between workers' lives at work and their private lives, to a large extent excluding family. This dichotomous view of the "work-family narrative" (Padavic, Ely, & Reid, 2019) can detract from and obstruct the career advancement of men, but particularly women, because women have been largely responsible for family and the wellbeing of children. This artificial dichotomy infringes on people's autonomy, hinders the wellbeing of working people, compromises work engagement and hinders work performance thereby detracting from organizational and societal productivity (Lepeley, 2017; Ochoa, Lepeley, & Essens, 2019).

In the specialized "work-family" literature, family and work are treated as separate and often conflicting "domains" in people's lives (e.g., Greenhaus & Beutell, 1985), with discrete expectations and behaviors, often unrelated and disconnected. The artificial separation of work from family emerged during the First Industrial Revolution, creating separate "spaces" for family, anchored in the home, and work, rooted in the workplace and organizations, presenting geographical and psychological separation of family and work. To large extent this dichotomy persists today, embedded in the traditional resource-focused management, considering humans as resources, presenting a distorted image that does not represent changing patterns of family and work which are increasingly connected and interdependent.

From the HCM perspective, management focused on resources overlooks the crucial role of people and their wellbeing as necessary conditions for continuously improving performance with quality standards by securing long-term organizational sustainability, igniting job creation, stimulating economic progress and ensuring social prosperity (Lepeley, 2017). Management anchored in "people as organizational resources" ignores the importance of family that emerged in the last decades demonstrating a positive correlation between family wellbeing and work performance (Jaskiewicz et al., 2017). Traditional resource-focused management research disregards the impact of the family and the way that working people influence organizational culture, performance and sustainability. Research often excludes "family variables" that neglect critical conflicts between family and work (Greenhaus & Beutell, 1985). Moreover, creating boundaries separating these "domains" based on structural differences that are often psychological, but are treated as real, harms important life integration that working people must have. Emerging studies of synergies between work and family, that transcend divisions between family and work, support an integrated LWC (e.g., Beutell & Gopalan, 2019).

Scholars are struggling with these dichotomies because "family" and "work" are not separate domains in a person's life. Family and work involve different tasks and responsibilities but are complementary dimensions of human life. Therefore, it is unrealistic to ignore and obstruct needed research presenting a more integrated and holistic perspective on life.

To properly address this apparent dilemma and offer a unified and integrated perspective on life, scholars developed the LWC (Beutell, Kuschel, & Lepeley, 2021) that is tightly aligned with fundamental principles and practices of HCM (Lepeley, 2017). LWC is built on the human development conceptualization that life's wellbeing largely depends on family, nuclear and extended, with work achievements *supplementing wellbeing*. Under the assumption that most, if not all, people live in family groupings, and many are also working in paid jobs, the LWC is universally applicable.

Organizations become productive and sustainable when the people who work in the organization at all levels, are able use their knowledge, skills and talents to produce goods and services that the organization delivers, in exchange for wages and salary required to meet living expenses. Financial security of employees converges with financial solvency and security necessary for organizational survival and sustainability. Paid jobs are a human activity that people undertake to secure resources necessary to support family expenses. LWC is gaining momentum after the pandemic because ongoing crises causing management and organizations to recognize that people's wellbeing is crucial in sustainable workplaces.

The effects of the pandemic have sharpened the focus on LWC because, during lockdown mandates, family activities were centered in the home. Despite consistent evidence that LWC has always been a central theme, it took a global crisis for organizations to understand the implications of the life and work continuity framing human life. The transition of management and organization from the resource focus to one that places humans at the center has been slow, to large extent, because it requires a deep understanding of causes and effects prompting the paradigm shift that the current crises have exposed with irrevocable determination. Present conditions are driving the consolidation of human centered cultural transformation in organizations (Lepeley et al., 2021a) supported by realistic LWC synchronizing the needs of employees as "whole persons" (Behson, 2021) with integrated lives.

Family stress theory

Prior to discussing family resilience, it is necessary to address how families are affected by crises. In this regard, FST (Hill, 1949) provides a sustainable framework showing how crises affect and disrupt families by focusing on interactions of crisis-related demands and resources that determine family outcomes (Prime, Wade, & Browne, 2020). FST has been foundational in the family resilience literature.

The basic idea of FST is the ABC-X model, where A refers to an external stressor/crisis event, B to available resources, C represents perceptions of the event and X is related to outcomes. The ABC-X model has produced a large diversity of studies, including military families, expatriate families, new venture creation by entrepreneurs, forced family relocation, migration and family resilience levels. Under normal circumstances, a working parent performs his or her duties *at work* with a separate family system *at home* with separate yet permeable boundaries. However, during the Covid pandemic, permeable home-work boundaries represented an unprecedented experience for many families because of constant interactions constraining all family and work activities to be completed simultaneously, in the same space and time, at home. This arrangement reveals the connection advanced by the LWC whereby family and work are integrated for most working parents who were simultaneously acting as parents, employees, caregivers, teachers, etc.

FST facilitates the integration of demands (A) and resources (B) in a family system coping with stress and striving for wellbeing outcomes (X) (Hill, 1949). FST acts as a framework that examines causes and effects of demands and the use of resources while considering individual differences in dealing with disruptions related to the Covid pandemic or other disruptions emerging at the local, national or global level.

At this juncture it is important to mention that stress in general, but particularly family stress, is not simply and only the result of a "major disruption" because it is possible that a family will be subject to simultaneous disruptions challenging their resource base. Thus, the family needs to build resilience capacity for dealing successfully with a variety of crisis scenarios that are happening with increasing frequency and intensity.

Family as practice for life

We all have a past. That past is largely shaped by family, one of the primary ways that children are socialized. Consider the following quote from the *Harvard Business Review*:

> Fundamental attitudes and behaviors that evolved from the family dynamics of your childhood have traveled with you into the present—and into the office. Those dynamics taught you a lot about authority, mastery, and identity. So when similar ones assert themselves in the office, it's easy to revert to childhood patterns.
>
> (Ancona & Perkins, 2022)

This quote directs our attention to the influence of family dynamics on the development of personal characteristics and attributes that persist for a lifetime. This component of human wellbeing is largely ignored by management and organizations. Gaps persist despite important models proposed by pioneering scholars like Alfred Adler (1870–1932), an Austrian philosopher and psychiatrist, who emphasized the search for meaning (significance) as important component of lifestyle and the attainment of wellbeing in life. His theory explains how children make sense of life beginning with early experiences by advancing the idea that family is preparation for life because it shapes behavior that lasts a lifetime (Lombardi, 1975). Adler highlighted the individual in the social context, distinguishing the family as the initial and profound formative experience. Adler focused on the life of children finding their way after being born as helpless creatures, totally dependent on parents for survival, nurturance and to thrive in life. Interactions between parents and siblings allow children to experience reality that overtime shapes their lifestyle, consistent with patterns for dealing with life challenges. Each child constructs reality based on individual experiences derived from family interactions.

Adler posed that the birth order of children influences their development. Considering that the first born or oldest child receives undivided parental attention because the first child is a unique experience for parents. Because parents are learning how to be parents, they tend to overprotect the child providing lots of care and attention to the newborn. So first born children tend to carry along similar responsibility of parental authority and achievement consistent with social norms incorporating parental values to a larger extend than younger siblings. Studies have shown that most NASA astronauts were either first-born or only children. First-born children tend to pursue traditional careers and occupations in science, medicine and law in conformity with family expectations and social norms. When a first-born child has siblings there are impending constraints of sharing parental attention, a situation Adler termed "dethronement" or removal from power. The way that first-born children handle this conflict is one of the first crises they face in life. First-borns can embrace the new sibling by accepting shared power or reject them attempting to maintain their superior position in the family constellation. The resolution of this conflict has long-lasting consequences impacting subsequent interpersonal situations, including work behaviors.

Adler's theory explains how childhood dynamics are foundational for lifestyle development for adult behaviors that start shaping at early age and persist in recollections of experiences, dreams and expressive behaviors, such as art, dance and musical inclinations. He argues that each child searches for significance forming a personal lifestyle. And once formed, lifestyles shape relationships, occupational choices, social interests and developing affection and concern for other people with important effects on life-long wellbeing.

Family resilience

Family resilience is the capacity of a family, as a social unit, to withstand shocks induced by stressful life challenges. Successful responses can strengthen the family making it more resourceful and better prepared to face further disruptions. Family resilience considers family systems as transactional processes in well functioning families, where resilience focuses on adaptive family functional to face disruptions and crisis. Effective coping and adaptation depend on the nature of the crises, resources available and the goals of the family in the social context. In the case of the pandemic, family resilience was anchored in adjustment, family cohesion, good communication and adequate financial management (Chen & Bonanno, 2020).

Family resilience is a dynamic process that consists of strengths and resources that family members can mobilize within the family system and the social environment dealing with disruptions. Family flexibility and agility in responding to situational shifts enhance family resilience (Gayatri & Irawaty, 2022). The processes emerge from cultural norms and family preferences in situations of adversity that craft unique family responses. Families create resilience pathways stemming from resources, challenges, values and goals.

Family resilience is essential for strengthening the wellbeing of family members. Resilience is a major support mechanism for people to advance human centered organizations, given that family resilience affects wellbeing of employees. Lepeley's study on the multiplier effect of women in entrepreneurship (Lepeley, 2020) highlights family responsibilities of women, with children's education as a value-added element, for the improvement of societies with direct and indirect support for organizations. Further, the multiplier effect impacts work, employment opportunities and ultimately performance and organizational sustainability when the demands of work are well aligned with other life responsibilities in the family, the community and society. A fundamental principle underlying LWC is that family resilience supports people at work who become advocates for workplace wellbeing necessary for long-term organizational sustainability (Beutell, Kuschel, & Lepeley, 2021).

Resilience spirals and social resilience

A central component of FST is the use of resources during crises. This is part of the resilience-building process for families and individual family members. The conservation of resources (COR) theory explains that resources are secured and protected, a major motivator of human behavior (Hobfoll, 1989). We propose that resources, that under normal conditions would be maintained and enhanced, must be used in response to crises. However, such resources are not used arbitrarily, but in the expectation that those resources will be a down payment toward garnering additional resources in the future after the crisis passes. Resources are deployed in the service of increasing family resilience. Considering this "resilience in the face of adversity" scenario, resilience serves as a springboard, a "trajectory of adaptation", whereby resilient behavior yields outcomes beyond what might otherwise be expected (Henley, 2010). Thus, the family system integrates the resources of family members as the family system increases its resilience efficacy in confronting crises successfully. Previous responses to a crisis become the best predictor of family behavior in a new crisis (Hill, 1949).

In effect, the family's repeated attempts to deal with crises inoculate the family against future crises by creating resilience capabilities that we term "resilience spirals". This means that families become increasingly competent in fending off crises using accumulated wisdom and resources. In effect, families deal with the crisis, but they also learn lessons for handling the next crisis. "Spirals are deviation-amplifying loops in which the positive, cyclic relationship between perceived efficacy and performance builds upon itself" (Lindsley, Brass, & Thomas, 1995) thus increasing family resilience capabilities. This is consistent with the impact of family efficacy beliefs on effective family functioning (Bandura et al., 2011).

However, such resilience spirals are necessary but insufficient because families do not live in isolation. They live in neighborhoods, towns, cities and society. What connects family resilience spirals to the broader community? Henley (2010) advanced the concept of multilayered social resilience to explain how resilience is connected in hierarchical ecosystems. Collective efficacy is defined including upward and downward resilience spirals. Family resilience enhances community resilience which, in turn, increases societal resilience. More work needs to be done on multilayered social resilience, but Henley's work is a promising start. Identifying how family resilience affects community resilience, for example, would be a major step forward in understanding crisis management.

Family resilience and wellbeing

The global pandemic threatened the wellbeing of families worldwide because it was an unprecedented event with pervasive consequences for humankind. Despite the challenges that families endured during the pandemic and other ongoing disruptions, many families have survived and are bouncing back from the crisis. Human resilience and family resilience played a considerable role in facing these unprecedented disruptions and crises as families have struggled to maintain their level of wellbeing.

Family wellbeing flows from effective and innovative responses to disruptions. Family wellbeing fosters family resilience allowing families to bounce back after confronting crises. Family wellbeing is more complex than personal wellbeing because it is built up by multiple family member coordinating efforts as a group (Fahey et al., 2012). Family wellbeing goes beyond a simple summing of the wellbeing of its members, and as such, can fluctuate and temporarily decline in times of crisis.

Wellbeing has been subjected to different interpretations and it is frequently confused with happiness. Embedded in HCM principles and practices, Lepeley (2021a) differentiates between wellbeing, as a sustainable condition overtime, contrasting with happiness, as a temporal and circumstantial event of joy or pleasure and absence of pain. Lepeley describes wellbeing as a multivariate framework that builds up overtime and is integrated by the following 7 *Complementary and Interactive Life Dimensions* (Lepeley, 2021a): life purpose, autonomy, love and affection, good health and physical fitness, financial security, long-life learning supporting intellectual/spiritual growth and contributions to society.

All the dimensions of wellbeing were disrupted for individuals and families during the pandemic. Parents play a particularly important role maintaining wellbeing during disruptions because their behavior has direct impact on children and the emotional responses of the family. Children react to a crisis based on cues from their parents because children model parental behaviors. Parents create a sense of life purpose by enacting the LWC, showing their love and affection to children, maintaining adequate financial resources and staying active and engaged. Practicing acts of gratitude can increase family wellbeing. Quality family time, doing positive activities together, can build intimacy, trust and cohesion that strengthen wellbeing. Social support from friends, members of the extended family, neighbors and community activities can help when parents or family members need additional assistance. Seeking social support using technology can keep families connected by offering mutual support during crisis disruptions.

Integration of individual, family, organizational and social wellbeing is an important dimension for effective deployment of HCM. These multilevels of wellbeing are ignored in "humans as resources" models of management. However, resilience capacity is built on the resilience of children, families, schools and communities suggesting that multilevel resilience emerges overtime and has evolved collectively (Masten & Motti-Stefanidi, 2020). This outcome is more apparent during crises because families are compelled to implement new strategies building on all dimensions and levels of wellbeing.

Concluding comments

This chapter explored family resilience and wellbeing during disruptions and crises. Family resilience is a necessary condition for effective responses to disruptions that are occurring with increasing frequency and intensity. FST underlines family resilience by conceptualizing threats to family systems using a resource-based approach. Resources are necessary for managing disruption effectively. The concept of *resilience spirals* helped to explain the integration of individual resilience, family resilience and community resilience. The multilayered nature of social resilience capacity and shared resources expedites crisis management and crisis resolution.

The discussion explored children's lifestyle development, including birth order effects, in dealing with parents, siblings and adults in general. Childhood resilience is shaped and developed as the child discovers how to navigate the environment by interacting with parents and siblings. The lifestyle that is formed in childhood becomes the resilience model for dealing with disruptions throughout life. Childhood "ghosts" and "angels" (Ancona & Perkins, 2022) exert their influence at critical times but particularly during crisis. Moreover, as adults, people can change their behaviors by recognizing that their parents and siblings played an important role in their development, shaping their resilience and wellbeing.

Resilient family members contribute to strengthen family resilience and family resilience transcends the resilience of individual family members when coping with disruptions and crises. Disruptions caused by the pandemic, war in Europe, hyperinflation and increasing threats of global recession are tests of endurance, fortitude and resolution to build resilience and bounce back better. To date, there is more information on dealing with the immediate impact of crises but much more needs to be known about dealing with long-term consequences of disruptions.

Family resilience can help families to face and manage disruptions. Family resilience spirals can help families transcend crises connecting families to the community to achieve collective wellbeing. HCM is anchored in the wellbeing of people in organizations that aligns with family dynamics and resilience by enhancing workers' performance, organizational success and long-term sustainability.

References

Ancona, D., & Perkins, D. N. T. (2022, January-February). Family ghosts in the executive suite. *Harvard Business Review*. https://hbr.org/2022/01/family-ghosts-in-the-executive-suite

Bandura, A., Caprara, G. V., Barbaranelli, C., Regalia, C., & Scabini, E. (2011). Impact of family efficacy beliefs on quality of family functioning and satisfaction with family life. *Applied Psychology*, 60(3), 421–448. 10.1111/j.1464-0597.2010.00442.x

Behson, S. (2021). *The whole-person workplace: Building better workplaces through work-life, wellness, and employee support*. Authors Place Press.

Beutell, N. J., Kuschel, K., & Lepeley, M. T. (2021). Life–Work continuum: The new organizational culture. In Lepeley, M. T., Morales, O., Essens, P., Beutell, N. J., & Majluf, N. (Eds.), *Human centered organizational culture: Global dimensions* (pp. 23–33). Routledge.

Beutell, N. J., & Gopalan, N. (2019). Pathways to work-family synergy: Resources, affect and wellbeing. *Journal of Family Studies*, 27(4), 556–572. 10.1080/13229400.2019.1656664

Chen, S., & Bonanno, G. A. (2020). Psychological adjustment during the global outbreak of Covid-19: A resilience perspective. *Psychological Trauma: Theory, Research, Practice, and Policy*, 12(S1), S51–S54. 10.1037/tra0000685

Gayatri, M., & Irawaty, D. K. (2022). Family resilience during Covid-19 pandemic: A literature review. *The Family Journal*, 30(2), 132–138. 10.1177/10664807211023875

Greenhaus, J. H., & Beutell, N. J. (1985). Sources of conflict between work and family roles. *The Academy of Management Review*, 10(1), 76–88. 10.2307/258214

Fahey, T., Keilthy, P., & Polek, E. (2012). Family Relationships and Family Well-Being : A Study of the Families of Nine Year-Olds in Ireland. Retrieved from http://hdl.handle.net/10197/5102

Henley, R. (2010). Resilience enhancing psychosocial programmes for youth in different cultural contexts: Evaluation and research. *Progress in Development Studies*, 10(4), 295–307. 10.1177/146499340901000403

Hill, R. (1949). *Families under stress: Adjustment to the crises of war separation and return*. Harper.

Hobfoll, S. E. (1989). Conservation of resources: A new attempt at conceptualizing stress. *American Psychologist*, 44(3), 513–524. 10.1037/0003-066x.44.3.513

Jaskiewicz, P., Combs, J. G., Shanine, K. K., & Kacmar, K. M. (2017). Introducing the family: A review of family science with implications for management research. *Academy of Management Annals*, 11(1), 309–341. 10.5465/annals.2014.0053

Lepeley, M. T. (2021a). Soft skills: The lingua franca of human centered management in the global VUCA environment. In Lepeley, M. T., Beutell, N. J., Abarca, N., & Majful, N. (Eds.), *Soft skills for human centered management and global sustainability* (pp. 3–22). Routledge.

Lepeley, M. T. (2021b). Master soft skills: The resilience – agility umbrella model. In Lepeley, M. T., Beutell, N. J., Abarca, N., & Majful, N. (Eds.), *Soft skills for human centered management and global sustainability* (pp. 23–37). Routledge.

Lepeley, M. T., Morales, O., Essens, P., Beutell, N. J., & Majluf, N. (Eds.). (2021). *Human centered organizational culture: Global dimensions*. Routledge.

Lepeley, M. T. (2020). The multiplier effect of wellbeing of women entrepreneurs: A practical approach and personal account. In Lepeley M. T., Kuchel, K., Beutell, N. J., Pouw, N., & Eijdenberg, E. L. (Eds.), *The wellbeing of women in entrepreneurship: A global perspective* (pp. 3–22). Routledge.

Lepeley, M. T. (2017). *Human centered management: 5 pillars of organizational quality and global sustainability*. Routledge.

Lindsley, D. H., Brass, D. J., & Thomas, J. B. (1995). Efficacy-performing spirals: A multilevel perspective. *Academy of Management Review*, 20(3), 645–678. 10.5465/amr.1995.9508080333

Lombardi, D. (1975). *Search for significance*. Nelson-Hall.

Masten, A. S., & Motti-Stefanidi, F. (2020). Multisystem resilience for children and youth in disaster: Reflections in the context of Covid-19. *Adversity and Resilience Science*, 1(2), 95–106. 10.1007/s42844-020-00010-w

Ochoa, P., Lepeley, M. T., & Essens, P. (Eds.). (2019). *Wellbeing for sustainability in the global workplace*. Routledge.

Padavic, I., Ely, R. J., & Reid, E. M. (2019). Explaining the persistence of gender inequality: The work–family narrative as a social defense against the 24/7 work culture. *Administrative Science Quarterly*, 65(1), 61–111. 10.1177/0001839219832310

Pew Research Center. (2010, November 18). *The decline of marriage and rise of new families*. https://www.pewresearch.org/social-trends/2010/11/18/vi-new-family-types/

Prime, H., Wade, M., & Browne, D. T. (2020). Risk and resilience in family well-being during the Covid-19 pandemic. *American Psychologist*, 75(5), 631–643. 10.1037/amp0000660

Smith, S. R., Hamon, R. R., Ingoldsby, B. B., & Miller, J. E. (2009). *Exploring family theories*. Oxford University Press.

5 Integrative HCM View of Resilience and Wellbeing

Peter Essens, Maria-Teresa Lepeley, and Nicholas J. Beutell

Introduction

One of the most outstanding consequences of the disruptions caused by the Covid-19 pandemic is the long-lasting effects on people's lives and working conditions. These are critical concerns of Human Centered Management (HCM) in general, and of this book on Human Centered Management and crisis in particular. This chapter addresses the following four critical dimensions for promoting people's wellbeing in a workplace challenged by the global VUCA environment: Resilience, needed to bounce back from difficult times; Empowerment, to create space for creativity and responsiveness promoting engagement, active participation and self-determination; Talent Management (TM), aiming to incentivize work engagement and satisfaction in organizations and the Life–Work Continuum (LWC), which views life and work as an integrated sequence of events rather than an ongoing confrontation between separate and often conflicting domains. The argument is that these key factors need to be addressed not only in policies but also in action ensuring people's wellbeing and organizational sustainability.

We live in a complex and dynamic world where disruptions that affect people, such as the Covid pandemic and other crises, have a dramatic impact across societies. Social and technical systems are interconnected to such an extent that local disasters have regional and global spillover effects. Studies show that disruptions are increasing in number and magnitude (UNDRR, 2020). The increasing interdependence of economic, social and security systems, supply chains, infrastructures and information systems increases vulnerability because of intensive urbanization, dependence on vital and virtual infrastructures, raw materials and climate change.

All systems face difficulties in remaining operational when unexpected and sudden changes in conditions occur. Systems are designed and prepared for known and expected disruptions, but when disruptions fall outside these boundaries, functioning can easily break down, which can compromise sustainability, affect interconnected systems and generally affect the wellbeing of the people they serve.

DOI: 10.4324/9781003330011-6

Some studies suggest that the economic impacts of disasters are relatively small from a macroeconomic perspective. However, the timing of the recovery and reconstruction strategies has proved crucial. Simulation analyses (input–output models) with existing data have shown that while total impacts of disasters are significant and complex domestically, if recovery and reconstruction strategies had not been deployed in the year following the disaster, the global effects would have been much more negative (Okuyama, 2010). Thus, the time window of measurement of effectiveness is relevant. This macroeconomic result illustrates the benefits and the need for people and organizations at the organizational and microeconomic levels to be better prepared for the impact and associated costs of unexpected disruptions.

HCM organizations promote a positive and constructive orientation through a strong sense of purpose and core values based on a culture that fosters high employee engagement and effective trust-based relationships necessary to shape the organization's social capital.

Resilience strategies

Organizations, as social systems, have a critical role in responding to emergencies and crises in society. So maintaining functionality and resilience is not only in their self-interest, but also a public obligation for maintaining services that provide products to communities and other organizations in their supply chain. HCM emphasizes that organizations can only achieve this important social responsibility goal by first meeting the needs of society and supporting their employees (Lepeley, 2017).

Strategies to withstand and adapt to changing circumstances, recover from shocks and stresses and learn from them, are known as resilience strategies. The literature on resilience is growing very rapidly. A search yielded 42,000,000 hits on Google and 31,561 hits in the academic literature (Web of Science; May 7, 2022). Peer-reviewed academic publications with "resilience" in the title (as a proxy for relevance) increased from 80 to nearly 6,000 between 2000 and 2021, indicating exponential growth. But the distribution of sources and applications is diverse: environmental leadership (43%); health/personal studies (41%); engineering (7%) and management (7%). Organizational resilience as a topic represents 8% of this set and shows rapid growth from 30 to 605 between 2010 and 2021.

The number of publications on resilience is increasing and most note that definitions range from sustaining and recovering to preparing or thriving in response to shocks. And this occurs at different levels of analysis, including individuals, teams, organizations, communities, regions, nations and in diverse systems that include but are not limited to financial, ecological, supply chains and migrations. Moreover, disruptions, shocks and disasters are of diverse nature, with diverse consequences. ISO quality standards define organizational resilience as the "ability of an organization to absorb and adapt in a changing environment" (International Organization for Standardization, 2017). Clarity about what resilience is, is a pending academic need with great relevance to practitioners who need a deeper understanding of processes that affect resilience, particularly from the moment a shock occurs, to the recovery phase and ultimately to a new level of functioning.

The bathtub as a resilience model

A process view of the level of functioning of a system after a disruption provides a detailed account of the resilience response of the system, which facilitates the identification of effective assessment of interventions. This chapter presents a generic model of a resilience process used in HCM practice. Called the "Bathtub", the model, shaped like a bathtub, represents the various levels of crisis response in relation to performance. Derived from an infrastructural systems context (see Goodwin, Essens & Smith, 2012), the "Bathtub" represents a generic system response that researchers and users can apply in labeling and discussing prototypical phases in the resilience process.

The initial response to disruptions (thick arrow) is to resist a change using known routines and quick fixes (B). When effects pose a potentially higher risk of greater system failure, other interacting parts of the system must be smoothly degraded (C) to a steady state that allows as many essential functions as possible (D). In this state, some level of recovery performance can be achieved while repairing, reorganizing and planning for gradual recovery (E). Getting the system back to the desired level of performance requires adaptation to new conditions. An important feature of the model is the consideration of time. Because time intervals become a crucial component, the faster the system can return to normal operation, the greater the benefits of resilience. Based on practice, this model assumes that recovery

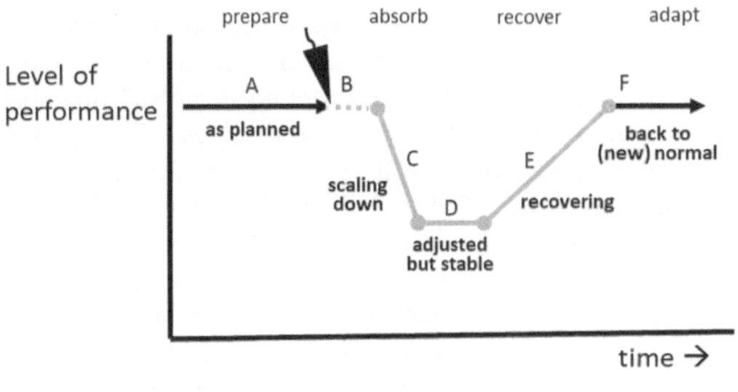

Figure 5.1 Phases of the Bathtub Model.

takes more time when the relapse is greater – downscaling, stabilization and recovery are strongly related.

From a systems' perspective, resilience encompasses multiple interactions within, between and across subsystems and levels of analysis that are common in organizations increasing the complexity of resilience. Variants of the Bathtub model have been used to describe the response profile following disruptions, often depicting a minimum stability period with immediate recovery (OECD, 2020). The Covid-19 crisis experience has shown that creating a (short) stable period is important for reorganizing the organization to cope with a persistent threat (see hospital example, Chapter 1 of this book).

Networks are relational resources that connect workers and interaction patterns in organizations. Networks transcend hierarchies and silos, enable rapid exchange of information and creative ideas with situation-specific responses. Networks connect different levels of the organization enabling a fluid exchange of people's knowledge with organizational-level skills and abilities that form the cognitive, behavioral and relational capabilities to deal with crises resulting from disruption. Essential behavioral elements of resilience are learned resourcefulness, ingenuity and initiative (Lengnick-Hall et al., 2011).

The bathtub model reinforces the critical dimension of time in dealing with disruptions. It reveals essential aspects of crises that might have differential effects at different levels: individual, team, organization and social system. Although resilience at all levels must be considered, we believe that resilience is a necessary, but insufficient condition for fully responding to crises overtime. We advance several other factors that help to complete the picture, factors that are bolstered by resilience but that go beyond resilience for successful crisis management. These factors include empowerment, TM and the LWC.

Integrating empowerment, TM and LWC with resilience

Among ongoing challenges, old management approaches no longer offer solutions. To counteract and overcome obstacles in the current environment, 4 complementary topics have become critical for advancing, restoring and strengthening organizations to ensure long-term sustainability in the highly volatile conditions of disruptions and crises. The analysis integrates Resilience, one of HCM's 5 Pillars[1] (Lepeley, 2017), with 3 other key concepts: Empowerment, TM and the LWC (see Figure 5.2).

Empowerment focuses on involvement, engagement, active participation and self-determination, seeking to link the individual's wellbeing to his or her social context (Perkins & Zimmerman, 1995). Supporting empowerment at work means providing the means to do work effectively, particularly through competency development, providing meaningful and challenging work and enabling influence over work-related decisions. TM,

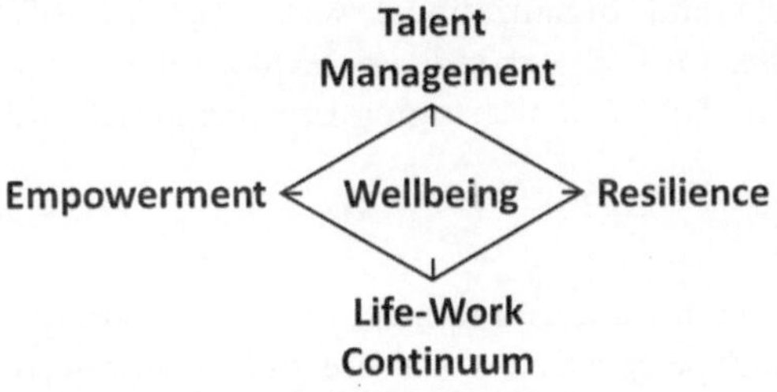

Figure 5.2 Resilience with empowerment, talent management and Life–Work Continuum contributing to wellbeing.

as the third Pillar of HCM, comes to the fore as a systematic approach to bring together those factors that optimize individual contributions and performance of each person in the organization by building resilience, as the pursuit of wellbeing is a common denominator for people and the workplace.

We argue that empowerment provides a solid foundation for resilience (see also Chapter 1). Both empowerment and resilience are strength-based approaches that utilize personal and structural resources for individuals to develop and grow despite obstacles, crises and setbacks. Empowerment provides the desired flexibility in the LWC to align life and work demands with organizational performance needs. Empowerment with its focus on engagement, individual development, growth and wellbeing is also a driver for TM. Personal and organizational strength is the collection of talent, competencies, skills and knowledge that employees have accumulated overtime, that are enacted when dealing with complex situations, either alone or by cooperating with colleagues.

Figure 5.2 shows the relationships that connect Resilience with Empowerment, TM and the LWC to increase wellbeing in HC organizations. TM in turn provides inputs to the other 3 components that are sources of people's wellbeing. In HCM, people's wellbeing in the workplace is a critical component necessary for achieving quality standards that ultimately determine extraordinary organizational performance and long-term sustainability. (Ochoa, Lepeley, & Essens, 2019).

The correlation between personal and organizational wellbeing is the main objective of HCM. Studies on job satisfaction and life satisfaction (Beutell & Schneer, 2014) show that, on the positive side, 60% of a sample of managers and professionals show a spillover relationship (i.e., a positive association between job satisfaction and life satisfaction). This contrasts with 32% showing an inverse association, while 8% show little or no relationship between work and life satisfaction.

In the aging workforce, these relationships shift as people retire, seek "bridge work", or start new careers or businesses. Disruptions caused by the pandemic have affected and shifted people's priorities, including the relationship between individual and organizational wellbeing. In this environment, wellbeing analyses must be expanded to explore new dynamics as integral components of the LWC in a changing organizational reality.

New crises, old skills

A new HCM culture in organizations requires new skills along with receptivity to new ideas and perspectives to revise old assumptions and generate effective new solutions to crisis situations. In effect, this is a cultural transformation. Learning basic routines is essential as a first response to crisis situations. Moreover, new circumstances may require a different course of action than the usual norms. Change increases the likelihood of chaotic situations when it is unexpected, and responses are not well synchronized. At all organizational levels, this requires a thorough understanding of the situation and how organizational processes adapt to related actions. Communication and information sharing combined with guidance to coordinate initiatives are essential. Relational capabilities within and outside the organization are based on feeling safe to ask questions, seek information, discuss organizational performance and then take shared responsibility for responding to the crisis. These interactions are essential for developing joint actions and accomplishments (Weick, 1993). Empowerment, delegation of power and responsibility are important attributes in an organizational culture where employees are engaged in and accept higher levels of personal responsibility to adapt more quickly to overcome shocks and disruptions.

Organizations and individuals are better prepared to manage shocks based on 3 critical elements that underlie a resilient organization:

1 functional and effective networks and relationships,
2 ability to change, agility to move forward and innovate and recognize and effectively respond to threats, and
3 leadership that can provide the trust needed for collective cohesion and collaboration which foster a culture of respectful interactions that are essential as foundational elements of a resilient organization.

Related approaches to building organizational resilience emphasize that resilience requires a strategic approach that integrates resilience thinking into organizational planning. Building on the experience of disasters in New Zealand, Vargo, Sullivan and Parsons (2013) developed a resilience scorecard with 13 indicators that represent 3 key clusters of organizational factors that represent "the ability to survive a crisis and thrive in a world of uncertainty": leadership and culture, networks and relationships and change readiness.

Achieving change readiness and preparedness for handling shocks requires the development and deployment of Soft Skills as core requirements for effective human interactions in HCM organizations (Lepeley, 2021b). Alexandra Samuel, who works with leading global companies to understand online customers and create data-driven reports, highlights the importance of the following Soft Skills in the article The Soft Skills of Great Digital Organizations: goal-oriented thinking, collaboration skills, communication skills, learning skills, trouble shooting skills, playfulness and sense of humor (Samuel, 2016).

Optimizing TM in disruptive times

The disruptions caused by the Covid-19 pandemic (starting in early 2020), including but not limited to social distancing and prolonged lockdowns to stop the spread of the deadly disease, profoundly changed organizational structures and strategies in the traditional workplace. Two years later, that change is ongoing and uncertainty is compounded by war in Europe and energy, economic and financial crises affecting organizations in countries around the world, the costs of which threaten organizational sustainability and the wellbeing of people.

Of the many disruptions associated with the pandemic, one that has received much attention is a tidal wave of workers quitting their jobs in the United States and around the world. This unusual trend dubbed the "Great Resignation" is leading to more research to better understand the causes of the phenomenon. In addition to pandemic disruptions, it has widespread implications for employers and organizations in all sectors and industries who are perplexed by the causes that lead massive numbers of employees to resign. Organizations need data-driven knowledge to create targeted retention programs and adjust management principles and practices if necessary (i.e., a culture shift).

The Great Resignation is covered in other chapters of this book (see Chapters 2 and 6). Here, suffice it to say that from the HCM perspective on TM, the Great Resignation is not surprising. On the contrary, it emerged as a natural response and natural reaction by employees to traditional organizational cultures and management strategies focused on resources, often at the expense of and ignoring the wellbeing of people, that have prevailed unchanged for more than a century. The Great Resignation ultimately provides proof that old tactics are no longer effective. Today, working people have access to vast amounts of information and opportunities to compare and decide on the best employment opportunities in organizations that match their needs, interests and values. In other words, people can more easily identify organizations that can value their talents, utilize them and promote their wellbeing.

However, recent studies show that, in many cases, the Great Resignation results in Great Regret (Tanzi, 2022). As the wave of resignations related to Covid risks in the workplace and new opportunities to work from home have prompted working people to reassess their work and lives amid the turmoil of a pandemic, but sources show that some of those who quit their jobs are having second thoughts and reconsidering. Of those who found a new job after quitting, a significant percentage say the new job did not meet their expectations. Job changers also say they miss colleagues and social contacts. Since many people spend as much time at work as they do with family and friends, those who build strong personal relationships with co-workers have a major impact on how they view the new job and how likely they are to stay or regret it. The disruptions that precipitated the Great Resignation took a long time to build up in the workplace, and they will take a long time to resolve unless the "people-centered" paradigm prevails.

Anthony C. Klotz, professor of management at University College London's School of Management, who coined the term "Great Resignation", believes the rate of quitting will remain high in the short term, but an impending economic downturn and general uncertainty in labor markets could change things. A global recession would slow the quit rate because during a recession, labor markets deteriorate and opportunities for workers to change jobs decrease. Klotz estimates that resignation rates may not be as high as they were during the pandemic, but the rates will fall. Yet there are already signs that rising costs of living and inflation are affecting worker behavior. The United Kingdom has coined the term "Great Unretirement", in which older people return to the workforce under pressure to cope with the rising cost of living. Other authors say it is unclear whether even a global financial crisis could reverse the tide of Great Resignation.

Managing talent

What makes organizations sustainable in the long run and ensures that employees stay at work are organizational conditions embedded in a people-centered culture that promotes empowerment for increasing people's wellbeing. This means that organizations make efforts, not only implicitly but explicitly, to discover, appreciate, value and use the talents of all employees, regardless of their level of responsibility in the organization. TM is 1 of the 5 Pillars of HCM in the framework that consolidates this model. In times of crisis, the above discussion identified challenges that confirm that the approach organizations take to manage people's talent is a critical element of sustainability.

HCM uses the term talent because unlike mere "work", talent represents value-added personal contributions that result in heightened job performance and work engagement enhancing job satisfaction. The sum of individual talents in an organization is a key input for continuous improvement, quality standards and organizational productivity that determine long-term sustainability.

The talent of working people is rooted in their human capital formed by education, experiences, skills, natural and acquired abilities, beliefs and values that contribute to optimal performance by using their personal abilities when given the opportunity. Human Capital is a Pillar of HCM, a personal asset that people have in deploying their talents or abilities that optimize critical thinking and problem-solving. It could be said that human capital is an inert asset until people activate it to solve problems in life and at work. Talents contribute to the development of resilience and agility needed for continuous performance improvement to achieve quality standards at the personal and organizational levels.

In HCM, talent is strongly related to Soft Skills. In terms of human capital, the difference between hard skills achieved through cognitive knowledge and formal education and Soft Skills, which are more intuitive and closely related to special personal talents, is largely related to informal education, observation and imitation. Lepeley (2021a) defines Soft Skills as personal attributes and traits possessed by people that enable them to interact effectively and harmoniously with other people. Soft Skills include self-esteem, emotional intelligence, autonomy, empathy, patience, self-awareness, effective listening and collaborative skills. Soft Skills are acquired or learned by different means via experiences at all ages. The earlier, the better to consolidate social interactions later in life and at work. In HCM, Soft Skills are highly associated with resilience, which, at the organizational level, prepares people for understanding and moving forward at various stages in the Bathtub Model (see Figure 5.1).

Organizational structures for TM

Human resources (HR) offices traditionally play an important personnel administration role in organizations – working hours must be recorded and salaries paid. In addition, functions such as developing career paths and designing compensation strategies emerged. A major shift in HR since the 1990s is the responsibility of line management for the implementation of HR policies in the workplace (Paauwe, 2007). Line managers are often less equipped for handling this role, because they have identified with the traditional human resource perspective, viewing people as a factor of production, rather than talent that enhances longer term benefits of employee wellbeing.

To reverse this trend and put employee wellbeing at the center of organizational change, HCM organizations must establish a dedicated TM entity, led and managed by multidisciplinary teams, supported by networks of psychologists, economists, educators and other specialties, aligned with organizational objectives. TM teams are responsible for optimal matching of job requirements with employee interests, talents and responsibilities. Efforts are made to systematically develop and methodically assess progress to identify areas in need of improvement in accordance with HCM Pillar 5, Sustainable Quality Management specifications.

To achieve TM optimization, TM team leaders develop design tools, ideally internally, to ensure that such tools are manageable and easy to use throughout the organization. This facilitates keeping realistic records of progress with intentional awareness for ensuring that the appraisal system does not overwhelm personal responsibilities, autonomy, or employee performance levels.

TM Team actions and processes include, but are not limited to, the following:

- Identify/design effective instruments to assess the talent of people at all levels of the organization.
- Secure empowerment strategies, with optimal alignment of responsibilities with personal talents, aimed at promoting autonomy, empowerment at work, commitment and satisfaction at work.
- Assess and provide training and education opportunities for personal improvement to support Human Capital, talent development, Resilience and Agility.
- Train employees with leadership potential to advance in the organization and serve as mentors to other employees.
- Reward and recognition systems that provide constant feedback leading to personal performance improvement and greater connection with the organization's mission, vision and goals.
- Promote connectivity, collaboration and cooperation among the organizations that share and enhance wellbeing in the workplace.
- Hire people with talent congruent with HCM.
- Provide support for employees that are laid off, to expedite the transition for the departing employee, to maintain organizational stability.
- Promote wellbeing in the workplace.

Actions and processes of employees' responsibility include the following:

- Assume responsibility for job requirements that secure knowledge and the conviction to be fulfilled.
- When unsure about actions to follow and move forward, seek advice from organizational leaders and colleagues. Don't wait and never waste time seeking improvement.
- Make sure personal resilience skills match those of the organization or seek help to synchronize them.
- Apply empowering strategies to colleagues, clients and customers for respectful interaction and trusting relationships.
- Assume personal responsibility that life and work are a continuum in the same life experience, not separate, discrete and conflicting life dimensions.
- Strive for smooth integration between work responsibilities, life tasks and leisure as critical elements of holistic personal wellbeing (Lepeley, 2021a).

The LWC and wellbeing for sustainability

LWC was developed by HCM scholars as an analytical framework to monitor life and work as integral dimensions of the holistic life experience of working people (Beutell, Kuschel, & Lepeley, 2021). Rather than separate and disconnected domains, LWC helps to assess the effectiveness and continuous improvement of wellbeing that affects life, work and people's ability to engage in work so that organizations optimize their talents as a necessary condition to achieve high performance leading to long-term sustainability.

Talented people use Soft Skills effectively to assess their impact during disruptions and crises inside and outside the workplace. This is the new imperative for organizational cultures as the pandemic has reinforced the deep connections between personal wellbeing, life, family and work. The LWC is a concept, aligned with HCM, that shows that people's lives are not dualistic with a clear separation between family and work, but instead recognizes a highly integrated and holistic approach to life. In this environment, Soft Skills play an important role in helping people understand the inevitable connection of their lives with a greater awareness of personal needs in life and at work, in sync with the needs of other people within an expanded social context.

Recent trends, consistent with HCM, demonstrate the importance of a successful LWC transformation by implementing new ways of working during crises. There is considerable evidence that few organizations have implemented organizational requirements in a way that closely matches employee needs. In large part, this is due to ignoring and overlooking the complex connectivity that exists between personal life and work responsibilities contained of individuals. This is an essential focus as companies and their employees negotiate new expectations. During the pandemic, when all but the "essential workers" reported to the workplace on site, most employees began working from home. The new work environment underwent radical changes, increasing health risks and safety concerns. In this new and challenging environment, the role of Soft Skills in remote and hybrid forms of work must be expanded.

Relating to the "Great Resignation", discussed above, LWC argues that employees largely decide to resign from jobs because their work responsibilities interfere with their personal life and family priorities, confident that they will get a better job, viewing life and work as a continuum, rather than as opposing dimensions or parts in one person's life, as is traditionally considered in organizations where management focuses on resources at the expense of people's needs. LWC is a consideration in layoff decisions. The emphasis companies place on "workism" and the belief that working more hours automatically leads to higher productivity is an illusion that has been perpetuated but is unfounded.

Consider the following quote from Huffington and Fisher (2022):

> *But it's not flexibility for its own sake—behind the desire for flexibility is a desire to recalibrate our relationship between our lives and our work. That's what's at the heart of the Great Reevaluation. People want their lives to come first.*

The multidimensional disruptions caused by the confluence of recent crises require people and organizations to reassess their life expectations, rethink organizational structures and workplaces, and create new strategies to manage the future. Solutions are unlikely to come from traditional resource-based approaches of the industrial past, but rather from human centered organizational strategies that will shape resilience strength in emerging sustainable organizational cultures.

Concluding comments

The disruptive effects of the Covid pandemic have exposed subcutaneous shortcomings of management models that focus on prioritizing resources over the wellbeing of people by exposing the exponential challenges facing organizations in the global VUCA environment. The "Bathtub" model shows how time influences crisis responses in mobilizing individuals, teams and organizations. Unprecedented phenomena such as the Great Resignation confirm that large numbers of workers worldwide are dissatisfied with the work they perform daily. Employees are searching for workplaces where people's wellbeing is reflected not only in policies but also in actions. Despite growing evidence of the need for change, the transition to the human centered paradigm is slow and increasingly challenged by new crises.

Disruptions provide compelling evidence of the importance of paying attention to the development of resilience in people and organizations. This focus strengthens and continuously improves the LWC approach and empowerment strategies as essential components of effective human centered TM needed for achieving and maintaining sustainability in organizations. In HCM, TM is essential for the accumulation of human capital because the growth of individual and collective talent depends on effective organizational structures and strategies in a stimulating human centered environment for overcoming the long-term effects of ongoing crises. HCM is needed for ensuring organizational sustainability.

Note

1 The five pillars aimed at developing essential elements of Human Centered Management are (1) Human Capital; (2) Disruption Resilience; (3) Talent Management; (4) Agility and (5) Sustainable Quality Model.

References

Beutell, N.J., Kuschel, K., & Lepeley, M.T. (2021). Life–work continuum: The new organizational culture. In Lepeley, M.T., Morales, O., Essens, P., Beutell, N.J., & Majluf, N. (Eds.), *Human centered organizational culture: Global dimensions* (pp. 23–33). Routledge.

Beutell, N.J., & Schneer, J.A. (2014). Job and life attitudes of managers and professionals. *Journal of Psychological Issues in Organizational Culture*, 4(4), 18–32. 10.1002/jpoc.21123

Goodwin, G. F., Essens, P. J. M. D., & Smith, D. (2012). Multiteam systems in the public sector. In S. J. Zaccaro , M. A., Marks, & L. A. DeChurch (Eds.), *Multiteam systems: An organization form for dynamic and complex environments*: 53–78. New York: Routledge.

Huffington, A., & Fisher, J. (2022, January 24). It's time to replace work-life balance with 'life-work integration'. *Fortune*. https://fortune.com/2022/01/24/great-resignation-life-work-integration-thrive-global/

International Organization for Standardization. (2017). Security and resilience — Organizational resilience — Principles and attributes. (standard No. 22316). Retrieved from https://www.iso.org/obp/ui#iso:std:iso:22316:ed-1:v1:en

Lengnick-Hall, C.A., Beck, T.E., & Lengnick-Hall, M.L. (2011). Developing a capacity for organizational resilience through strategic human resource management. *Human Resource Management Review*, 21(3), 243–255. 10.1016/j.hrmr.2010.07.001

Lepeley, M.T. (2021a). Soft skills. The lingua franca of human centered management in the global VUCA environment. In Lepeley, M.T., Beutell, N.J., Abarca, N., & Majful, N. (Eds.). *Soft skills for human centered management and global sustainability* (pp. 3–22). Routledge.

Lepeley, M.T. (2021b). Master soft skills: The resilience – agility umbrella model. In Lepeley, M.T., Beutell, N. J., Abarca, N., & Majful, N. (Eds.). *Soft skills for human centered management and global sustainability* (pp. 23–37). Routledge.

Lepeley, M.T., Beutell, N.J., Abarca, N., & Majful, N. (Eds.). (2021). *Soft skills for human centered management and global sustainability*. Routledge.

Lepeley, M.T. (2017). *Human centered management: Five pillars of organization quality and global sustainability*. Routledge.

Ochoa, P., Lepeley, M.T., & Essens, P. (Eds.). (2019). *Wellbeing for sustainability in the global workforce*. Routledge.

OECD (2020, April 28). *A systemic resilience approach to dealing with Covid-19 and future shocks*. https://www.oecd.org/coronavirus/policy-responses/a-systemic-resilience-approach-to-dealing-with-Covid-19-and-future-shocks

Okuyama, Y. (2010). Globalization and localization of disaster impacts: An empirical examination. In *CESifo Forum* (11) 2, 56–66. München: ifo Institut für Wirtschaftsforschung an der Universität München.

Paauwe, J. (2007). *HRM and Performance: In search of balance*. Tilburg University.

Perkins, D.D., & Zimmerman, M.A. (1995). Empowerment theory, research, and application. *American Journal of Community Psychology*, 23(5), 569–579. 10.1007/bf02506982

Samuel, A. (2016, February 5). The soft skills of great digital organizations. *Harvard Business Review*. https://hbr.org/2016/02/the-soft-skills-of-great-digital-organizations

Tanzi, A. (2022, July 12). *Millions of Americans regret the great resignation. Bloomberg*. https://www.bloomberg.com/news/articles/2022-07-12/millions-of-americans-regret-quitting-in-the-great-resignation

UNDRR (2020). *The human cost of disasters: an overview of the last 20 years (2000-2019)*. https://www.undrr.org/publication/human-cost-disasters-overview-last-20-years-2000-2019

Vargo, J., Sullivan, J., & Parsons, D. (2013). *Benchmarking resilience: Organisational resilience in the Australian water industry*. University of Canterbury. Department of Accounting and Information Systems https://ir.canterbury.ac.nz/handle/10092/11238

Weick, K.E. (1993). The collapse of sensemaking in organizations: The Mann Gulch disaster. *Administrative Science Quarterly*, 38(4), 628–652. 10.2307/2393339

Part 2

HCM and Crisis: Workplace Disruptions and Solutions

6 The Great Resignation in South Africa

Linda Ronnie

Introduction

This chapter examines the phenomenon known as the Great Resignation (GR). It explores the origin, causes and consequences of the GR as part of the global crisis affecting organizations at micro and meso levels, particularly the effects impacting employer–employee relations related to organizational performance and sustainability. The GR is identified as a disruption derived from the Covid-19 pandemic and the socio-economic crisis impacting organizations globally. South Africa was no exception. South African organizations were caught unaware by the effects of the pandemic disruptions, moving from traditional organizational structures and practices to extensive use of technology compelled through lockdowns and employees switching to online work (Bussin & Swart-Opperman, 2021). Organizations had to reconsider sustainability under these new conditions making difficult decisions in a changing and highly volatile environment driven by ongoing crises.

The GR is a term coined by US professor Anthony Klotz (Cohen, 2021), referring to one of the multiple consequences of the crisis affecting organizations worldwide. Although GR was led by voluntary employee turnover, it became a challenge for organizations unaware of the causes and unable to understand the phenomenon. GR is also known as the Big Quit (Curtis, 2021) and the Great Attrition (de Smet et al., 2021), descriptions intended to represent large numbers of employees leaving their organizations voluntarily in the middle of the pandemic. This chapter looks at the phenomenon globally and explores consequences in the South African context. It examines events that triggered the massive employee exodus and suggests proposals to mitigate its effects drawing on Human Centered Management (HCM) principles and practices.

The global GR

Since 2019, when the Covid-19 pandemic started, organizations across sectors worldwide began experiencing an unusual exodus of employees exiting their jobs by their own accord. Some authors argue that more than a

DOI: 10.4324/9781003330011-8

GR, it is a Great Reshuffle (Birinci & Amburgey, 2022), implying that individuals are searching for the best employment available and taking advantage of increased opportunities arising as effects of the pandemic were subsiding. Either way, this trend needs to be understood to discover the reasons employees are providing for their exit.

"Push and pull" theory proposes that voluntary turnover happens because of a) the desire to exit (the "push" factor/s) typically as a result of job dissatisfaction and/or b) being drawn to other organizations (the "pull" factor/s) where potential employment alternatives are more attractive in terms of benefits and opportunities (MacGregor & Wood, 2009). Push factors typically drive employees away from the organization, while pull factors draw employees towards other organizations.

GR research has been conducted in the medical field related to trends induced by work stress, burnout, depression and anxiety as major psychological factors (Ksinan, 2022; Linzer, Griffiths, & Feldman, 2022). Across job categories, reasons for employee exit include "pull" factors such as increasing workplace flexibility (Curtis, 2021), increased remuneration, job security and remote work alternatives (Foster, 2021). Across countries, a McKinsey study (De Smet et al., 2021) found that many employees experienced a series of "push out" factors including a lack of being valued by the organizations or managers or did not experience a sense of belonging at work. Alarmingly, the same study noted that more than a third of employees were intending to leave their jobs without having alternative employment, signaling a sense of discord with their work. More recent research highlights that the GR is part of a wider phenomenon – which the authors ascribe to the modern alienation of work (Kuzior, Kettler, & Rąb, 2022) – resulting in employees leaving their jobs for ethical, cultural, relations and personal factors.

The GR in South Africa

In South Africa, the forced Covid-19 pandemic lockdowns lead to a recession that, coupled with health concerns, drastically increased economic uncertainty. Working South Africans also experienced uncertainty whether to remain in their organizations or seek opportunities elsewhere. Facing 35 percent unemployment, it would appear unlikely that South Africa would participate in the GR phenomenon, but the country is showing a variant of the phenomenon that prevailed in the United States and the United Kingdom.

A Salary and Wage Survey conducted in South Africa found that, in 2022, resignations in organizations are at the highest level of all termination categories in the last decade (Richter, 2022). Among the main reasons respondents cited: 53 percent seek better working environments, improved career opportunities and avoid a toxic environment (bullying, harassment, burnout and stress), 20 percent left seeking better work-life balance, 19 percent seeking better pay and 8 percent cited emigration.

The sectors most affected were people management personnel, Sales and Marketing, Information Technology, the academic sector and Financial Services.

Results from a follow-up survey showed that respondents expressed an explicit wish for work-life balance and telework. The majority (70 percent of the respondents) were teleworking with hybrid alternatives, with 35 percent reporting unhappiness being physically back at their workplaces while 28 percent of employees resisted such a move (Richter, 2022). Employee prerequisites for remaining with their employer included an enabling organizational culture, trust, better communication and empowerment.

It appears that South African employees, or rather those in professional and senior management categories, are not concerned about the consequences of organizational exit, especially if their skills are highly sought after. When organizations fail to address the root causes of the turnover, institutional knowledge is lost and problem-solving solutions are depleted. Some problems in particular present more potential to damage organizations with negative impacts also affecting a country's economy: disruptions affecting business succession planning, factors hindering business processes and efficiency, depletion of relational capital and difficulty with attracting suitable staff – all of them harming national human capital (Serenko, 2022). How organizations and their employees address the underlying reasons causing the GR and understand its consequences is therefore critical.

HCM: Solutions for organizations in transition

A discussion with HCM scholars confirms that, based on its fundamental principles and practices, employees choose to leave their job when the organization fails to meet their needs and the workplace overlooks concerns for employee wellbeing.

HCM represents a paradigm shift away from the traditional resource focus to putting people at the center of organizations (Lepeley, 2017). The HCM framework is built on 5 pillars:

1. Human capital
2. Disruption resilience
3. Talent management (TM)
4. Agility
5. Sustainable Quality Management (SQM).

Human capital refers to development of people's attributes, knowledge, education and skills (hard and Soft Skills) (Lepeley et al., 2021a) driving collaboration and coordination with colleagues and leaders at work. *Disruption resilience* focuses on capacity to forecast and external disruptions that affect organizations to advance solutions. *TM* pursues optimal use of people's creativity and innovation required for organizations to move forward. *Agility* refers to the capacity to design effective strategies to advance. *SQM* is the methodology necessary to attain continuous improvement and quality standards essential for organizations to secure sustainability in the VUCA (volatile, uncertain, complex, ambiguous) environment. SQM, a critical component of HCM, includes 3 areas directly related to responsibility and wellbeing of people in organizations, namely customers, employees and leadership. HCM provides a holistic framework to assess the causes and effects of disruptions to find realistic solutions for the workplace. Crises are not unusual for organizations but current global disruptions that started with the pandemic are exacerbated by ongoing crises with consequences paralleled to those after World War II.

The following sections discuss selected dimensions of the HCM model that facilitate understanding of the GR problem and potential solutions.

Organizational resilience

Resilience is not a natural organizational attribute; it is a condition organizations develop overtime to effectively manage disruptions and bounce back from difficult events. Organizations become resilient when their employees are resilient. Considering that it is people who inject resilience in organizational culture – because organizations are inert objects that become alive only with people's actions and interactions (Lepeley, 2017) – resilient talented employees are central to the development of organizational resilience. In return, an organizational culture encourages attraction and retention of talented resilient individuals. A common denominator of organizations most affected during the GR is lack of resilience.

Personal fragility and organizational vulnerability constitute strong forces obstructing organizational efforts to increase performance, productivity, competitiveness and sustainability. Crises offer opportunities to start anew, creating opportunities for organizational renewal. Resilience is then the capacity to advance reconstruction and innovation including organizational values, practices and behaviors (Hamel & Välikangas, 2003).

Life–Work Continuum

The GR has exposed employees growing dissatisfaction with work schedules inconsistent and incompatible with personal life responsibilities. While Fetherston et al. (2020) refer to this as "work-life merge", Beutell, Kuschel and Lepeley (2021), in high alignment with HCM principles and practice, identify the Life–Work Continuum (LWC). This discussion is extremely relevant to the consequences of lockdowns imposed in South Africa and worldwide, where home spaces had to merge with workspace when employees became home bound and worked remotely. Under lockdown conditions, childcare and home assistance were limited and, in line with Crook (2020), school closures and the unavailability of childcare services increased employees' workload in South Africa. Beutell, Kuschel, & Lepeley (2021) explain that the new routine of life that started during the pandemic boosted the life component of the LWC that is frequently in contrast and conflict with the work dimensions.

Talent management

TM is curtailed by insufficient knowledge of the organization's human capital and its potential and problems of internal practice inconsistencies. In the absence of consistent processes and strategies, employees are forced to rely on resource availability. The GR exposes the need for an inclusive TM approach as a necessary condition to optimize TM in organizations. This would ensure useful and meaningful employee contribution to the organization boosting employment and the labor force (Anlesinya & Amponsah-Tawiah, 2020). TM can only be optimized with the talent of people. A recent South African survey showed that recruitment costs are $US 18,000 per South African organization (Richter, 2022). Therefore, it is critical that TM strategies are optimized to avoid damaging financial outcomes that threaten people's wellbeing and organizational sustainability.

Wellbeing

Lepeley (2021) presents a wellbeing model integrating 7 complementary life dimensions, namely: life purpose, freedom and autonomy, physical fitness and good health, love and affection and contribution to society. Wellbeing is reached when a person works continuously to improve each dimension harmonizing complement. This discussion uses 3 of the 7 complementary life dimensions – life purpose, freedom and autonomy and financial security – to analyze the GR trends in South Africa to better understand reasons for employee exit. Trends show that employees mainly mention lack of life purpose, often conflicting with organizational purpose and mission. More specifically, employees either are unclear about the concepts of freedom and autonomy or feel it is undermined when they experience lack of support and empathy and perceive they are inadequately remunerated. The importance of personal wellbeing is drastically impaired with pandemic disruptions hampering employees' ability to plan beyond the immediate term (Islam et al., 2020; Settersten et al., 2020).

Practical implications for organizations to manage the GR trend

The discussion has implications for organizations in South Africa and more broadly, beyond dealing with challenges of the GR. To ensure organizational stainability, practical strategies to address gaps in organizational approaches are suggested to advance shifts needed in the short and long terms.

Synchronizing employer and employee wellbeing

The GR has provided evidence that the "one-size-fits-all" approach does not work; especially in the case of employees with skills in high demand in the marketplace. Idiosyncratic deals (i-deals) are a subcategory of psychological contracts in employer–employee relationships. Idiosyncratic employment arrangements refer to distinct terms of employment negotiated between individual employees and management that consider, satisfy and synchronize the needs of both parties (Liao, Wayne, & Rousseau, 2016). Therefore, the outcome of a well-negotiated i-deal is based on the organization attracting and retaining valued employees who, in exchange, get employment that meets well-being needs (Rousseau, Ho, & Greenberg, 2006). I-deals acknowledge and meet individual needs of employees which are pre-requisite for continuous improvement of organizational performance and productivity to attain and deliver quality standards.

Importance of the LWC

The pandemic lockdown gave people a unique opportunity to compare and contrast life and work preferences and responsibilities, which to a large extent ignited the GR. Organizations had advanced in some way to address the work-life balance in pre-pandemic times, but it is argued that institutional structures make it difficult to balance work and life dimensions (Kanter, 2012). Lepeley (2017) recognizes the difficulty, but emphasizes that resource-focused organizations, using obsolete approaches dating from the beginning of the 20th century, are unable to synchronize organizational needs with people's needs. Lepeley advises that it is critical to recognize that the problem is not the organization, but shortcomings and ignorance or negligence to learn about newer strategies and to deploy HCM. Beutell, Kuschel, & Lepeley (2021) caution that organizations that ignore the needs of employees as an integral part of employees' lives and consider them instead as separate components of human wellbeing are encountering surmounting challenges to attain sustainability.

Agility in the workplace

The GR highlighted the interest of employees in increasing autonomy in their jobs. Agility is Pillar 4 of HCM and refers to the autonomy employees are granted when organizations trust their knowledge, talent and skills and let them assume personal responsibility for excellent outcomes (Lepeley, 2017; Lepeley, 2021a, b). Agile organizations work to achieve trust as the condition for autonomy that benefits workers of all ages, including young people with multiple interests, older workers, parents and caregivers, people with disabilities and those with current or long-term health conditions (Davies, 2021). Additional technology and telework support organizational transformation. Studies have found that remote workers are happier and more engaged with the work they do (Rahman & Arif, 2021), have significantly reduced commuting time and travel costs (Aczel et al., 2021) and appreciate how the absence of commuting reduces stress allowing them to enjoy more family and leisure time to recuperate (International Labour Organization, 2020). HCM emphasizes the importance of agility in innovation, increased performance and productivity required for sustainability (Lepeley, 2017). Other studies report that work flexibility opens access to scarce talent (Matli, 2020). Howe, Jachimowicz and Menges (2022) suggest that flexibility impacts employees' non-work-related interests. The authors argue that providing flexibility aligned with social and financial resources encourages employees to undertake out-of-work activities including sport and travel. Work flexibility encourages employee's commitment, creates a more appealing workplace to attract new entrants and offers a healthier environment that boosts wellbeing and promotes retention.

Concluding comments

This chapter discusses the impact of one of the notorious effects of pandemic-induced disruptions, the GR. It presents the case of South Africa. The analysis and recommendations are drawn predominantly from US and European research, but with global relevance for organizations and employees. It is, however, important to consider the importance of contextual realities to design and target solutions adjusted to local conditions. The proposals for improvement are related to the HCM pillars and elements related to its core that provide the background of the analysis and multidimensional strategy.

The rapid movement of skills and knowledge out of organizations is an unprecedented, although not entirely unexpected, crisis and its impact on the labor market is significant. The GR is not unexpected for HCM scholars who emphasize the need to focus on people's wellbeing, their human capital and talent. The main problems are rooted in organizations – anchored in traditional, increasingly ineffective resource-focused management approaches – unable to recognize those shortcomings and unfamiliar with HCM. The present time is a good moment to assess organizational needs and advance the transition of putting people at the center of organizations. In this case, HCM principles and practices are optimal to deploy a people-centered comprehensive organizational culture with practical implications to create sustainable and inclusive organizations that are resilient, agile and innovative and offer employees, customers and broader communities the benefits they are seeking to mitigate the effects of pandemic disruptions.

References

Aczel, B., Kovacs, M., Van Der Lippe, T., & Szaszi, B. (2021). Researchers working from home: Benefits and challenges. *PLoS One*, 16(3). 10.1371/journal.pone.0249127

Anlesinya, A., & Amponsah-Tawiah, K. (2020). Towards a responsible talent management model. *European Journal of Training and Development*, 44(2/3), 279–303. 10.1108/ejtd-07-2019-0114

Beutell, N., Kuschel, K., & Lepeley, M.T. (2021). Life-work continuum. The new organizational culture. In Lepeley, M. T., Morales, O., Essens, P., Beutell, N., & Majluf, N. (Eds.). *Human centered organizational culture: Global dimensions* (pp. 23–33). Routledge.

Birinci, S., & Amburgey, A. (2022). The great resignation vs. the great reallocation: Industry-level evidence. *Economic Synopses. Federal Reserve Bank of St. Louis*, 4, 1–2. 10.20955/es.2022.4

Bussin, M. H. R., & Swart-Opperman, C. (2021). Covid-19: Considering impacts to employees and the workplace. *SA Journal of Human Resource Management*, 19(0), a1384. 10.4102/sajhrm.v19i0.1384

Cohen, A. (2021, May 10). How to quit your job in the great post-pandemic resignation boom. *Bloomberg Businessweek*. https://www.bloomberg.com/news/articles/2021-05-10/quit-your-job-how-to-resign-after-covid-pandemic?leadSource=uverify%20wall

Crook, S. (2020). Parenting during the Covid-19 pandemic of 2020: Academia, labour and care work. *Women's History Review*, 29(7), 1226–1238. 10.1080/09612025.2020.1807690

Curtis, L. (2021, June 30). Why the Big Quit is happening and why every boss should embrace it. *Forbes*. https://www.forbes.com/sites/lisacurtis/2021/06/30/why-the-big-quit-is-happening-and-why-every-boss-should-embrace-it/?sh=ca100c601c32

Davies, G. (2021). *Addressing skills and labour shortages post-Brexit*. Chartered Institute of Personnel and Development. https://www.cipd.co.uk/Images/addressing-skills-labour-shortages-post-brexit_tcm18-102313.pdf

De Smet, A., Dowling, B., Mugayar-Baldocchi, M., & Schaninger, B. (2021, September 8). "Great Attrition" or "Great Attraction"? The choice is yours. *McKinsey Quarterly*. https://www.mckinsey.com/business-functions/people-and-organizational-performance/our-insights/great-attrition-or-great-attraction-the-choice-is-yours

Fetherston, C., Fetherston, A., Batt, S., Sully, M., & Wei, R. (2020). Wellbeing and work-life merge in Australian and UK academics. *Studies in Higher Education*, 46 (12), 2774–2788. 10.1080/03075079.2020.1828326

Foster, S. (2021, August 23). Survey: 55% of Americans expect to search for a new job over the next 12 months. *Bankrate*. https://www.bankrate.com/personal-finance/job-seekers-survey-august-2021/

Hamel, G., & Välikangas, L. (2003). The quest for resilience. *Harvard Business Review*, 81(9), 52–63.

Howe, L.C., Jachimowicz, J.M., & Menges, J.I. (2022, March 30). To retain employees, support their passions outside work. *Harvard Business Review*. https://hbr.org/2022/03/to-retain-employees-support-their-passions-outside-work

International Labour Organization. (2020). Teleworking during the COVID-19 pandemic and beyond: A practical guide. International Labour Organization.

Islam, S.M.D.-U., Bodrud-Doza, M., Khan, R.M., Haque, M.A., & Mamun, M.A. (2020). Exploring Covid-19 stress and its factors in Bangladesh: A perception-based study. *Heliyon*, 6(7), e04399. 10.1016/j.heliyon.2020.e04399

Kanter, R.M. (2012, August 28). The imperfect balance between work and life. Harvard Business Review. https://hbr.org/2012/08/the-imperfect-balance-between.html

Ksinan, J.G. (2022). Impact of Covid-19 pandemic on the workforce: From psychological distress to the Great Resignation. *Journal of Epidemiology and Community Health*, 76(6), 525–526. 10.1136/jech-2022-218826

Kuzior, A., Kettler, K., & Rąb, Ł. (2022). Great Resignation – Ethical, cultural, relational, and personal dimensions of generation Y and Z employees' engagement. *Sustainability*, 14(11), 6764. 10.3390/su14116764

Lepeley, M.T. (2021). Soft skills: The lingua franca of human centered management in the global VUCA environment. In Lepeley, M. T., Beutell, N., Abarca, N., & Majful, N. (Eds.). *Soft skills for human centered management and global sustainability* (pp. 3–22). Routledge.

Lepeley, M.T., Beutell, N.J., Abarca, N., & Majful, N. (Eds.). (2021a). *Soft skills for human centered management and global sustainability*. Routledge.

Lepeley, M.T., Morales, O., Essens, P., Beutell, N.J., & Majluf, N. (Eds.). (2021b). *Human centered organizational culture: Global dimensions*. Routledge.

Lepeley, M.T., Kuschel, K., Beutell, N., Pouw, N., & Eijdenberg, E. (Eds.). (2020). *Wellbeing of women in entrepreneurship: A global perspective. Routledge.*

Lepeley, M.T. (2017). *Human centered management: 5 pillars of organizational quality and global sustainability*. Routledge.

Liao, C., Wayne, S.J., & Rousseau, D.M. (2016). Idiosyncratic deals in contemporary organizations: A qualitative and meta-analytical review. *Journal of Organizational Behavior*, 37(S1), 9–29. 10.1002/job.1959

Linzer, M., Griffiths, E.P., & Feldman, M.D. (2022). Responding to the Great Resignation: Detoxify and rebuild the culture. *Journal of General Internal Medicine*. 10.1007/s11606-022-07703-1

MacGregor, T., & Wood, P. (2009, September/October). How to keep your best people. *Employment Today*, 28–30. https://psytech.com/Content/Media/employment_today_exit_interviewing_sept2009.pdf

Matli, W. (2020). The changing work landscape as a result of the Covid-19 pandemic: Insights from remote workers life situations in South Africa. *International Journal of Sociology and Social Practice*, 40(9/10), 1237–1256. 10.1108/ijssp-08-2020-0386

Rahman, K.T., & Arif, Z.U. (2021). Working from home during the Covid-19 pandemic: Satisfaction, challenges, and productivity of employees. *International Journal of Trade and Commerce*, 9(2), 282–294. 10.46333/ijtc/9/2/3

Richter, R. (2022, June 27). Employers are under pressure as salary increases fall below inflation. *Old Mutual*. https://www.oldmutual.co.za/corporate/resource-hub/all-articles/employers-are-under-pressure-as-salary-increases-fall-below-inflation/

Rousseau, D.M., Ho, V.T., & Greenberg, J. (2006). I-deals: Idiosyncratic terms in employment relationships. *Academy of Management Review*, 31(4), 977–994. 10.5465/amr.2006.22527470

Serenko, A. (2022). The great resignation: The great knowledge exodus or the onset of the great knowledge revolution? *Journal of Knowledge Management*. 10.1108/jkm-12-2021-0920

Settersten Jr., R.A., Bernardi, L., Härkönen, J., Antonucci, T.C., Dykstrae, P.A., Heckhausen, J., Kuhg, D., Mayer, K.U., Moen, P., Mortimer, J.T., Mulder, C.H., Smeeding, T.M., van der Lippe, T., Hagestad, G.O., Kohli, M., Levy, R., Schoon, I., & Thomson, E. (2020). Understanding the effects of Covid-19 through a life course lens. *Advances in Life Course Research*, 45, 100360. 10.1016/j.alcr.2020.100360

7 Emotional Creativity, Resilience and Work Performance

Anielson Barbosa da Silva and José Wilker Macêdo

Introduction

In the last decade, management has been subject to continuous disruptions with significant effects on people's wellbeing and impacting work performance. Emerging disruptions are pressing organizations in all sectors and worldwide, conducting extensive, effective and continuous assessment of current practices with the aim of finding new approaches to improve people's performance in the workplace as an essential condition for organizations to attain long-term sustainability in the global volatile, uncertain, complex, ambiguous (VUCA) environment. The Covid-19 pandemic is one among many world disruptions inflicting emotional reactions in people that affect their work performance and hindering their ability to manage uncertainty induced by ongoing crises.

In the current environment, studies indicate that improving people's emotional creativity (EC) and resilience (R) increases potential to improve performance in the workplace and manage disruptions, optimizing opportunities and minimizing negative effects of disruptions and crisis mobilizing creative strategies to solve problems, adapt to circumstances and recover from difficulties.

Creating learning environments aimed to foster shared experiences and strategies needs to pay more attention to emotional, physical, social and technological dimensions of management in organizations. To stimulate collaboration, trust and teamwork are keys to counterbalance the effects of crises and seeking solutions developing and promoting EC and R.

This chapter analyzes correlations beindustries in Brazil, educatween EC and R and their effects on performance among professionals in 3 industries in Brazil, education, healthcare and technology, during the Covid-19 pandemic to assess preparedness to face crisis and counterbalance disruptions affecting the wellbeing of people in the workplace.

The discussion introduces the concept of EC as a Soft Skill thighly impacting work performance, particularly during times of crisis necessary to secure organizational sustainability. In this context, managing emotions creatively is essential to reduce negative interferences that play a central role

DOI: 10.4324/9781003330011-9

in managing disruptions with agility in the workplace (Lepeley, 2017; Lepeley, 2021a, b).

Lepeley states that resilient people tend to be more optimistic, proactive and easy to adapt to the new circumstances with more agility (Lepeley, 2021a, b). According to Fernández-Díaz et al. (2021), people with high levels of creativity and resilience show a higher-than-normal "innovative spirit" of tenacity and enthusiasm to move on in spite of failures and crisis.

A 2020 Eurofound report (2020) indicates that resilience is a personal trait helping people manage problems caused by the pandemic. Assessment of personal and organizations, resilience in times of crises can help organizations identify actions to assist people to expedite recovery. Lepeley (2017, 2021a, b) argues that building personal resilience helps people to respond better when facing complex and unpredictable disruptions and crises.

Emotional creativity

EC is defined as a set of cognitive abilities and personality traits based on originality to foster emotional experiences. The EC concept was developed by James R. Averil in 1999 along with an inventory called emotional creativity inventory (ECI). ECI includes 30 self-perception items aimed to evaluate the ability to express emotions in ingenious and authentic ways. Studies show that creative and resilient people have a greater capacity to face difficulties and adversities in life (Ochoa & Blanch, 2019) and can adapt faster to changing demands and stressful experiences (Tugade & Fredrickson, 2004). Therefore, understanding links and interactions between EC, R and work performance is an important step to deal with disruptive effects.

People have innate abilities and traits, including interests to explore new experiences, excitement and geniality that contribute to the development of EC. Research shows that emotional experiences and the ability to plan adaptive actions in emotionally complex environments are largely associated with personal levels of EC. This chapter argues that EC is a Soft Skill that can be learned (Averill, 1999).

In this chapter, EC is considered as a Soft Skill that requires ability to reflect on emotional experiences in innovative ways. People develop EC by managing emotions creatively, exploring causes and consequences during processes of decision making, problem solving and setting goals to improve professional practices in different situations and contexts. EC can be learned through reflective processes in specific contexts aiming to enhance well-being as an essential variable needed to improve individual performance (Lepeley, 2017; Lepeley et al., 2021a, b).

In the workplace, EC is strengthened through optimal integration of knowledge and actions, including experiences in life, in the family (Beutell, chapter in this book), in education, organizations, the economy and society. EC is also considered a coping strategy based on self-understanding, intrinsic motivation and increased awareness of professional roles, professional identity, leadership styles and innovative performance (Kuška et al., 2020).

Macêdo (2022) developed an EC scale for the workplace – ECSW in Brazil built on 2 dimensions: *reflecting-on-emotions* (RE) and *acting-on-emotions* (AE).

RE is the ability to assess causes and effects of the emotions during idea generation, decision-making, goal-setting and problem-solving processes in the workplace. AE is the ability to develop creative strategies and put them into action and express positive emotions in different situations and contexts. AE is an adaptive behavior aiming to generate individual and collective benefits.

The relationship between reflection and action is related to Schön (1983) notion of reflective practice of personal emotional experience through reflection on practice immediately following an action or event.

Measuring EC effectiveness as a Soft Skill requires identifying actions in a specific context related to people's life and work. Table 7.1 identifies attributes of EC in the workplace in terms of dimensions and attributes.

For the purpose of this study, EC is a construct aligned with human centered management (HCM) principles and practices aimed to help people using creativity and ingenuity to solve problems, make decisions and focus on professional goals with agility built on the capacity to reflect and act. For Lepeley, agility is a function of imagination, creativity and courage to undertake educated risks to advance from the present condition to a better situation (Lepeley, 2017, 2021a, b). Emotionally creative people are more agile to find solutions during disruptions and crises and experience positive emotions, leading to enhanced wellbeing and improving performance in life and the workplace.

Table 7.1 EC dimensions and attributes in the workplace

Dimension	*Attributes*
Reflections-on-emotion	I analyze the causes and consequences of emotions in decision making. I reflect on the emotions involved in problem solving. I reflect on emotional experience related to current problems. I reflect on emotions related to my professional goals. I reflect on emotions to improve my professional performance.
Action-on-emotion	I develop strategies to avoid harming myself when experiencing intense emotions. I make efforts to creatively express emotions in different situations and contexts. I make efforts to create ways to express my emotions in a positive way.

Note: Adapted from Macêdo (2022).

Resilience

Coutu (2002) posed that resilience is a dynamic capacity of people confronted with life's hardship that can bounce back. Faced with disruptions, like the pandemic followed by economic crises, resilient people bounce back and become stronger, healthier and more successful after living hard experiences.

Fernández-Díaz et al. (2021) associate resilience to positive adaptation to complex circumstances, psychological capacity to recover quickly from difficulties, problems, constraints and unavoidable disruptions with willpower, determination, empowerment and stamina to improve continuously. Resilience integrates complex, dynamic and context-dependent interactions between an individual and their teams in changing environments involving neurobiological and cultural processes, promoting personal thriving and wellbeing (Kaye-Kauderer et al., 2021). Essens, in this book (Chapter 1), discusses the link between resilience and empowerment.

EC, R and performance in the workplace

EC is commonly linked to emotional intelligence (EI) in the workplace, as discussed by Majluf and Abarca (2021) in the *Sensible Leadership* book of the HCM Series. Disruption resilience is 1 of the 5 Pillars of HCM Model (Lepeley, 2017). Lepeley emphasizes that human capital Pillar 1 can be optimized in organizations when people develop capacity to identify external and internal disruption and act with resilience. Lepeley builds up on the importance of resilience in her chapters in the Soft Skills book (2021a, b), where resilience plays a central role as one of the Master Soft Skills shaping the *Resilience – Agility Umbrella* model to strengthen performance in the workplace as a necessary condition for organizations to attain long-term sustainability in the global VUCA environment counterbalancing effects of disruptions and crises.

EC and R can be developed through experiences encompassing cognitive, social and emotional dimensions. Resilience practices presented by Greindl (2014) can boost creativity using relaxation techniques, encouraging collaborative work, building EI in teams and clarify values and purposes of all activities.

Fernández-Díaz et al. (2021) express career success and performance related to individual levels of EC and R. They posed that EC is a personal ability people must continuously stimulate to thrive in life and at work. They found that resilience increases with age and practice, lifelong learning and the diversity of life experiences, rather than exclusively in the workplace.

It is important to note that in the workplace, people focus on work and do not have time to reflect on own or others' emotions with the intent to make decisions and solve problems. This evidence points out the need to plan actions ahead to helping self and other workers is referred as "emotionally intelligent", as indicated by Herland (2021).

The study

The study was intended to advance knowledge about the relationship between EC and R and their effects on performance in 3 industries in Brazil. This empirical study collected a sample of 655 workers in education (N:243), healthcare (N:202) and technology (N:210) in Brazil. The main hypothesis was that EC and R affect individual performance differently in the 3 industries. The study was conducted in 2022 as part of an academic project to develop and validate an EC measure scale in Brazil and analyze the relationship among EC, R, individual performance, wellbeing and emotional exhaustion.

The sample

The average age of the participants was 38 years; 49 percent female and 51 percent male; 46 percent were parents with children; 57 were married or living in a stable relationship with another person; 35 percent were paid low salaries and 65 percent had average salaries. Sixty-eight percent resided in the Northeast region of Brazil. It is important to highlight that gender distribution differs by industry. Eighty percent of the sample in technology industry was men, contrasting with 49 percent in education and 22 percent in healthcare.

Data collection and analysis

Data were collected using a survey of professional workers in the 3 industries mentioned. EC variables were assessed using the ECSW - Emotional Creativity Scale in the Workplace validated by Macêdo (2022). Resilience variables were assessed by the scales of Lopes and Martins (2011). Performance was assessed with the Employee Performance Scale (Rodwell, Kienzle, & Shadur, 1998).

Professional workers from all regions of Brazil were invited to participate using email messages and through LinkedIn. Data analysis tested whether EC and R affect individual performance at work using structural equations analysis. The effect of gender on the variables was also investigated.

Findings and implications

Results presented in Table 7.2 show that professionals in healthcare report higher level of EC while education professionals are more resilient than in the other industries. Performance at work depends on higher levels of EC and R. Comparing the 3 industries, technology workers showed the lowest levels of EC, R and in job performance.

The results show that experiences of healthcare workers, dealing with pain and suffering on a daily basis, are consistent with higher EC and

Table 7.2 EC, R and performance in healthcare, education and technology

Industry	*Emotional creativity*	*Resilience*	*Performance*
Healthcare	Highest level of EC than professionals in other industries.	Perceive themselves as less resilient than education professionals and more resilient than technology professionals.	Higher levels of EC and R correlate with higher work performance.
Education	Higher levels of EC than technology professionals.	Perceive themselves as more resilient than professionals from other industries.	
Technology	Lowest level of EC and R.		Lowest levels of EC and R report lower self-perception of performance.

abilities to find creative solutions leading to actions necessary to improve work performance coinciding with Herland (2021).

In education, resilience drives performance and capacity to bounce back to counterbalance disruptions of the pandemic, pressing professionals to learn fast to adapt and adopt new teaching and learning strategies associated with restrictions in physical distancing and lockdowns imposing intense use of remote and hybrid teaching, consistent with Naidu (2021).

Professionals in the technology industry rated themselves less resilient, less emotionally creative and with lower self-perception of performance. This result seems to suggest that professionals in the technology industry were less affected by pandemic disruptions than professionals in healthcare and education. It may suggest that intensive use of technology and teleworking impacting professionals is a regular activity for tech people but more disruptive among education and health professionals, suggesting the importance of researching the effects of contextual factors on EC, R and performance.

Findings show that resilience affects EC. When workers are resilient, they seem to be more emotionally creative and open to new ideas and strategies to face crises. Workers with EC and R perceive they have better performance.

To face disruptive events, people tend to display EC and R that, as our results show, positively affect work performance in healthcare and education more than in tech industry. Findings suggest that organizations need to encourage employees to invest more in personal efforts improving Soft Skills to improve EC and R, which positively impact wellbeing at work and consequently performance in human led organizations, to a higher extent than in the technology industry.

The study showed no effect of gender on performance and EC, even though women had higher levels of resilience. This may indicate that results for both cohorts are the same on analyzing data by professional cohort. It may also imply that men and women perceive work performance in a similar way and subject to similar evaluation standards. But when the purpose was to evaluate the performance of others, the results of men were evaluated better than those of women. This intriguing result may be explained by patriarchal social culture present in organizations in Brazil.

Concluding comments

The objective of this study was to assess levels of correlations between EC, R and work performance in healthcare, education and the technology industry in Brazil. EC was introduced by the authors as an additional construct complementary to supporting HCM to enhance people's wellbeing in organizations. The study expanded the discussion of resilience, Pillar 2 among the 5 Pillars of HCM associated with EC and performance in the workplace.

Increasing numbers of studies are reporting the importance of effective management of emotions to increase the wellbeing. This study supports the assumption that developing ability to practice and reflect on emotional experiences, and specifically related to human ingenuity and creativity, may improve wellbeing, strengthen decision-making processes resulting in improved personal performance and productivity leading to organizational sustainability. The results confirm that EC has major effect on improving performance in healthcare, where workers deal daily with vulnerable patients in need of special care, and resilience is more prevalent in education.

Results show that resilience is an important Soft Skill to improve work performance among educators, particularly in times of pandemic crisis, leading to benefits associated with the forced, fast and deep transition from face-to-face interactions with students in a classroom to remote and hybrid work using technology and internet communications.

Neither EC nor R has a significant effect on performance in the technological industry. This seems to support that analytical skills, such as rationality and technical knowledge, which are priorities to improve performance in this industry intensely populated by men today, have higher effects on performance than EC or R. Findings are worth receiving attention and further research.

It would be useful to relate this study with another study conducted by Barbosa da Silva included in this book about mindfulness to strengthen implications of developing complementary programs aimed to support students during times of crisis, separating by context and industries in terms of different Soft Skills needed to improve wellbeing and performance in different industries.

References

Averill, J. R. (1999). Individual differences in emotional creativity: Structure and correlates. *Journal of Personality*, 67 (2), 331–371. 10.1111/1467-6494.00058

Beutell, N. J., Kuschel, K., & Lepeley, M. T. (2021a). Life-work continuum: The new organizational culture. In Lepeley, M. T., Morales, O., Essens, P., Beutell, N., & Majluf, N. (Eds.). *Human centered organizational culture: Global dimensions* (pp. 23–33). Routledge.

Beutell, N. J., Kuschel, K., & Lepeley, M. T. (2021b). Learning from failure: Soft skills for sustainability in the VUCA environment. In Lepeley, M. T., Beutell, N., Abarca, N., & Majful, N. (Eds.). *Soft skills for human centered management and global sustainability* (pp. 41–55). Routledge.

Coutu, D. L. (2002). How resilience works. *Harvard Business Review*, 80(5), 46–55. https://hbr.org/2002/05/how-resilience-works

Eurofound (2020, November 6), *Living, working and Covid-19*. Covid-19 series. Publications Office of the European Union, Luxembourg. https://www.eurofound.europa.eu/publications/report/2020/living-working-and-covid-19

Fernández-Díaz, J. R., Gutiérrez-Ortega, M., Llamas-Salguero, F., & Cantón-Mayo, I. (2021). Creativity and resilience as predictors of career success. *Sustainability*, 13(8), 4489. 10.3390/su13084489

Greindl, B. (2014). Creativity and esilience. *The resilience institute, 1-4*. https://resiliencei.com/2014/01/creativity-and-resilience/

Herland, M. D. (2021). Emotional intelligence as a part of critical reflection in social work practice and research. *Qualitative Social Work*, 21(4), 662–678. 10.1177/14733250211024734

Kaye-Kauderer, H., Feingold, J., Feder, A., Southwick, S., & Charney, D. (2021). Resilience in the age of Covid-19. *BJPsych Advances*, 27(3), 166–178. 10.1192/bja.2021.5

Kuška, M., Trnka, R., Mana, J., & Nikolai, T. (2020). Emotional creativity: A meta-analysis and integrative review. *Creativity Research Journal*, 32(2), 151–160. 10.1080/10400419.2020.1751541

Lepeley, M. T. (2021a). Soft Skills: The lingua franca of human centered management in the global VUCA environment. In Lepeley, M. T., Beutell, N. J., Abarca, N., & Majluf, N. (Eds.). *Soft Skills for human centered management and global sustainability* (pp. 3–22). Routledge.

Lepeley, M. T. (2021b). Master soft skills: The resilience – agility umbrella model. In Lepeley, M. T., Beutell, N. J., Abarca, N., & Majful, N. (Eds.). *Soft skills for human centered management and global sustainability* (pp. 23–37). Routledge.

Lepeley, M. T. (2017). *Human centered management: 5 pillars of organizational quality and global sustainability*. Routledge.

Lopes, V. R., & Martins, M. D. C. F. (2011). Factorial validation of the Connor-Davidson resilience scale (Cd-Risc-10) for Brazilians (Original title: Validação fatorial da escala de resiliência de Connor-Davidson (Cd-Risc-10) para brasileiros). *Revista Psicologia: Organizações e Trabalho*, 11(2), 36–50.

Macêdo, J. W. L. (2022). Emotional creativity at work: Contributions for well-being (Original title: Criatividade emocional no trabalho: contribuições para o bem-estar) [Doctoral dissertation, University Federal of Paraíba].

McGill, I., & Brockbank, A. (2004). *The action learning handbook*. Routledge.

Majluf, N., & Abarca, N. (2021). *Sensible leadership: Human centered, insightful and prudent*. Routledge.

Naidu, S. (2021). Building resilience in education systems post-Covid-19. *Distance Education*, 42(1), 1–4. 10.1080/01587919.2021.1885092

Ochoa, P., & Blanch, J. M. (2019). Psychosocial wellbeing at work: Reasons to invest in healthy employees and workplaces. In Ochoa, P., Lepeley, M. T., & Essens, P. (Eds.). *Wellbeing for sustainability in the global workplace* (pp. 3–14). Routledge.

Rodwell, J. J., Kienzle, R., & Shadur, M. A. (1998). The relationship among work-related perceptions, employee attitudes, and employee performance: The integral role of communications. *Human Resource Management*, 37(3-4), 277–293. 10.1002/(SICI)1099-050X(199823/24)37:3/4<277::AID-HRM9>3.0.CO;2-E

Schön, D. A. (1983). *The reflective practitioner: How professionals think in action*. Basic Books.

Tugade, M. M., & Fredrickson, B. L. (2004). Resilient individuals use positive emotions to bounce back from negative emotional experiences. *Journal of Personality and Social Psychology*, 86(2), 320–333. 10.1037/0022-3514.86.2.320

8 Psychosocial Dimensions of Telework Overload during the Covid-19 Pandemic

Paola Ochoa, David Coello-Montecel, and Josep M. Blanch

Introduction

The consequences of surmounting disruptions the Covid pandemic imposed on people in general and the workplace in particular are still led by uncertainty and unknowns. The consequences for work appear increasingly complex, diverse and to large extent daunting. In the still volatile and uncertain global environment, a most significant change organizations are detecting is rapid and broad base adoption of telework with intensive use of digital technologies.

The Covid pandemic pressed for transformations in multiple dimensions of life, including health, social interactions and traditional work patterns. In the workplace, changes have been deep and significant. Not only in physical environment where workers carry out their activities, but also how people relate to each other and to other members of the organization as well as channels they use to communicate. These are pressing factors that obstruct clear understanding of pandemic disruptions and their impact re-configuring working conditions. Rapid change has revealed emergence of psychosocial risks that need to be addressed to find solutions effective to counterbalance negative effects to strengthen the wellbeing of people in the workplace (Lepeley, 2017, 2021a, 2021b) and impacts on their families and communities (Ochoa & Blanch, 2019).

Telework: evolution or revolution?

In March 2020, OECD reported that in the United Kingdom and Australia about 47% of employees were teleworking. In Japan, a country that did not impose nationwide lockdowns, the percentage was 28%. The same report indicates that the percentage of remote workers was higher in large firms and this work arrangement was more common among individuals with higher qualifications (OECD, 2021). In Latin America, the International Labor Organization (ILO) reported that during the second 2020 quarter, approximately 23 million employees were teleworking, representing between 20 and 30% of the working population. A breakdown by country

DOI: 10.4324/9781003330011-10

shows teleworking rate was higher in Argentina (22%), Costa Rica (20%) and Chile (19%). They contrasted with lower rates in Brazil and Ecuador at 11% (ILO, 2020a). Before the Covid-19 pandemic, teleworking percentages in Latin American countries averaged 3% (ILO, 2021).

Consistent with exponential growth in teleworking, this chapter identifies and analyzes characteristics, causes and effects of telework overload, online fatigue and permanent online connectivity. The discussion offers suggestions to minimize psychosocial risks associated with these health conditions. The first section presents the theoretical framework of the three key concepts, followed by comprehensive discussion relating to new psychosocial risks identified and the closing comments offer suggestions to help professionals and organizations solve pending challenges.

Telework and new psychosocial risks factors

Telework overload

Telework has numerous definitions (e.g., ILO, 2020b; Brunelle & Fortin, 2021; Kumar et al., 2021). However, the most consistent with this study is one proposed by Bailey and Kurland (2002). They state that telework involves using computer technology to work from home or another place outside the traditional workplace during part of the week.

Telework became the most popular work arrangement from the beginning of the pandemic. It was one of the very limited options to guarantee continuity of operations in rapid response to confinement restrictions forcing distance work from the traditional workplace. Nevertheless, pandemic challenges prolonged and telework continued as the preferred option in many organizations. Telework dilemmas emerged related to occupational health (Felstead & Henseke, 2017; Palumbo, 2020). The issue became stronger when conditions of coexistence to work at home pressed people to share space in a nonvoluntary way to follow confinement biosafety protocols. Increasing demands and conflicts added to original demands of families with children.

Work overload is the perception of having too much work to do in limited time (Leiter & Schaufeli, 1996; Schaufeli & Van Dierendonck, 1993). Work overload emerged and increased as one of the consequences of the loss of limits between two vital workers' spheres, family and work, in the teleworking context.

Research documents consequences of telework overload associated with increasing work–life and family–work conflicts impacting workers' wellbeing during the pandemic (Barriga et al., 2021; Soubelet-Fagoaga et al., 2022). Negative consequences of telework overload result from role conflict, frustration because of not meeting duties in either dimension, and working unlimited numbers of hours beyond regular office schedules. Negative consequences grew with health concerns increasing signs of sadness, sickness or loss of loved ones and significant uncertainty about the future exacerbated by the pandemic but extended by ongoing global crises.

In spite of negative telework outcomes, studies identify telework advantages that improve the Life–Work Continuum (Beutell, Kuschel, & Lepeley, 2021). Among them are flexibility, increased autonomy, less commuting, saving energy resources (Karia & Asaari, 2016), socioeconomic benefits (savings) and increased family contact. To large extent telework is a valuable tool for conciliation between life and work balance, increasing voluntarism and more effective negotiations leading to agreements between workers and employers.

Online fatigue

During Covid 2020 confinement, videoconference apps were the main tools for telework. Between December 2019 and April 2020, Zoom reported an exponential increase in number of video calls, from 10 million to 300 million daily (Chawla, 2020). The pandemic-induced boom of videoconferencing was essential to work from home. However, it came with relevant issues and one of the most frequently reported was videoconference fatigue or Zoom fatigue, as it is commonly referred to in the literature. This type of fatigue cannot be understood only as exhaustion or tiredness from staring at a screen. Research findings show that this type of fatigue is caused by increased complexity of interpersonal interactions demanding extraordinary cognitive efforts (Nadler, 2020).

The pandemic imposed volumes of changes in many aspects of life. Digital technologies led the change as a main resource facilitating the transition. Video conferencing and social media have become part of daily life with intense use of Internet and digital technologies. The phenomenon gave rise to the pandemic-related fatigue, referred to as *online fatigue* (Bonanomi et al., 2021) and *digital fatigue* (Alvizou, 2020). Both relate to adverse effects of continuous use of digital technologies and Internet. In a broader sense, this fatigue is associated with feelings of overwhelm or overload spending excessive time online, looking at a screen and being connected online (Alvizou, 2020).

Permanent online connectivity

The *permanently online, permanently connected* adage gained relevance addressing psychosocial risks dimension of teleworking during the pandemic. Vorderer, Krömer and Schneider (2016) defined it as a behavior of continuous use of electronic media and a psychological state of permanent communicative vigilance. Extending this definition to an organizational context, Büchler, ter Hoeven and van Zoonen (2020) defined constant connection as the workers' continuous availability or 24/7 connected to the organization using work-related communication media during work time but also while out of work schedules.

Permanent connectivity is a "*double-edged sword*" given the ambivalent impact of digital technologies on workers' performance and wellbeing. The literature identifies 4 paradoxes related to job autonomy (Mazmanian, Orlikowski, & Yates, 2013), job satisfaction (Waizenegger, 2015), productivity and social interactions (Day, Barber, & Tonet, 2019). On the one hand digital technologies enhance feelings of autonomy and flexibility to decide when or where to work, improve communication and collaboration with coworkers and reduce the sense of isolation. On the other hand, the use of technology intensifies connectivity with potential to expose workers to a higher level of perceived obligation to respond, information overload and blurring the boundaries between work and personal life.

These paradoxes apply mostly to workers who must adopt telework as primary work arrangement and highlight the psychosocial risks associated with intense online connectivity (Büchler et al., 2020; Deloitte, 2021). Working from home allowed flexibility to organize the working day, time distribution with other responsibilities, including child care and children attending online classes, health care of relatives or dealing with routinely household responsibilities but commonly work extended beyond regular hours. This made workers feel permanently connected to work. And the overload contributed to perceptions of dissatisfaction, frustration and stress.

Digital technologies that allowed workers access to permanent connectivity with family, coworkers and friends prompt them to excessive consumption of information that included viral infections, deaths, crisis of healthcare systems and economic crisis caused by lockdowns. Adverse effects led to difficulty or reduced sleep time, difficulty focusing during workdays or relaxing during weekends, resulting in isolation, loneliness, fears and anxiety. In general, permanent connectivity became a warning sign of psychosocial risks. In order to face challenges, solutions need to advance in the Life–Work Continuum improving integration of work and family (Beutell et al., 2021) and workers' psychosocial wellbeing (Ochoa & Blanch, 2019).

Disruptions in telework

New psychosocial risks discovered during the pandemic and evolving social interactions imposed by confinements added to a precarious economy and changes in working conditions and organizational priorities were underlined by unprecedented global uncertainty of the lethal virus.

The concepts telework, teleworking overload, online fatigue and permanent online connectivity are related, but there are distinctions that require special attention. Teleworking overload and permanent online connectivity are considered psychosocial risks. However, online fatigue, tiredness and worries related to work activities, including video calls, are effects and outcomes of psychosocial risks. The similarity between actual risks and effects is that both take place using digital technologies and tools.

Both were magnified and got greater visibility during the pandemic. Effects go beyond what is commonly known as *technostress*, which refers from the stress workers experience because of constant connectivity, information overload and problems associated with the use of multiple types of technologies (Tarafdar, Cooper, & Stich, 2019; Scaramuzzino & Martinell Barfoed, 2021).

The pandemic affected people in general and particularly workers imposing social, health and technological disruptions that exposed new digital psychosocial risks with potential for developing other consequences. The psychological implications and consequences of telework overload and permanent online connectivity are presented in Table 8.1.

Psychosocial risks in management and the workplace

Large amounts of unprecedented disruptions affecting the workplace during the pandemic pressed need to reassess effectiveness of management models to evaluate effects on wellbeing given growing evidence of limitations of the traditional resource – focused management to solve work-related problems in a rapidly changing workplace transitioning from physical buildings to online distance telework.

In this turbulent context, Human Centered Management (HCM) (Lepeley, 2017; Lepeley et al., 2021a, 2021b; Ochoa et al., 2019), centered on people's wellbeing, provided the highest convergence with psychosocial analysis. In particular Agility, Pillar 4 in HCM, expedited support for organizations and professionals seeking systematic assessment and improvement of the emerging work environment compared with presenteeism, given high

Table 8.1 New psychosocial risks resulting from the pandemic disruptions

Phenomenon	*Psychological implications*	*Effects on work and family*
Teleworking overload	• Perception of accumulated telework • Feeling of never-ending pending telework tasks	• Role conflict • Work-family conflict • Fears of deficiencies in digital competencies • Exhaustion/Burnout • Low productivity • Online fatigue
Permanent online connectivity	• Permanent digital connection.	• Difficulty to disconnect work and family environment • Tiredness and fatigue • Disconnection with reality • Online fatigue • Reality evasion • Low productivity

alignment and complementarity with the Life–Work Continuum that has important effects on wellbeing (Beutell et al., 2021) to attain long-term sustainability.

Sustainability is a critical issue. According to Lepeley (2017), long-term organizational sustainability is secured when organizations work to achieve the wellbeing of people in the workplace and effectively deploy Quality Management as a necessary condition to continuously improve performance and productivity driving sustainability. Khan, Ahmad and Majava (2021) refer to sustainability as the triple bottom line (TBL). According to Giovannoni and Fabietti (2013), sustainability can be defined as the capability of an organization to last in time, in terms of profitability, financial performance, productivity aligned with social and environmental dimensions impacting its capital.

HCM scholars emphasize the need for human wellbeing and deployment of quality standards are sine qua non conditions for organizational sustainability. To secure human wellbeing in the workplace, however, it is necessary to continuously assess and compare effectiveness of different management approaches. And adopt those that put the wellbeing of people at the center of organizations (Lepeley, 2017; Ochoa, Lepeley, & Essens, 2019; Lepeley et al., 2021a, 2021b).

The following are suggestions to support improvement in the workplace aiming to diminish causes and effects of psychosocial risks on wellbeing based on the experience and research of the authors of this chapter:

1 Organizations need to continuously assess levels of wellbeing in the workplace aiming to diminish or eliminating negative effects of ongoing pandemic disruptions, with special attention on the transition from face-to-face work to telework and hybrid options. Organizational policies need closer alignment with principles of healthy work, quality of life and resilient and agile work models (HCM Pillars 2 and 4) and continuous assessment and improvement (Pillar 5) of wellbeing in the workplace (Ochoa et al., 2019; Lepeley, 2017, ILO, 2022).
2 Deployment of organizational policies that encourage technology disconnection as strategies to prevent psychosocial risks, stress and permanent online connectivity. Organizations need to create spaces not mediated by technology to allow rest and promote family–work balance. The cases of countries, such as Canada and Belgium with a framework for disconnection may serve as examples for Latin American countries (CBC, 2021). The European Parliament adopted a resolution on workers' right to digital disconnection and encouraged the European Commission to address it legislatively (Cremades, 2021).
3 Promotion of metrics and indicators to establish baseline on emerging risks related to connection–disconnection monitoring indicators of quality of life, occupational health, healthy and unhealthy habits and diseases due to incorrect use of technology.

4 Incentive design and application of resilient structures and agile strategies to face disruptions and crises, including systematic monitoring and correction of excessive workloads, psychosocial risks, connectivity measures, social interaction and adjustment to Life–Work Continuum.
5 Implementation of telework model that extends beyond organizations to a broader social context. The pandemic highlighted the importance of social and public policies' connection achievement of common goals. Organizations have a responsibility to monitor and meet needs and demands that emerge in the community where customers and users come from, considering responses to people's needs with innovative solutions for psychosocial problems.

Concluding discussion

This chapter provided insights needed to identify special features and differences between telework overload, online fatigue and permanent online connectivity negatively impacting psychosocial risks, harming most dimensions of life wellbeing. Solutions are pressing because these problems were exacerbated by unprecedented disruptions of the Covid pandemic and ongoing economic crisis affecting humanity at global level.

The discussion was aimed at providing support to organizational leaders to advance implementation of HCM structures and strategies to minimize negatives effects of pandemic disruptions to secure wellbeing of people, in high contingency with quality standards in the workplace required for sustainability aligned with Life–Work Continuum. If there is one positive thing of the pandemic, it is that pandemic has pressed organizations to improve, becoming resilient and agile in order to survive learning from failures during the disruptions, encouraging to create, redesign and enhance workers' health and quality of life.

References

Alevizou, G. (2020). Virtual schooling, Covid-gogy and digital fatigue April 8. *Blog of the London School of Economics*. https://blogs.lse.ac.uk/parenting4digitalfuture/2020/04/08/virtual-schooling-Covid-gogy/

Bailey, D. E., & Kurland, N. B. (2002). A review of telework research: Findings, new directions, and lessons for the study of modern work. *Journal of Organizational Behavior*, 23(4), 383–400. 10.1002/job.144

Barriga Medina, H. R., Campoverde Aguirre, R., Coello-Montecel, D., Ochoa Pacheco, P., & Paredes-Aguirre, M. I. (2021). The influence of work–family conflict on burnout during the Covid-19 pandemic: the effect of teleworking overload. *International Journal of Environmental Research and Public Health*, 18(19), 10302. 10.3390/ijerph181910302

Beutell, N. J., Kuschel, K., & Lepeley, M. T. (2021). Life–work continuum: The new organizational culture. In Lepeley, M. T., Morales, O., Essens, P., Beutell, N. J. & Majluf, N. (Eds.). *Human centered organizational culture: Global dimensions* (pp. 23–33). Routledge.

Bonanomi, A., Facchin, F., Barello, S., & Villani, D. (2021). Prevalence and health correlates of online fatigue: A cross-sectional study on the Italian academic community during the Covid-19 pandemic. *PloS ONE*, 16(10), e0255181. 10.1371/journal.pone.0255181

Brunelle, E., & Fortin, J. A. (2021). Distance makes the heart grow fonder: An examination of teleworkers' and office workers' job satisfaction through the lens of self-determination theory. *SAGE Open*, 11(1), 1–11. 10.1177/2158244020985516

Büchler, N., ter Hoeven, C. L., & van Zoonen, W. (2020). Understanding constant connectivity to work: How and for whom is constant connectivity related to employee wellbeing? *Information and Organization*, 30(3), 100302. 10.1016/j.infoandorg.2020.100302

Canadian Broadcasting Corporation (CBC). (2021, December 27). *Pandemic puts' right to disconnect' in spotlight as provinces inch toward policies.* https://www.cbc.ca/news/business/right-to-disconnect-policies-1.6298845

Chawla, A. (2020, May 21). *Coronavirus (Covid-19) – 'Zoom' Application Boon or Bane.* 10.2139/ssrn.3606716

Cremades, O. (2021, February 10). A small step towards regulating the digital disconnection in the European Union? (Original title: ¿Un pequeño paso hacia la regulación de la desconexión digital en la Unión Europea?). *Cinco Días, El País.* https://cincodias.elpais.com/cincodias/2021/02/09/legal/1612904590_958285.html

Day, A., Barber, L., & Tonet, J. (2019). Information communication technology and employee well-being: Understanding the "iParadox Triad" at work. In Landers, R. N. (Ed.). *The cambridge handbook of technology and employee behavior* (pp. 580–607). Cambridge University Press. 10.1017/9781108649636.022

Deloitte (2021). *How the pandemic stress-tested the increasingly crowded digital home.* Deloitte Center for Technology, Media and Telecommunications. https://www2.deloitte.com/content/dam/insights/articles/6978_TMT-Connectivity-and-mobile-trends/DI_TMT-Connectivity-and-mobile-trends.pdf

Giovannoni, E., & Fabietti, G. (2013). What is sustainability? A review of the concept and Its applications. In Busco, C., Frigo, M. L., Riccaboni, A., & Quattrone, P. (Eds.). *Integrated reporting* (pp. 21–40). Springer. https://link.springer.com/book/10.1007/978-3-319-02168-3

Felstead, A., & Henseke, G. (2017). Assessing the growth of remote working and its consequences for effort, wellbeing and work-life balance. *New Technology, Work and Employment*, 32(3), 195–212. 10.1111/ntwe.12097

International Labour Organization. (2022, June 10). *International labour conference adds safety and health to fundamental principles and rights at work.* https://www.ilo.org/global/about-the-ilo/newsroom/news/WCMS_848132/lang—en/index.htm

International Labour Organization. (2021). *Challenges and opportunities of teleworking in Latin America and the Caribbean (Technical Note).* https://www.ilo.org/wcmsp5/groups/public/---americas/---ro-lima/---sro-port_of_spain/documents/genericdocument/wcms_813472.pdf

International Labour Organization. (2020a). *From potential to practice: Preliminary findings on the numbers of workers working from home during the Covid-19 pandemic (Policy Brief).* www.ilo.org/wcmsp5/groups/public/---ed_protect/---protrav/---travail/documents/briefingnote/wcms_777896.pdf

International Labour Organization. (2020b). *Defining and measuring remote work, telework, work at home and home-based work (Technical Note).* https://www.ilo.org/wcmsp5/groups/public/---dgreports/---stat/documents/publication/wcms_747075.pdf

Karia, N., & Asaari, M. H. A. H. (2016). Innovation capability: the impact of teleworking on sustainable competitive advantage. *International Journal of Technology, Policy and Management*, 16(2), 181–194. 10.1504/IJTPM.2016.076318

Khan, I. S., Ahmad, M. O., & Majava, J. (2021). Industry 4.0 and sustainable development: A systematic mapping of triple bottom line, Circular Economy and Sustainable Business Models perspectives. *Journal of Cleaner Production*, 297, 126655. 10.1016/j.jclepro.2021.126655

Kumar, P., Kumar, N., Aggarwal, P., & Yeap, J. A. (2021). Working in lockdown: The relationship between Covid-19 induced work stressors, job performance, distress, and life satisfaction. *Current Psychology*, 40(12), 6308–6323. 10.1007/s12144-021-01567-0

Leiter, M. P., & Schaufeli, W. B. (1996). Consistency of the burnout construct across occupations. *Anxiety, Stress & Coping*, 9(3), 229–243. 10.1080/10615809608249404

Lepeley, M. T. (2021a). The human centered sustainable quality culture in organizations. In Lepeley, M. T., Morales, O., Essens, P., Beutell, N. J., & Majluf, N. (Eds.), *Human centered organizational culture: Global dimensions* (pp. 3–22). Routledge.

Lepeley, M. T. (2021b). Soft skills: The lingua franca of human centered management in the global VUCA environment. In Lepeley, M. T., Beutell, N. J., Abarca, N., & Majluf, N. (Eds.). *Soft skills for human centered management and global sustainability* (pp. 3–22). Routledge.

Lepeley, M. T., Morales, O., Essens, P., Beutell, N. J., & Majluf, N. (Eds.). (2021a). *Human centered organizational culture: Global dimensions*. Routledge.

Lepeley, M. T., Beutell, N., Abarca, N., & Majful, N. (Eds.). (2021b). *Soft skills for human centered management and global sustainability*. Routledge.

Lepeley, M. T. (2017). *Human centered management: 5 pillars of organizational quality and global sustainability*. Routledge.

Mazmanian, M., Orlikowski, W. J., & Yates, J. (2013). The autonomy paradox: The implications of mobile email devices for knowledge professionals. *Organization Science*, 24(5), 1337–1357. 10.1287/orsc.1120.0806

Nadler, R. (2020). Understanding "Zoom fatigue": Theorizing spatial dynamics as third skins in computer-mediated communication. *Computers and Composition*, 58, 102613. 10.1016/j.compcom.2020.102613

Ochoa, P. & Blanch, J. M. (2019). Psychosocial wellbeing at work: reasons to invest in healthy employees and workplaces. In Ochoa, P., Lepeley, M. T., & Essens, P. (Eds.). *Wellbeing for sustainability in the global workplace* (pp. 3–14). Routledge.

Ochoa, P., Lepeley, M. T., & Essens, P. (Eds). (2019). *Wellbeing for sustainability in the global workforce*. Routledge.

Organization for Economic Co-operation and Development (2021). *Teleworking in the Covid-19 pandemic: Trends and prospects*. https://www.oecd.org/coronavirus/policy-responses/teleworking-in-the-Covid-19-pandemic-trends-and-prospects-72a416b6/

Palumbo, R. (2020). Let me go to the office! An investigation into the side effects of working from home on work-life balance. *International Journal of Public Sector Management*, 33(6/7), 771–790. 10.1108/IJPSM-06-2020-0150

Scaramuzzino, G., & Martinell Barfoed, E. (2021). Swedish social workers' experiences of technostress. *Nordic Social Work Research*. 10.1080/2156857X.2021.1951335

Schaufeli, W. B., & Van Dierendonck, D. (1993). The construct validity of two burnout measures. *Journal of Organizational Behavior*, 14(7), 631–647. 10.1002/job.4030140703

Soubelet-Fagoaga, I., Arnoso-Martinez, M., Elgorriaga-Astondoa, E., & Martínez-Moreno, E. (2022). Telework and face-to-face work during Covid-19 confinement:

The predictive factors of work-related stress from a holistic point of view. *International Journal of Environmental Research and Public Health*, 19(7), 3837. 10.3390/ijerph19073837

Tarafdar, M., Cooper, C. L., & Stich, J. F. (2019). The technostress trifecta-techno eustress, techno distress and design: Theoretical directions and an agenda for research. *Information Systems Journal*, 29(1), 6–42. 10.1111/isj.12169

Vorderer, P., Krömer, N., & Schneider, F. M. (2016). Permanently online – Permanently connected: Explorations into university students' use of social media and mobile smart devices. *Computers in Human Behavior*, 63, 694–703. 10.1016/j.chb.2016.05.085

Waizenegger, L. (2015, March 4-6). *Connectivity as a Two-Edged Sword: Mirroring the Multifaceted Field of Constant Connectivity*. 12th International Conference on Wirtschaftsinformatik, Osnabrück, Germany.

Part 3

Higher Education: Disruptions and Solutions

9 Pandemic Disruptions Affecting Wellbeing of Academic Women in South Africa

Marieta du Plessis, Linda Ronnie, and Cyrill Walters

Introduction

The purpose of this book, titled *Human Centered Management and Crisis: Workplace Disruptions, Wellbeing and Organization Sustainability*, is to facilitate identification and analysis of unprecedented disruptions affecting organizational performance, wellbeing of people in the workplace and long-term sustainability across sectors, industries and countries. The book offers a comprehensive discussion of the challenges and restrictive conditions organizations and people have been exposed during the Covid-19 pandemic and other ongoing crises in the global VUCA (volatile, uncertain, complex, ambiguous) environment.

Although the effects of the pandemic are ongoing and it is leading to deeper organizational transformation across sectors, research studies of the consequences have received less attention in higher education, as the focus is commonly on the private sector. The Covid-19 pandemic resulted in unprecedented problems for academics and universities (Du Plessis et al., 2022). This chapter addresses effects of disruptions impacting universities in the public sector in South Africa focusing on women academics experiencing drastic changes in traditional work routines and life style during the pandemic lockdowns.

The pandemic crisis exacerbated an unsettling notion when academic women had to change office work routines to start working from home and remotely for the first time. The home environment suddenly became congested and a constrained place to work in. They were caught up in demands of competing roles as mothers comforting and teaching children, as care givers to extended family while simultaneously teaching online classes and helping students. Academic women in the study struggled to perform normal teaching and research activities. The new operations hindering wellbeing increased the need to develop resilience to keep pace with work; while being aware that the long-term sustainability of these universities depended on their academic performance.

DOI: 10.4324/9781003330011-12

This study presents the results of a cross-sectional study conducted in 26 universities in South Africa aiming to evaluate the effects of the Covid-19 pandemic disrupting work and wellbeing of academic women. It analyzed the experiences of 2,025 women during the pandemic-enforced lockdowns. The results showed evidence that the universities did not have adequate synchronicity between internal operations and external disruptions and threats. This gap led to internal tensions and challenges with significant impact on wellbeing.

The study relies on Human Centered Management (HCM) methodology anchored in the wellbeing of people in the workplace and organization as a precondition to secure sustainability (Lepeley, 2017). In contrast with management approaches focused on resources, HCM advances people's wellbeing in the workplace and the marketplace as a precondition to improve performance, productivity and long-term organizational sustainability (Lepeley, 2017).

Pre-pandemic environment in universities

The pandemic lockdown periods posed significant conflicts between academic work and family responsibilities (Fisher et al., 2020), especially for academic women in South Africa (Ronnie, Bam, & Walters, 2022), experimenting anew how to effectively balance the demands of childcare and family relationships with academic work. Blackmore (2020) expressed concerns that changing demands were increasing pressures across the academy and staff functions, where women already had precarious conditions associated with low paying, contract-based jobs in universities. Although changes in academia did not start with the Covid-19 pandemic, abrupt disruptions accelerated these problems demanding the attention to find solutions. Among them, to address and improve outcomes in terms of the Life-Work Continuum (LWC; Beutell et al., 2021a) in the academic environment prominently affecting the wellbeing of women.

Sample description and methodology

The study draws on data gathered from 2,025 women working in academia as faculty and academic managers in 26 public universities of South Africa during the period of Covid-19 lockdown. Ethical clearance was necessary and granted by the host institution Stellenbosch University, followed by clearance from the other 25 universities. The institutions conducted the study using an online survey sent to female academics with an introductory cover letter and the electronic link to the survey instrument.

The survey questionnaire consisted of 12 questions using the Likert scale followed by an open-ended section to collect detailed responses of the participants. This section provided a substantial volume of qualitative data that was coded by theme and analyzed. This chapter presents data collected in the open-ended section.

The total population of female academics in the 26 universities ranged between 24,332 and 25,857, depending on special nominations (Walters et al., 2022). The 2,025 full responses received showed 8.3 percent survey response. To protect privacy respondents were identified only by institution and responses were not attributed to any particular university, department or school. The career stages of respondents were evenly spread, with 30 percent of respondents in the 0–5 years range of academic appointment. The largest numbers of responses were from the University of South Africa (UNISA) with 286 responses, the University of Pretoria (UP) with 184, Stellenbosch University (SU) with 172 and the University of Cape Town (UCT) with 111, recognized as Africa's top university by the "World University Rankings (2020)".

Participants told about their experiences across pandemic stages from "hard" lockdown or Stage 5 to gradual easing of lockdown through the end of September 2020, Stage 2. Stages 5 and 4 represented restrictions of movement and services, including schools, domestic services and childcare, exacerbating demands of households and families. In Stages 3 and 2, schools were re-opened with social distancing measures, and learners attended school on a rotational basis, due to limited space to meet social distancing in classrooms. The re-opening of schools brought some relief for academic mothers, but care and home-schooling still needed to be provided on rotational days where children had to stay at home. For the most part South African universities eliminated face-to-face teaching, with minor exceptions subject to institutional permission for some professional fields, i.e., medical students' practicums and laboratory work.

Findings

Participants discussed the effects of the pandemic describing experiences leading to increasing stress at work and family demands, demonstrating traditional organizational culture entrenched on view of life and work as separate and mutually exclusive dimensions of personal life and wellbeing (Beutell, Kuschel, & Lepeley, 2021a). Forty-one percent of the participants expressed increasing emotional impact affecting academic work that required more support. Twenty-six percent indicated the need for the same support as before the pandemic. Caring for children, as caregivers and homeschooling teachers, was a primary stressor voiced by respondents. Other home challenges included caring for elderly dependents, managing routine chores, like home maintenance, shopping and meal preparation.

There is abundant literature showing that even in dual-career families, care burdens and domestic work overwhelmingly rested on women during pandemic lockdowns (Chemaly, 2020; Featherstone, 2020; Zamberlan, Gioachin, & Gritti, 2021). This problem was confirmed in our study in the responses of academic women and mothers that struggled between work responsibilities and felt guilty for the care of their children when they were working (Ahmad, 2020; De Coster, 2020). In terms of work responsibilities, the most stressful professional challenges included teaching online to large groups of students, conducting research along with administrative demands from the department, attending large number of online meetings and responding to increasing numbers of email messages.

Findings showed constraints women faced to adapt to the deep transformation in work structures from the traditional face-to-face classroom to distance and hybrid work formats.

Wellbeing dimensions

New work patterns emphasizing work at home instead of working at the university offices interfered significantly with the lifestyles of academic women. These results fell short of meeting HCM practices embedded in LWC (Beutell et al., 2021a) model and the 7 complementary dimensions of life wellbeing (Lepeley, 2019). A summary of the results is presented in Table 9.1 summarizes the disruptions participants experienced in each dimension of wellbeing as effect of disruptions and resilience mechanisms used to counter effect of the pandemic.

The study results suggest that universities had to focus on the pandemic crisis that resulted in emergency shifts from classroom teaching to distance and remote teaching and learning. Ongoing pressures to face unprecedented disruptions forced higher education institutions to undertake drastic changes that often overlooked the detrimental effects on the wellbeing of people, hindered work engagement and performance, and jeopardized sustainability.

Life purpose dimension

Academic women who identify with professional roles align personal achievements with successful research, teaching outputs and supporting students. The study shows evidence of negative experiences draining personal resources due to the escalation of workload through working from their homes with simultaneous family duties, including children and extended care of other family members.

An experienced academic, mother of two young children, summarized her experience: "I still feel pressured and guilty for not being able to effectively manage all my duties and able to find balance between being productive at work and fulfilling all my family responsibilities".

A mid-career academic woman with no children described her case:

> I feel bad if I don't do everything in my power to support my students. But I have nobody to support my work-related emotional strain and burnout. I am very tired. I have been working seven days a week since lockdown started.

Table 9.1 Summary of findings of effects on academic women wellbeing and resilience mechanisms.

Wellbeing dimension	*Disruptions*	*Effects*	*Resilience mechanisms*
Life purpose	Difficult to manage competing demands of work and family	Struggling to cope; emotional strain and burnout	
Income/financial security	Fear of losing job	Stress; stunted career progression	Emotional intelligence
Physical fitness/good health	Overwhelming emotions impacting (mental) health	Emotional strain; depression; suicidal thoughts	Collaboration skills Problem-solving techniques
Love/affection/meaningful relationships	Lack of access to support of grandparents, childcare, managers	Loneliness and isolation; coping alone	Patience Bouncing back from failure
Contribution to society	Recognizing students' needs and providing financial support	Feeling powerless to change systemic problem	

A mid-career academic with a toddler and a child in primary school:

> I am proud of what I was able to accomplish, but I also need to acknowledge that it came at a price on my health, family's wellbeing, and I feel guilty for not meeting the demands of all my multiple roles, as I would have wanted.

An early-career academic, mother of a preschool child:

> I'm extremely frustrated and barely coping. I'm not as productive as I'd like to be even on days where I have time. I need rest and don't feel mentally strong to do my work. I fear I might lose my job or my contract would not be renewed because I feel I am underperforming. I feel guilty and very disappointed in myself for not being able to manage.

Income/financial security dimension

A challenge for some participants was job security, over decreasing work productivity or performance. They feared they would lose their jobs or that the work they did was no longer required in online programs. The problem was particularly acute for faculty members with short-term contracts, exposed to higher risks of their careers and threats to their financial security (Crook, 2020).

An early career faculty mother of a toddler said: "I worry the lockdown will hinder my academic progress impacting my reputation as [a] reliable and capable faculty member".

Physical fitness/good health dimension

Although the survey did not include information about physical fitness, concerns with mental health and fitness were evident. Several participants expressed concerns in the following ways.

An established faculty member with a primary school and a high-school child expressed: "I am not longer sure of my value".

A woman in an established academic career, mother of a high school child said: "I have been able to keep my sanity due to medication and therapy".

Mid-career academic woman with no children stated: "I have suicidal thoughts constantly".

It is critically important for institutions to be aware of academics in this mental health condition because the feelings demonstrate she is drained of all meaning and purpose and in need of immediate help.

Love/affection/meaningful relationships dimension

The study shows that personal relationships took strain during the Covid-19 pandemic. Women in traditional family units expressed distress and discomfort. Single mothers reported significant levels of distress, emotionally strained with little support and opportunity for self-care.

Early-career academic with a child in primary school: "Lockdown is particularly stressful for single parents because support structures such as friends, elderly family members, are no longer accessible".

The study showed that living alone was convenient is some circumstances but particularly challenging for faculty new to a university and unfamiliar with the city.

Early-career academic without children:

> The emotional stress and trauma of hard lockdown was extremely difficult to cope with. I was relatively new to the university and to the area and had no local support system at all. It is difficult to concentrate on academic work stuck at home and coping with multiple challenges alone.

Lack of meaningful and trusting communications made participants feel vulnerable and unable to share their needs and feelings with others.

Early-career academic without children: "My experience in higher education is that being overwhelmed [and expressing those feelings] is covertly perceived as a weakness and an impediment to achieving results. There has been no adjustment to expectations [in terms of performance]".

Contribution to society

Academic women in the sample frequently conveyed feelings that even when they felt burnt out, they forced themselves to deliver and continued working. Further inquiries showed that they were motivated by their work and commitment as students at the expense of other dimensions of well-being including financial security. These are some examples:

An established academic woman with no children:

> I spent my money buying mobile data for students to connect to the internet; I have no regrets. But I feel regret for students who experience inequality with regard access to resources, despite the enormous effort my university had put in place to try and support the students – the need was just too great.

An established academic, mother of two teenagers:

> As most of their data availability was after midnight, they got immediate support from me as I was still awake working e.g., students asking via WhatsApp about the work at 2 am, got an answer within seconds to minutes from me. This of course came at the cost of sleep.

Resilience: the positive side of adversity among academic women

In terms of resilience, meaning capacity to adapt to change and thrive in the face of adversity (Folke et al., 2005), and in reaction to negative effects of the pandemic, participants exhibited resilience-related skills. The extracts below show expressions of emotional intelligence, collaboration skills, problem-solving techniques, patience and bouncing back from failure to cope with the pandemic-related crisis.

Mid-career academic with two children in primary school:

> I did little research, by choice, because I preferred to pay special attention to my children's school performance. Switching to online learning helped me because I am technology savvy and was able to make the transition quite seamlessly. I believe that using well-established social media forums with my students allowed me to offer them emotional and academic support necessary to pull through what could be described as new and trying times.

Established academic woman with three adult children:

> When the lockdown was implemented, I was in my new job for only one month. I had 18 postgraduate students who started their experiments when restrictions were issued. So, all went back home, leaving 50 individual studies running. I had to take over their work, managing trials and completing the experiments. Lockdown tested my abilities and patience.

Mid-career academic with no children: "Support from fellow colleagues using WhatsApp messages/groups and online Google meetings were very helpful. We were able to discuss new way of working online and support one another, professionally and personally".

Early career academic with one child in primary school:

> The lockdown has been an eye-opener, especially considering the multiple roles that women have to take on. However, at the same time, it displays the resilience of women, although it is overwhelming, we adapt, manage and get what needs to be done completed.

Mid-career academic with no children:

> What women are good at is problem solving and we get better as providing the productive and intimate labour as we get older. My computer is good but internet access in my area is slow, so the system brought a lot of stress for I could not deliver fast enough. [But] women are tough and resilient! You will be surprised.

Established academic with no children:

> I found that experience sharing was done more frequently online than in a face-to-face environment. I had a chance to share with international colleagues experiencing the same issues and finding common ground. And everybody is willing to share professional knowledge. This second semester has been easier, and it feels like 'the new normal' is able to achieve the needs of higher education.

Concluding discussion

The results of this study of 2,025 faculty women confirm that reaching LWC requires optimal combination of the seven dimensions of wellbeing embedded in HCM to advance organizational sustainability during crises and in the global VUCA environment. Moreover, personal progress is highly aligned with personal capacity of "learning from failure" that leads to positive outcomes. To respond to disruptive situations, it is necessary to develop and deploy specific Soft Skills (to learn from failure and deal effectively with guilt; transforming negative experiences into positive driving forces). In terms of resilience, this study shows that despite resilient behavior exhibited by faculty women in some instances stress is a strengthening mechanism.

The study showed that academic women were disproportionately negatively affected during the pandemic due to an overload of professional duties and personal responsibilities and findings indicate similar challenges across different career stages. Our proposals for improvement is that in order to be effective university polices addressing ongoing issues need to apply equally to women and men academics, including men and women holding institutional leadership roles.

As result of this study, our team of researchers proposes that institutions in the public higher education system in South Africa adopt Human Centered Management practices aimed at continuous assessment to improve institutional performance and sustainability with higher reliance on continuous improvement on the wellbeing of people – students, faculty and related personnel.

The following is a list of practical suggestions to address issues aiming to improve the wellbeing and resilience of academic members and is adaptable to higher education worldwide:

1 Emphasize management centered on people – resulting in optimal use of resources to improve educational service and programs to all students.
2 Revise and update institutional policies to make provision for the emotional health of academics including counseling resources.
3 Develop systematic assessment of institutional planning, academic performance, management plans and programs considering different needs and responsibilities of women faculty aiming to optimize gender parity.

4 Deploy systematic assessment of continuous improvement of institutional processes and practices obstructing parity and equal opportunity in the workplace.

The proposed plan has potential to develop a systemic effort to attain higher academic performance based on the wellbeing of academics and university personnel at all levels. This should be supported through enhancing resilience securing long-term sustainability of South African educational institutions.

References

Ahmad, A. S. (2020, March 27). Why you should ignore all that coronavirus-inspired productivity pressure. *The Chronicle of Higher Education*. https://www.chronicle.com/article/Why-You-Should-Ignore-All-That/248366

Beutell, N. J., Kuschel, K., & Lepeley, M. T. (2021a). Life–work continuum: The new organizational culture. In Lepeley, M. T., Morales, O., Essens, P., Beutell, N., & Majluf, N. (Eds.) (2021), *Human centered organizational culture: Global dimensions* (pp. 23–33). Routledge, UK.

Beutell, N., Kuschel, K., & Lepeley, M. T. (2021b). Learning from failure: Soft skills for sustainability in the VUCA environment. In Lepeley, M. T., Beutell, N., Melo, N. A., & Majful, N. (Eds.), *Soft skills for human centered management and global sustainability* (pp. 41–55). Routledge.

Blackmore, J. (2020). The carelessness of entrepreneurial universities in a world risk society: A feminist reflection on the impact of Covid-19 in Australia. *Higher Education Research & Development*, 39(7), 1332–1336. 10.1080/07294360.2020.1825348

Chemaly, S. (2020, April 20). Coronavirus could hurt women the most. Here's how to prevent a patriarchal pandemic. *Think: Opinion, Analysis, Essays*. https://www.nbcnews.com/think/opinion/coronavirus-could-hurt-womenmost-here-s-how-prevent-patriarchal-ncna1186581

Crook, S. (2020). Parenting during the Covid-19 pandemic of 2020: Academia, labour and care work. *Women's History Review*, 29(7), 1226–1238. 10.1080/09612025.2020.1807690

De Coster, M. (2020). Towards a relational ethics in pandemic times and beyond Limited accountability, collective performativity and new subjectivity. *Gender, Work & Organization*, 1–6. 10.1111/gwao.12467

Du Plessis, M., Jansen van Vuuren, C. J., Simons, A., Frantz, J., Roman, N. V., & Andipatin, M. (2022). South African higher education institutions at the beginning of the Covid-19 pandemic: Sense-making and lessons learnt. *Frontiers in Education*, 6, 740016. 10.3389/feduc.2021.740016

Featherstone, L. (2020, May 7). The pandemic is a family emergency. *The New Republic*. https://newrepublic.com/article/157528/coronavirus-pandemic-family-care-work-crisis-social-reproduction-theory

Fisher, J., Languilaire, J.-C., Lawthom, R., Nieuwenhuis, R., Petts, R. J., Runswick-Cole, K., & Yerkes, M. A. (2020). Community, work, and family in times of Covid-19. *Community, Work & Family*, 23(3), 247–252. 10.1080/13668803.2020.1756568

Folke, C., Hahn, T., Olsson, P., & Norberg, J. (2005). Adaptive governance of social-ecological systems. *Annual Review of Environment and Resources*, 30, 441–473 10.1146/annurev.energy.30.050504.144511

Lepeley, M. T. (2017). *Human centered management: 5 pillars of organizational quality and global sustainability*. Routledge.

Lepeley, M. T. (2019) *EDUQUALITY: Human centered quality management in education: A model for deployment, assessment and sustainability*. Information Age Publishing.

Ronnie, L., Bam, A., & Walters, C. (2022). Emotional wellbeing: The impact of the Covid-19 pandemic on women academics in South Africa. *Frontiers in Education*, 7, 770447. 10.3389/feduc.2022.770447

Walters, C., Mehl, G., Piraino, P., Jansen, J., & Kriger, S. (2022). The impact of the pandemic-enforced lockdown on the scholarly productivity of women academics in South Africa. *Research Policy*, 51(1). 10.1016/j.respol.2021.104403

World University Rankings. (2020). https://www.timeshighereducation.com/world-university-rankings/2020/world-ranking

Zamberlan, A., Gioachin, F., & Gritti, D. (2021). Work less, help out more? The persistence of gender inequality in housework and childcare during UK Covid-19. *Research in Social Stratification and Mobility*, 73, 100583. 10.1016/j.rssm.2021.100583

10 Mindfulness Program to Strengthen Mental Health during Crises

Anielson Barbosa da Silva

Introduction

The Covid-19 pandemic exposed people worldwide to unprecedented disruptions harming multiple dimensions of wellbeing. Long and recurrent lockdown mandates kept people distant and isolated in their homes and away from regular social contacts besides the family. Disruptions took a significant toll in education. Students in higher education in particular suffered the consequences of institutions facing unparalleled disruptions that caught them unprepared to handle a surmounting crisis and failing to deliver adequate services and support.

To address the ongoing changes and challenges, I designed a Program on Mindfulness for students. This chapter discusses implications and results of the Mindfulness Program (MP) implemented in 2021. The program was designed to support students develop Soft Skills to cope with effects of the pandemic improving management of personal emotions to confront situations impacting wellbeing and consequently their lives and work.

Pandemic disruptions caused deep changes in teaching processes and the professional context, hindering people's cognitive and emotional development. In this context, Soft Skills become important resources to restore and maintain effectiveness in training, professional performance and to pursue wellbeing (Lepeley, 2021, Lepeley et al., 2021; Cullen & Brito, 2015).

Studies show that mindfulness and socio-emotional programs help improve to manage emotions, decrease stress (Mazolla & Rustenhol, 2018), and improve collaboration leading to constructive conflict resolution. In my experience as professor at a public university in Brazil I found that students in a business administration class were facing increasing difficulty managing emotions, especially in processes of communications and social interactions during the pandemic. An assessment of the situation made me realize that some kind of support was needed. Research in emotional education EE reports that Mindfulness is helpful to face disruptions and manage emotions more effectively. I decided to take Mindfulness training.

DOI: 10.4324/9781003330011-13

I realized how much it can contribute to improve mental health and dimensions of wellbeing. This was necessary motivation to design a Mindfulness emotional education program for my students.

The program took place in 2021. It was offered as a strategy to support students deal with disruptive events. The program presented in this chapter can be used as a strategy to counteract the effects of disruptions and crises.

Mindfulness

Mindfulness is a conscious state of deliberate attention, focused on the present, without judgment (Kabat-Zinn, 2009), that helps people to cooperate paying attention to the needs of the other party in communications and conflict situations, avoiding a natural tendency to make inaccurate judgments about other people (Gupta et al., 2021).

Mindfulness emotional education programs are a complementary approach to develop people's ability to manage emotions using Soft Skills to restore and enhance wellbeing in educational and organizational settings.

Learning to manage emotions

Managing emotions is a complex process that requires a person to think and identify how emotions interfere with behavior. It involves a process of emotional awareness, which commonly starts identifying how emotions impact on physical sensations, thoughts and actions in personal and professional life.

Organizational and social environments are subject to intense challenges and constant pressures since the pandemic started. Managing distressful situations requires cognitive knowledge and overall active use of Soft Skills. Despite their importance in social relations, communications and increasing demands by organizations and the workplace, Soft Skills have not become a common subject of studies in education until now and their delivery is pending. Lepeley, who has worked and published extensively on Soft Skills and applications in executive business education, entrepreneurship and Quality Management (2021) defines Soft Skills as *personal attributes and traits people possess that enable them to interact effectively and harmoniously with other people.* Lepeley and other HCM scholars emphasize a high positive correlation between Emotional Intelligence and use of Soft Skills (Lepeley et al., 2021).

Emotional intelligence

Emotional Intelligence (EI) is the capacity to identify personal emotions, to such extent as to positively impact also the emotions of others. A large variety of Soft Skills are used to express EI and among them empathy, good listening, critical thinking, problem-solving to stimulate resilience and agility, two of the five Pillars of HCM (Lepeley, 2017) and central elements of this book. The EI theory was introduced by Peter Salovey and John Mayer in the 1990s and it was further developed and brought to lay public by Harvard professor Daniel Goleman in the mid-1990s. EI has also been known as Emotional Quotient (EQ), intended to measure similar to Intellectual Quotient (IQ). However, some psychologists argue that EQ lacks explanatory power. An argument that is increasingly debatable, overall from the HCM perspective. Salovey and Mayer (1990) identify the following basic skills to advance EI: *perceiving* and *understanding* emotions, *using* emotions in thoughts and *managing* emotions. Important EI components are self-awareness, self-regulation, motivation, empathy and social skills. All impact professional performance, some directly in work activities, or indirectly improving mental health, stamina and quality of life that increase wellbeing.

Emotional Management (EM) is one of the derivatives of EI applying to work environments stimulating high performance and job satisfaction (Bar-On, 2010). Social Emotional Learning (SEL) is another concept related to EI and a field of study that emerged in recent decades (Weissberg et al., 2015). Its definition is derived from and very similar to EI.

EI and SEL in educational settings

In the educational contexts, students and future professionals faced several challenges associated increasing pressure for high performance, work intensity, use of technology and constant connectivity that requires new behaviors. In this case again, Soft Skills help to expand individual and interpersonal awareness of emotional experiences (Conley, 2015).

The development of SEL programs is rather new. The programs are intended to recognize and manage emotions developing ability to think clearly and feel more competent in studies and work (Zins et al., 2004). A well-known SEL program is CASEL (*Collaborative for Academic, Social and Emotional Learning*), it serves as a guide for improving personal development, promoting satisfying relationships and stimulating ethical and productive work. The basic Soft Skills used in CASEL are Self-awareness, Self-management, Social awareness, Relationship skills and Responsible decision-making (CASEL, 2015).

Mindfulness and socio-emotional programs

In terms of Mindfulness, programs are gaining popularity lately. The best-known are MBSR (mindfulness-based stress reduction), MBCT (mindfulness-based Cognitive Therapy for Depression) and MSC (mindful Self-Compassion). Other programs use these protocols to develop sets of formal and informal practices.

Mindfulness is effective to managing tensions and stress using emotional self-awareness and self-regulation Soft Skills. MPs are built of the following principles (Mazzola & Rostenhol, 2018):

- Focus on actions taking place in the present with full attention to act.
- Capacity to describe feelings, experiences and communicate personal feelings to others.
- Remain calm in conflicting situations to avoid conflict.
- Accept personal feelings, physical sensations and ideas without judging or classifying into categories.
- Record sensations and physical signs, feelings and ideas, perceive effects on behavior and mood.

The Programs that incentivize, active participation is more effective to develop participants' capacity to manage adversity in complex environments (Reitz et al., 2016). Institutionalization of Mindfulness intervention programs help people prepare to get resilient and agile to overcome crisis. High levels of mindfulness are associated with high levels of EI, positive affect and life satisfaction and low levels of negative feelings indicating the benefits of mindfulness for students (Shutte & Malouff, 2011).

MP design

The Program aimed to support students improve self-knowledge techniques, developing strategies to manage emotions and using Soft Skills aligned with personal interests in life and work.

The program objectives were:

- help students develop capacity to pay attention and deal with thoughts effectively.
- improve communications and social interactions.
- cultivate *self-compassion* to increase emotional and social awareness.
- recognize the role of emotions in self-knowledge (personal abilities, feelings, beliefs, preferences, motivations.
- identify levels of mental health, quality of life and wellbeing.

Self-compassion refers to accept instances of perceived inadequacies, failure or suffering as normal states. It represents interactions between key elements of self-kindness, self-judgment, common humanity, isolation, mindfulness and overidentification. In organizations, self-compassion helps employees search for self-acceptance of imperfections that can be improved to improve job satisfaction, performance and wellbeing (Neff, 2016; Dodson & Heng, 2022).

I designed the MP based in experience in Mindfulness Expert Course in the University-Company Foundation at University of Valencia, Spain and following training in the Mindful Self-Compassion program necessary to develop program activities. The Program lasted eight weeks. The main subjects covered in classes were awaking mindfulness; recovering basic emotions; managing thoughts; cultivating self-compassion; communicating and relating with compassion, recognizing difficult emotions and taking care of self. The program was delivered online with 2 hours meetings every week including experiential and interactive practices. Independent activities were distributed and practiced in Google® platform. The total Program lasted 32 hours.

Formal meditation practices included reading poems and specific narratives on mindfulness have been recorded by me and shared in a podcast channel on the Spotify platform.

One of the practical activities was to write a gratitude journal recording practices of gratitude about the following questions: How do I feel today? What new experiences have you had? What are thankful for today? Participants were asked to record gratitude for three situations/experiences/facts that occurred during the day. A study on the effects of gratitude revealed that simple reflective writing about gratitude showed significantly greater and lasting neural sensitivity to gratitude in the medial prefrontal cortex of participants' brains after three months of activity (Kini et al., 2016).

Methodology

Sample

A total of 141 undergraduate and graduate students were invited to participate in the Program. Fifty-five students or 39 percent completed both questionnaires. The sample included 71 percent women, 29 percent men, 66 percent were single, average age 32 years old. The low men participation can be explained because MPs in Brazil arouse more interest among women.

The instrument

Before and after the Program, participants had to answer questionnaires to identify interests and objectives (beginning of program) and after the program reports on perception of life satisfaction and quality of life, general mental health, anxiety, depression and stress and development and application of Soft Skills.

The Program included objective evaluation on MP implications in the development of Soft Skills and wellbeing improvement. The following Soft Skills were included (Silva and Macêdo, 2020):

- *Self-awareness*: ability to recognize and understand personal emotions and those of others, associated with compassion and empathy.
- *Emotional regulation*: ability to manage emotions to maintain satisfactory performance in situations of stress and flexibility to adapt to changing circumstances.

- *Social consciousness*: ability to cooperate working in teams, assuming responsibility for actions, acting with empathy and collaboration recognizing the difficulties of others.
- *Self-control*: ability to manage personal emotions in stressful situations.
- *Emotional creativity*: ability to use emotions creatively to solve problems, manage conflict constructively, create opportunities to experience positive emotions and establish partnerships in favor of collective interest and social wellbeing.

Findings

Responses to the post-program questionnaire about participants' mental health and quality of life indicated average improvement of 18 percent and 10 percent, respectively. A more significant impact was observed in specific mental health, reporting on average decreases in depression 33 percent, anxiety 32 percent and stress 23 percent.

Undergraduate and graduate participants documented perceptions after taking of the MP as follows:

> *"I improved a lot after the program and I continue doing the daily meditations. I am advancing controlling irritability. Breathing techniques keep me in the present, I realized that I was doing things on automatic mode I changed and my anxiety level has decreased" (undergraduate student).*
>
> *"I learned a great deal and specific techniques help me to work better with my emotions, particularly I use them a tools to manage anxiety, fears and procrastinations" (undergraduate student).*
>
> *"The program was very meaningful for me. I acquired skills that allow me to have greater self-knowledge that improve wellbeing". (graduate student).*
>
> *"I didn't notice changes during the Program, but when it ended. Probably because I was facing a stressful situation (academic works, seminar and Valentine's Day all in the same week). After the program I am able to manage my emotions much better" (undergraduate student).*
>
> *"The meditations helped to reduce anxiety and reach more reflections of self-knowledge, which brought me more acceptance and attention to certain feelings and emotions that I had and of which I was not aware" (graduate student).*

Reported average improvement in Soft Skills were 15 percent in emotional creativity, 13 percent emotional regulation, 10 percent self-awareness, 8 percent social consciousness and 7 percent emotional self-control. Although results show low improvement in Soft Skills, this may be explained by the complexity of the five Soft Skills and insufficient time to process and internalize them.

Table 10.1 Benefits of the MP in self-knowledge and wellbeing

Benefits for Self-knowledge	*Benefits for Wellbeing*
• Finding a meaning in life. • Improving ways to advance • Changing situations to feel better. • Relearn to live and discover new things. • Be aware of personal limitations to reduce stress. • Increase awareness of inner fears and frustrations. • Greater diligence and actions for moments devoted to self-care. • Recognizing need to live in the present moment. • Higher awareness of life experiences increasing more balance and gratitude.	• Improve sleep quality. • Capacity to meditate during periods of anxiety or panic attacks. • Improve breathing to find calm and reduce anxiety. • Practice to calm down techniques in moments of distress. • Taking breaks between activities to reduce stress. • Carrying out small actions resulting in positive emotions. • Learn to recognize emotions (positive and negative) to manage them. • Calming thoughts and emotions to develop patience and tolerance.

Program benefits

Table 10.1 identifies specific benefits for the students who participated in the program cited in alignment with Demarzo and Campayo (2015) studies on effectiveness of mindfulness training in health care, education and business organizations related to self-knowledge and wellbeing.

The benefits of self-knowledge are linked to the following: changes in lifestyle, higher awareness of fears, actions to improve self-care to find balance and gratitude, living in the present moment, finding life purpose.

Benefits for physical and emotional wellbeing were achieved through relaxation practices, meditation, breaks between activities leading to improvement in sleep quality, reduced anxiety and stress, learning to cultivate positive emotions and manage positive and negative emotions. Practice thoughts that calm the mind, increasing patience and tolerance with self and with other people.

Concluding discussion

Emotional education helps people manage challenges from disruptions reducing anxiety, depression and stress. In general, programs aimed to help students improve general physical and mental health result in support improvements in academic performance and better preparation to face incoming challenges when they enter the workforce.

In particular, MP, as the one presented in this chapter, shows potential to benefit students in the short run, but particularly overtime because it takes time for people to process and internalize new mental models to improve stress management and other situations that affect personal achievements in life and work as much as social interactions.

MPs are still uncommon but will be increasingly needed to help people confront challenges during periods of unprecedented disruptions and crises, including, but not limited to the Covid pandemic and other ongoing crises that are extensively hindering people's stability and wellbeing. In the present global VUCA (volatile, uncertain, complex, ambiguous) environment, disruptions and crises are most likely to become the norm rather than the exception. From this dimension of surmounting world uncertainty, the Human Centered Management advice is to pay continuous attention to the development of resilience to face disruptions as an essential element to secure wellbeing of people in organizations seeking to secure long-term sustainability.

References

Bar-On, R. (2010). Emotional intelligence: an integral part of positive psychology. *South African Journal of Psychology*, 40(1), 54–62. 10.1177/008124631004000106

Casel - Collaborative for Academic, Social, and Emotional Learning (2015). *CASEL guide: Effective social and emotional learning programs.* https://static1.squarespace.com/static/5532b947e4b0edee99477d27/t/5d0948b6a78e0100015f652f/1560889545559/CASEL+Secondary+Guide+2015.pdf

Conley, C. S. (2015) SEL in higher education. In: Durlak, J. A., Domitrovich, C. E., Weissberg, R. P., & Gullotta, T. P. (Eds.). *Handbook of social and emotional learning: research and practice* (pp. 197–212). The Guilford Press.

Cullen, M., & Brito, G. (2015). Mindfulness and emotional balance (Original title: *Mindfulness y equilibrio emocional*). Editorial Sirio.

Demarzo, M., & Campayo, J. G. (2015). Mindfulness handbook: Curiosity and acceptance. (Original title: *Manual prático de mindfulness: curiosidade e aceitação*). Palas Athena.

Dodson, S. J., & Heng, Y. T. (2022). Self-compassion in organizations: A review and future research agenda. *Journal of Organizational Behavior*, 43(2), 168–196. 10.1002/job.2556

Gupta, V., Bhattacharya, S., & Gopalan, N. (2021) Emotions, emotional intelligence and conflict management: A conceptual framework to optimize soft skills in the workplace. In Lepeley, M. T., Beutell, N. J., Abarca, N., & Majluf, N. (Eds.). *Soft skills for human centered management and global sustainability* (pp. 56–66). Routledge.

Kabat-Zinn, J. (2009). *Mindfulness in Daily Life: wherever you go, there you are* (Original title: *Mindfulness en la Vida Cotidiana*: donde quiera que vayas, ahí estás). Paidós.

Kini, P., Wong, J., Mclnnis, S., Gabana, N., & Brown, J. W. (2016). The effects of gratitude expression on neural activity. *Neuroimage*, 128, 1–10. 10.1016/j.neuroimage.2015.12.040

Lepeley, M. T. (2021). Soft skills: The lingua franca of human centered management in the global VUCA environment. In Lepeley, M. T., Beutell, N. J., Abarca, N. & Majluf, N. (Eds.). *Soft skills for human centered management and global sustainability* (pp. 3–22). Routledge.

Lepeley, M. T., Beutell, N. J., Abarca, N., & Majluf, N. (Eds.) (2021). *Soft skills for human centered management and global sustainability*. Routledge.

Lepeley, M.T. (2017). *Human Centered Management: The 5 Pillars of Organizational Quality and Global Sustainability*. Routledge.

Macêdo, J. W. L., & Silva, A. B. (2020). Construction and validation of a socio-emotional competence scale in Brazil (Original title: Construção e validação de uma escala de competências socioemocionais no Brasil). *Revista Psicologia: Organizações e Trabalho*, 20(2), 883–890. 10.17652/rpot/2020.2.17382

Mazzola, N., & Rusterholz, B. (2018). Mindfulness for teachers (Original title: *Mindfulness para profesores)* (2nd ed.). Editorial Desclee de Brouwer.

Neff, K. D. (2016). The self-compassion scale is a valid and theoretically coherent measure of self-compassion. *Mindfulness*, 7(1), 264–274. 10.1007/s12671-015-0479-3

Reitz, M., Chaskalson, M., Olivier, S., & Waller, L. (2016). *The mindful leader*. Ashridge Hult.

Salovey, P., & Mayer, J. D. (1990). Emotional intelligence. *Imagination, Cognition and Personality*, 9(3), 185–211. 10.2190/dugg-p24e-52wk-6cdg

Schutte, N. S., & Malouff, J. M. (2011). Emotional intelligence mediates the relationship between mindfulness band subjective well-being. *Personality and Individual Differences*, 50, 1116–1119. 10.1016/j.paid.2011.01.037

Silva, A.B. & Macêdo, J.W. (2020). Management of emotions in the workplace of public servants (A Gestão das emoções no trabalho dosservidores públicos).In. Silva, A.B. (Ed.). *Competency-based People Management in Public Organizations in Brazil (Gestão de Pessoas por Competências nas Instituições Públicas Brasileiras)* 2nd ed. (pp. 554–595). Editorial UFPB. http://www.editora.ufpb.br/sistema/press5/index.php/UFPB/catalog/book/806

Teasdale, J., Williams, M., & Segal, Z. (2016). *Mindfulness handbook: an eight-week program to free you from depression, anxiety and emotional stress* (Original title: *Manual prático de mindfulness: um programa de oito semanas para libertar você da depressão, da ansiedade e do estresse emocional)*. Pensamento.

Vignola, R. C. B., & Tucci, A. M. (2014). Adaptation and validation of the depression, anxiety and stress scale (DASS) to Brazilian Portuguese. *Journal of Affective Disorders*, 155, 104–109. 10.1016/j.jad.2013.10.031

Weissberg, R. P., Durlak, J. A., Domitrovich, C. E., & Gullotta, T. P. (2015) Social and emotional learning: past, present and future. In Durlak, J. A., Domitrovich, C. E., Weissberg, R. P., & Gullotta, T. P. (Eds.). *Handbook of social and emotional learning: research and practice* (pp. 3–19). The Guilford Press.

Zins, J. E., Bloodworth, M. R., Weissberg, R. P., & Walberg, H. J. (2004) The scientific base linking social and emotional learning to school success. In: Zins, J. E., Weissberg, R. P., Wang, M. C., & Walberg, H. J. (Eds.), *Building academic success in social and emotional learning: what does the research say?* (pp. 3–32). Teachers College Press.

11 Transition to Telework in an Academic Setting in Peru

Oswaldo Morales, Sergio Morales, and Gareth H. Rees

Introduction

Since 2019, the Covid-19 pandemic generated a broad range of disruptions with detrimental effects on people's wellbeing and exposed organizations to unprecedented threats for sustainability and survival. The problems replicated rapidly, distressing organizations across industries unprepared for a surmounting crisis impacting performance and productivity in the workplace and the marketplace. Health care systems imposed mitigation measures restricting mobility and gatherings enforcing social distancing, mask wearing, personal hygiene routines, Covid testing and national vaccination programs (OECD, 2020).

In Peru, some mitigation measures were mandated and some were voluntary. All created operational challenges for organizations routinely involved in in-person delivery and face-to-face (f2f) contacts. Operations of educational institutions at all levels were deeply disrupted. Classes were canceled and educational institutions had to substitute f2f with intense use of technology and video conferences to continue providing educational services in the unprecedented environment deeply disrupted by the pandemic. The shift from in-person teaching and learning to virtual environments disrupted the normal lives and work of academics and students. Overtime it became clear that universities were unprepared for this rapid and drastic change and so were forced to improvise strategies to adapt to new conditions. It became evident that some strategies were more effective than others. Factors such as instructor and student characteristics, learning environment and instructional design, support mechanisms, information technology, diversity of course materials played a role in successful change and adaptation to teleworking and distance education, as did training of instructors and students, institutional support, student understanding of virtual learning environments to speed up the transition (Alqahtani & Rajkhan, 2020).

ESAN and HCM

In the 2017 book *Human Centered Management: 5 Pillars of Organizational Quality and Global Sustainability*, Lepeley's keen forecasting vision of the

DOI: 10.4324/9781003330011-14

global VUCA (volatile, uncertain, complex, ambiguous) environment built the Human Centered Management (HCM) framework on 5 pillars. In order to study the transition to online education and professors' teleworking in ESAN's organizational culture, we selected 2 of the 5 pillars, disruptions resilience – Pillar 2 and agility – Pillar 4 to analyze if these expedited or obstructed the transition process. At this point in time, the inclusion of Pillar 2 in HCM appears not only premonitory, but it is a call for attention to the urgency that people and organizations develop resilience to identify and gain capacity to deal with disruptions optimizing benefits and minimizing costs. This study focuses on assessment of an organization's culture building on the experience of one of the authors of this chapter as one of the editors of the book *Human Centered Organizational Culture: Global Dimension* (2021), which is part of the Routledge HCM Series.

Assessment of results of the transition in ESAN University showed that in general application of HCM principles expedited identification of incoming challenges and decision-making processes necessary to deal with pandemic disruptions. The chapter discusses changes in organizational culture in ESAN from the perspective of professors and their wellbeing and how it impacted results during the transition.

Methodology

Data to conduct this study were provided by ESAN's Directorate of Distance Education (DDE) to observe Organizational Culture (OC) and assess levels of resilience and agility impacting performance and wellbeing of professors and teaching staff during the pandemic.

OC is defined as an organizational dimension that synchronizes practices, beliefs, norms and values of people leading organizational behavior and management (Morales, Rees, & Morales, 2021) to support organizational structure and strategies. The assumption is that OC is developed overtime and it is continuously adapting to changing environments (Schein, 2017).

This study used the Hofstede Organization Culture Dimension Model to assess OC special features impacting and modifying the resilience and agility components of HCM. Resilience refers to the vision necessary to identity and anticipate effects of disruptions increasingly affecting people and organizations associated with capacity to bounce back to get stronger to advance in the shortest possible time period. Agility refers to the development and deployment of creative ability needed to innovate and move forward to continuous performance improvement required to secure long-term sustainability. It is important to note that Resilience and Agility do depend on rational knowledge but to the large extent are influenced by effective deployment of Soft Skills (Lepeley, 2021; Lepeley et al., 2021b).

The telework transition

The pandemic disruptions forced universities to substitute office research work and f2f teaching with telework and distance learning, compensating inflexible office and classroom work with more flexible online alternatives in teleworking in terms of time and space (Heiden et al., 2021) as a powerful tool to overcome difficulties driven by pandemic effects (Burgos, Tlili, & Tabacco, 2021). In most respects, use of telework led to increased demand for efficiency to rise productivity. Kazekami (2020) argues that telework tends to increase job satisfaction and productivity due to flexible work hours as technology use spreads out and teleworking is increasingly impacting coworker interactions, work schedules and job responsibility in the workplace.

In this disruptive environment, a pressing challenge for universities is to assess the wellbeing of professors and teaching assistants to stimulate high performance in educational outcomes aligned with desirable balance between work and family lives (Beutell, Kuschel, & Lepeley, 2021; Wolor et al., 2020). Rapid shifts to telework often have lacked the necessary planning needed to deploy optimal approaches (Cuerdo-Vilches et al., 2021) and assimilate changes in the use of technologies (Schmitt et al., 2021). These conditions had a negative effect on job satisfaction, productivity and the balance of work and family life (Ono & Mori, 2021).

Pandemic effect on education

The pandemic forced universities to deeper change than organizations in other sectors to react and adapt quickly with limited time and resources (Burgos et al., 2021). Studies report that sudden changes had positive and negative effects on the work and life and wellbeing of professors, students and nonacademic staff (White & McCallum, 2021). On the positive side, some studies reveal that job satisfaction was associated with acquiring new skills, more autonomy and different patterns of socialization (De Los Heros Rondenil et al., 2020). Negative aspects were primarily associated with unexpected disruptions hindering balance between work and family life (Ilic-Kosanovic, 2021) and moving to telework was stressful, affecting wellbeing (Heiden et al., 2021).

In Peru, pandemic disruptions were similar to the rest of the world. Peruvian education workers reported that contracting Covid-19 was a major concern for faculty members, their families and friends. Difficulties adapting to telework led to increases in work overload and job stress due to lack of resources and largely to lack of reliable internet connectivity in rural areas (Miranda, Bazán, & Nureña, 2021). So, universities in general face major problems developing strategies to adapt to the disruptions with new teaching and learning methods (Benites, 2021; Figallo, González, & Diestra, 2020).

Telework at ESAN University

ESAN was established in 1963 in Lima, the capital of Peru, as a graduate business school by an agreement between the Peruvian government and the United States' Stanford University Business School. Today ESAN is a private nonprofit business university. Its primary education focus continues to be graduate business university offering national and internationally recognized master and doctoral programs. ESAN recently established comprehensive undergraduate programs.

ESAN started to offer online programs in 2013, as a pioneer in Latin America. So, its distance education programs grew fast to meet growing national demand for business programs across the country. In 2012, ESAN established the DDE. Since then, it has trained 185 professors to teach online and manage required pedagogical, administrative and technological changes. In 2018, ESAN delivered 83 online courses in 1,100 teaching hours to 975 students.

DDE regularly conducts course assessment reports of students' satisfaction of courses, teaching methods, course contents and value of the experience. According to Oswaldo Morales, who in August 2022 assumed the position of ESAN's Vice President for Research, the results of the assessment activity are used to identify strengths and areas of improvement of the organizational culture to advance change in the university. Morales mentioned that DDE reports significantly anticipated effects of the pandemic disruptions and supported professors to adopt and adapt fast to the telework environments improving OC (Morales et al., 2016) as circumstances required.

ESAN organizational culture and study methodology

With respect to organizational cultures, one of the most commonly assessment methodologies used is the Hofstede dimensions (1990). The Hofstede Organizational Culture Model was developed by Geert Hofstede and Bob Waisfisz (Waisfisz, 2015). It is based on 6 dimensions to measure organizational culture and effectiveness. The dimensions assess OC as follows: means orientation versus goal orientation (D1), internally driven versus externally driven on customer orientation (D2), easy-going work environments versus strict work discipline as levels of control (D3), general versus professional focus (D4), open system versus closed system approachability (D5) and employee-orientated versus work-orientated management philosophy (D6) (Hofstede, 2022). This study chose 3 of the 6 dimensions of the Hofstede Model, D2, D3 and D4, to advance the discussion of convergence with 2 of the 5 pillars of HCM (Lepeley, 2017), namely, Pillar 2 – disruption resilience and Pillar 4 – agility.

Data were collected using an online survey based on three groups of questions: (i) 46 questions with opposite statements imposing forced choice on respondents, (ii) 26 multiple choice questions and (iii) 4 demographic questions. These data serve to develop reports associated with actual and optimal dimension scores, using software purchased from the hofstede-insights.com website.

Hofstede's D2 dimension measures internal versus external orientation. Internal orientation posits that workers say they know their customers' need but rarely ask customers directly. In externally directed organizations, workers maintain continuous dialog with customers to ensure they understand their needs and demands and integrate them in the design and production of products and service. The D3 dimension measures organizational structures and controls that range between easy-going organizations with open and permissive structures with low levels of control to strict work environments highly disciplined and rigorous. The D4 dimension measures social control ranging between workers identifying either with work divisions (e.g., Marketing Department) or identifying primarily with professional roles (e.g., profession first and foremost).

Assessing ESAN's OC

Data to evaluate ESAN's OC were collected as part of a training program of ESAN professors and personnel. A total of 21 professors completed the survey. These data were analyzed on 3 dimensions of the model D2 (score 56), D3 (score 34) and D4 (score 54). The results are shown in Figure 11.1 with a black arrow pointing to scores received in the 3 dimensions.

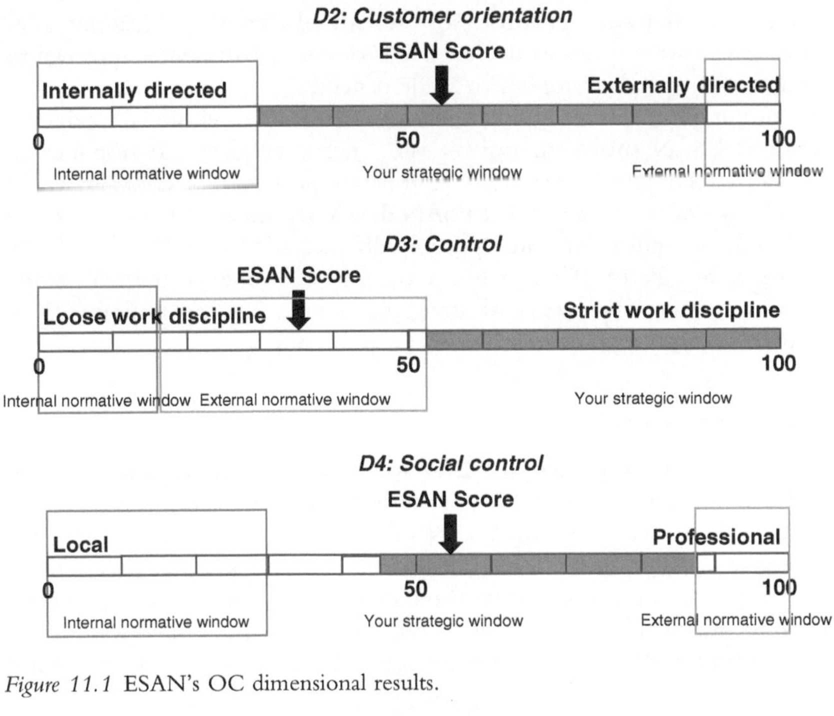

Figure 11.1 ESAN's OC dimensional results.

Results

D2. Customer orientation

Results show that ESAN's culture is more externally oriented, meaning that professors are paying attention to the needs of students. This result is consistent with ESAN's early delivery of online courses and programs and communications with students and the continuous performance assessments leading to customers' satisfaction in program that preceded the pandemic by many years.

D3. Control orientation

Results show an easy-going culture based on autonomy and flexibility, contrasting with high control and strict requirements. Lepeley (2017) indicates that autonomy and flexibility are necessary features to expedite the transition and strengthen development of Human Centered Organizational Culture (HC OC) (Lepeley, 2017; Lepeley et al., 2021a). Waisfisz (2015) points out that ESAN's score demonstrates adaptability and aptitude to deal with unexpected situations.

D4. Social control

Results reveal that ESAN's culture is more professional than locally oriented. Professional orientation is also associated with greater autonomy expressed in active and agile professor–student relationships, including faster responses because professors do not need to seek departmental approval to take action to speed up replies to student needs.

In summary, an externally oriented, easy-going and professionally oriented culture at ESAN shows an organization that is familiar and responds to customers' needs and expectations, stimulating professors to collaborate and innovate. Morales points out that ESAN developed these attributes overtime and significantly advanced and supported distance education (Morales, 2020; Morales et al., 2016). Thus, while Covid-19 was unexpected, this study identifies specific organizational strengths, supporting the importance of resilience and agility to deal with unexpected crises.

Telework and the pandemic

Barreda, Escalante and Picoy (2021a) and Cuenca, Huaman and Rimachi (2021) conducted studies to assess how pandemic mandates impacted that transition to telework among ESAN professors in relation to the balance between work and family life. The findings showed low negative effects; even when professors reported working more hours, this did not affect their ability to adequately balance work with family responsibilities. Further, their communications with colleagues remained active during transition routines and their work responsibilities were not significantly affected. Some professors indicated that after the transition to telework they felt more productive than before. Similarly, even though work overload, autonomy and stress were reported by some professors with negative impact, the transition in general was considered successful.

The decision to offer classes online was advanced based on ESAN's strategy to train professors using teaching platforms, keeping regular communication with supervisors and students and providing open access to the Graduate School Dean and professors. Results suggest that providing professors with the necessary resources to guide students through the transition with a commitment to high performance significantly facilitates telework deployment across the institution.

Resiliency and agility in ESAN OC

Although attributes associated with resilience and agility were not explicitly tested in the study, both concepts are a central focus of ESAN's OC contingent with long standing research collaboration between HCM Editors and ESAN professors, who have contributed to extensive advances of HCM.

Study findings allow to confirm evidence that ESAN has an OC that pays attention and promotes the wellbeing of professors converging with resilience and agility principles and practices embedded in Pillars 2 and 4 of HCM. ESAN supported professors with consistent approaches to adapt and adopt new conditions of telework. Additionally, the DDE, which directed the program, provided years of experience and investment in training aiming to meet students' needs that contributed to smooth the transition along with latest methods and pedagogical tools to design and manage change with resilience and agility. These efforts increased the institutional memory and knowledge capital with sensitivity on people's needs allowing professors to compensate negative effects that included finding adequate alignment along the Life–Work Continuum (Beutell et al., 2021). This suggests that organizations that embrace innovation in response to market changes may have advantages to confront challenges induced by pandemic effects.

Moreover, ESAN's experience suggests that educational institutions deploying people centered culture aligned with HCM's principles of resilience and agility are likely to provide more suitable support to university managers, professors and students needed to expedite successful transitions from in-person approaches to the online environment.

Concluding suggestions

The unprecedented local and global disruptions of the Covid-19 pandemic that expose people and organizations to one of the worst crises the world had not seen since the end of World War II led to difficult problems and detrimental effects for educational institutions. Although the pandemic affected organizations in all sectors and industries, education suffered deeper, more drastic and long-lasting transformation transitioning from f2f operations between instructors and students to practically total online environment in an extremely short time.

The study conducted at ESAN University to assess performance and adaptation to telework and online education showed that its HC OC oriented to meet the needs of people was most effective. In ESAN's case, professors were able to help students because they have a considerable level of autonomy to make decisions about work and interactions with students in a relaxed environment, more inclined to professional practice than administrative controls, expedited adaptation and the transition.

The research team anticipated the importance of resilience and agility embedded in HCM and found that ESAN's OC offered professors, students and personnel effective support develop resilience and act with agility to deal with the challenges increasing benefits and minimizing inherent costs of disruptions.

ESAN's early experience in online education offered significant advantages in times of need and confirmed the institution was well positioned the change to the telework environment. ESAN's experience confirms that organizations that develop resilience and agility support HCM culture with advantages to face crises by enabling academics and staff to advance their wellbeing along the Life-Work Continuum.

References

Alqahtani, A. Y., & Rajkhan, A. A. (2020). E-learning critical success factors during the Covid-19 pandemic: A comprehensive analysis of e-learning managerial perspectives. *Education Sciences*, 10(9), 216. 10.3390/educsci10090216

Barreda, S., Escalante, A., & Picoy, A. (2021). *Influence of the perception of remote work conditions on the job satisfaction of postgraduate professors during the Covid-19 pandemic.* (Original title: *Influencia de la percepción de las condiciones del trabajo no presencial en la satisfacción laboral de los profesores de posgrado durante la pandemia por la Covid-19*) [Unpublished master's thesis]. ESAN University.

Benites, R. (2021, April). *University higher education in post-pandemic Peru* (Original title: *La educación superior universitaria en el Perú post-pandemia).* Serie Políticas y Debates Públicos, PUCP.

Beutell, N. J., Kuschel, K., & Lepeley, M. T. (2021). Life–work continuum: The new organizational culture. In Lepeley, M. T., Morales, O., Essens, P., Beutell, N. J., & Majluf, N. (Eds.). *Human centered organizational culture: Global dimensions* (pp. 23–33). Routledge.

Burgos, D., Tlili, A., & Tabacco, A. (2021). *Radical solutions for education in a crisis context: Covid-19 as an opportunity for global learning.* Springer.

Cuenca, E., Huaman, M., & Rimachi, E. (2021). *The perception of teleworking and its influence on work-life balance in university professors during Covid-19* (Original title: *La percepción del teletrabajo y su influencia en el balance vida trabajo en profesores universitarios durante la Covid-19*) [Unpublished master's thesis]. ESAN University.

Cuerdo-Vilches, T., Navas-Martín, A., March, S., & Oteiza, I. (2021). Adequacy of telework spaces in homes during the lockdown in Madrid, according to socioeconomic factors and home features. *Sustainable Cities and Society*, 75, 103262. 10.1016/j.scs.2021.103262

De Los Heros Rondenil, M. G., Murillo López, S. C., & Solana Villanueva, N. (2020). Job satisfaction in times of pandemic: the case of university professors in the health area (Original title: Satisfacción laboral en tiempos de pandemia: El caso de docentes universitarios del área de salud. *Revista de Economía del Caribe*, 26. 10.14482/ecoca.26.158.7

Figallo, F., González, M., & Diestra V. (2020). Peru: Higher education in the context of the Covid-19 pandemic (Original title: Perú: Educación superior en el contexto de la pandemia por el Covid-19). *Revista de Educación Superior en América Latina*, 8, 20–28. 10.14482/esal.8.378.85

Heiden, M., Widar, L., Wiitavaara, B., & Borman, E. (2021). Telework in academia: Associations with health and well-being among staff. *Higher Education*, 81(4), 707–722. 10.1007/s10734-020-00569-4

Hofstede, G., Neuijen, B., Ohayv, D. D., & Sanders, G. (1990). Measuring organizational cultures: A qualitative and quantitative study across twenty cases. *Administrative Science Quarterly*, 35(2), 286–316. 10.2307/2393392

Hofstede Insights. (2022). *What Are the Dimensions of Organisational Culture?* https://hi.hofstede-insights.com/organisational-culture#step-5

Ilic-Kosanovic, T. (2021). Work-life balance of teaching staff at higher education during pandemic. *Serbian Journal of Engineering Management*, 6(1), 63–71. 10.5937/sjem2101064i

International Labour Organization (2020, May 18). *An employers' guide on working from home in response to the outbreak of Covid-19.* https://www.ilo.org/actemp/publications/WCMS_745024/lang–en/index.htm

Kazekami, S. (2020). Mechanisms to improve labor productivity by performing telework. *Telecommunications Policy*, 44(2), 101868. 10.1016/j.telpol.2019.101868

Lepeley, M. T., Morales, O., Essens, P., Beutell, N. J., & Majluf, N. (Eds.). (2021a). *Human centered organizational culture: Global dimensions*. Routledge.

Lepeley, M. T., Beutell, N. J., Abarca, N., & Majful, N. (Eds.). (2021b). *Soft skills for human centered management and global sustainability*. Routledge.

Lepeley, M. T. (2021). Master soft skills: The resilience–agility umbrella model. In Lepeley, M. T., Beutell, N. J., Abarca, N., & Majful, N. (Eds.). (2021). *Soft skills for human centered management and global sustainability* (pp. 23–37). Routledge.

Lepeley, M. T. (2017). *Human centered management: 5 pillars of organizational quality and global sustainability*. Routledge.

Miranda, R., Bazán, C., & Nureña, C. (2021). *Teacher well-being and the impact of the Covid-19 pandemic in rural multigrade schools* (Original title: *Bienestar docente e impacto de la pandemia de Covid-19 en escuelas rurales multigrado).* Proyecto CREER/GRADE. http://www.grade.org.pe/creer/recurso/bienestar-docente-e-impacto-de-la-pandemia-de-covid-19-en-escuelas-rurales-multigrado-un-estudio-cualitativo-con-docentes-de-tres-regiones-del-peru/

Morales, O., Rees, G., & Morales, S. (2021). Assessment of the theoretical evolution of organizational culture: Pending need for human focus. In Lepeley, M. T., Morales, O., Essens, P., Beutell, N. J., & Majluf, N. (Eds.). *Human centered organizational culture: Global dimensions* (pp. 93–103). Routledge.

Morales, O. (2020). Virtual education in ESAN: Cultural change in the adoption of new technologies associated with online education (Original title: La educación virtual en ESAN: Cambio cultural en la adopción de nuevas tecnologías asociadas a la educación online). In Sarabia, C. & Morales, O. (Eds.). *Case study in the use of technologies applied to university teaching (original title: Estudio de casos en el uso de tecnologías aplicadas a la docencia universitaria)* (pp. 201–224). McGraw-Hill.

Morales, O., Vértiz, H., & Puertas, J. (2016). Proposal for online people-centered management executive education: A case study at ESAN University. In M. Lepeley, E. Kimakowitz & R. Bardy (Eds.), *Human centered management in executive education* (pp. 258–272). Palgrave Macmillan.

Organisation for Economic Co-operation and Development – OECD. (2020). *Covid-19 in Latin America and the Caribbean: An overview of government responses to the crisis.* https://www.oecd.org/coronavirus/policy-responses/Covid-19-in-latin-america-and-the-caribbean-an-overview-of-government-responses-to-the-crisis-0a2dee41/

Ono, H., & Mori, T. (2021). Covid-19 and telework: An international comparison. *Journal of Quantitative Description: Digital Media*, 1, 1–35. 10.51685/jqd.2021.004

Schein, E. (2017). *Organizational culture and leadership.* Wiley.

Schmitt, J., Breuer, J., & Wulf, T. (2021). From cognitive overload to digital detox: Psychological implications of telework during the Covid-19 pandemic. *Computers in Human Behavior*, 24, 106899. 10.1016/j.chb.2021.106899

White, M., & McCallum, F. (Eds.). (2021). *Wellbeing and resilience education: Covid-19 and its impact on education.* Routledge.

Waisfisz, B. (2015). *Constructing the best culture to perform.* Itim International.

Wolor, C., Solikhah, S., Fidhyallah, N., & Lestari, D. (2020). Effectiveness of e-training, e-leadership, and work life balance on employee performance during Covid-19. *Journal of Asian Finance, Economics and Business*, 7(10), 443–450. 10.13106/jafeb.2020.vol7.no10.443

12 Online Higher Education and Pandemic Disruptions

Rosa Ulloa

Introduction

The Covid-19 pandemic had implications for people and organizations. The impacts are so deep that we have not had time to reflect on them. It will take a long time to understand what has changed and what needs to be changed to reinstate the Human Centered Perspective at the core of the current volatile and uncertain local and global environment.

Lockdowns forced us to implement technological tools and digital platforms for the continuity of work. Education was one of the sectors that rapidly switched to intensive use of technology and digital tools, leaving behind offices and buildings. Higher Education Institutions (HEI) adopted Online Education (OE) abruptly, and teachers, students and administrators were deeply disrupted without an adequate and complete technological adoption causing negative impacts on their perception of OE effectiveness and benefits.

Internally, the institutional shock was chaotic, difficult and resulted in a partial, incomplete and inadequate move. It caught faculty, students and administrators unprepared, ill-equipped and scared. Externally, many months of uncertainty and ambiguity, built up negative perceptions about HED vulnerabilities, liabilities and low capacity to face disruptions and deal with rapid change. In terms of management and leadership, the pandemic was an unparalleled trial of HED resilience and agility (Lepeley, 2017).

Beyond detrimental external perceptions, overtime the pandemic crisis brought to light the benefits of OE as new delivery formats with advantages that started to compensate for initial disadvantages and limitations. The pending challenge was to generate knowledge to increase understanding of such an unprecedented phenomenon by starting to identify the differences between existing and fast-emerging OE.

The rest of the chapter discussed the effects of imposed pandemic directives that steered negative perceptions of OE in contrast with positive outcomes. These negative perceptions of shortcomings are contrasted with evidence of benefits presented in research findings of the transition, evolution, gains and overall, new opportunities to foster human development and wellbeing for significantly larger numbers of students.

DOI: 10.4324/9781003330011-15

The concluding discussion presents emerging experiences increasing capacity to deal more effectively with disruptions and calls attention to the need to align HED management with Human Centered Management (HCM) principles and practices, integrating Disruption Resilience, 2nd Pillar of HCM (Lepeley, 2017) and Human Centered Leadership (Majluf & Abarca, 2021) as critical elements to deal effectively with complex and difficult disruptions and be prepared to face unexpected transitions protecting the wellbeing of people.

Online education in the pre-pandemic environment

In the decade previous to the Covid-19 pandemic, the resurgence and rapid growth of OE stimulated volumes of research focused on comparing it with traditional learning practices. Studies reported differences in students' demographics, age, marital and employment status, but student outcomes and achievements showed no differences (Paul & Jefferson, 2019; Vlachopoulos, Jan, & Lockyer, 2019). Findings also corroborated that traditional education materials and resources were outdated and resulted in unsuitable education materials and resources for developing distance education programs. Another significant problem to accept OE was that students felt a sense of isolation driving low motivation, resulting in high dropout rates from online courses.

Overtime a new body of theoretical knowledge emerged following several lines of research proposals. The Transactional Distance Theory (TDT) presented a framework to develop distance education programs following a systematic approach (Kukul, 2021), addressing issues related to instructional modality (Lister & McFarlane, 2021) and training OE professors to mediate with psychological and communicational challenges. At this point, the relevance of training teachers using a different method than traditional classroom education had become clear. And so did the growing need to instruct students on new online learning technics, communication skills and approaches required to be functional with technology in the digital environment, deeply contrasting with face-to-face classrooms.

TDT significantly facilitated the systematic deployment of OE driving its expansion, not exclusively in HEIs but also for other organizations providing training for work and continuing education. Research in the field provided effective guidance to implement OE efficiently and securely to prevent emotional issues, such as working linking learning and emotions (Immordino-Yang, 2015). Those studies resolved issues for instructional OE designers and course instructors that help to diminish psychological concerns and also geographical distance constraints (Moore, 1993).

Advances in technological developments that strengthen OE induced more people to register. OE growth trends revealed that while traditional in situ HED enrollments were decreasing those of OE showed steadily increases (Seaman, Allen, & Seaman, 2018). The flexibility of OE met a growing demand among people in the workforce and working in organizations that had been unable to participate in traditional learning instruction (Ghallagher, 2016). Overtime this growing trend led to society's acceptance of OE as legitimate education. People became confident and trusted OE delivering up-to-date education with time flexibility and deleting geographical distance concerns to reach schools and institutions.

In terms of learning outputs, studies documented personal motivation as the most relevant factor in high achievement (Giesbers et al., 2013; Castillo Merino & Serradell López, 2014; He et al., 2015) and use of advanced strategies aimed to improve and engage students in online courses.

Technological advances closed gaps in OE instructors' training, and communication processes became more efficient and effective. Discussions about the benefits of mixing modal instructions arose as a consequence and traditional learning was pressed to improve in parallel with online learning using more technological interactions (Picciano, Seaman, & Allen, 2010). Instructors improved students' guidance focusing less on course content and more on providing students with a significant experience for life. The experience using digital technologies led to more efficient educational processes and outcomes.

The benefits of OE expanded rapidly, acknowledged the practical implications for professional training, the achievement of 21st-century skills (Ferran-Ferrer, Minguillón, & Pérez-Montoro, 2013) and Soft Skills (Ulloa-Cazarez, 2021).

While acceptance of OE was growing, educational efforts worldwide were innovating classroom practices with digital technologies implementing novel synchronous and asynchronous communications, and introducing new teaching and learning dynamics that enriched settings supporting developments in OE and digital technologies as a parallel process.

Research on this topic is a work in progress, but it is helpful to identify disciplines and dynamics with the potential to add knowledge and information on complementary modalities. For instance, successful development of educational technology quickly raised interest in other scientific fields of human development, including psychology and health. Moreover, instructional technologies were seen as an approach that could reduce social and psychological problems and a solution for people unable to advance in traditional, highly controlled educational environments. Applying gamification strategies created new scenarios for younger ages and adding options for people with disabilities. OE developments yielded successful outputs and practices, and by the end of the last decade, online learning was an accepted educational scenario with fast-increasing new offerings of formats to meet almost any educational needs.

HED during the Covid-19 pandemic

At the beginning of the pandemic, organizations in different industries reacted differently to the mandatory measures, according to their capacities to handle the unknown and unexpected. Some businesses were forced to close, unable to deal with financial distress and health problems, technological shortcomings and fear and uncertainty in a rapidly changing and threatening environment (Bartik et al., 2020; Eurostat, 2020; Romero, 2020). In 2020, increasing numbers of organizations in all sectors and industries closed because of decreasing customers, supply chain issues, escalating inflation and price increases (Bogdan, 2022). Other organizations prevailed, transforming the way of conducting businesses and adopting new digital technology, platforms and telework.

In this environment, agility and innovative capacity became the key to sustainability. Some lessons are targeted, and some educational institutions are included in this group of survivors. There is evidence that most universities did not stop providing educational services to their communities, although many revealed important gaps in performance (The World Bank, UNESCO, & UNICEF, 2021) facing important negative pandemic effects. But institutions advanced the transition from traditional mode to distance education strategies and OE.

HEIs were pressed to manage and rearrange their intellectual and economic capital to solve pressing operational issues including supporting and re-training faculty and staff to deal with effects of pandemic lockdowns and the surmounting health risks. A most pressing issue was rapid access and adoption of new technology and technical knowledge to face drastically different scenarios and many obstacles that obstruct the technological transition.

In spite of increasing availability and access to new online tools and technics provided to educational institutions by international development organizations (like UNESCO and OECD), some universities went on lockdowns, unable to cope with technological infrastructure, training faculty and personnel in new information technologies (Hu, 2022).

It is important to recall that before the pandemic induced health risks and emergencies, educational systems were already struggling with persistent financial constraints, inefficient management, limited resources and insufficiently well trained personnel. The harming issues that existed before the pandemic increased after pandemic disruptions (The World Bank, UNESCO, & UNICEF, 2021), creating highly challenging scenarios for HEIs, considering the importance and magnitude of HED for the population at large and overall, for vulnerable groups assisted by institutions.

The pandemic exposed a persistent need to improve education and the responsibility of institutions to offer quality standards to all students in the system (Lepeley, 2017; Lepeley et al., 2021a,b). School and university closures deeply harmed students with significant learning losses and led to dropout rates among the most vulnerable. There are growing concerns about the long-lasting effects of ongoing problems in education and the urgent need for solutions to mitigate losses. In contrast, universities in countries without or with less restrictive pandemic mandates continued providing educational services and did not report significant differences in enrollments but increased capacity to escalate engaging faculty, students and communities in OE.

OE as an emergency pandemic response

During the start of the pandemic, OE surged as an emergency response, largely improvising, giving place to misconceptions about its relevance and quality standards. The abrupt implementation encountered many professors unwilling to incorporate Information and Communication Technologies (ICT) and OE in their teaching practices (Kamal & Illiyan, 2021). Consequently, concerns about OE utility were exacerbated by an ongoing debate about its effectiveness, appropriateness and doubtful contribution to improving people's wellbeing and performance levels. Prior to the pandemic the use of ICTs was optional for educators. But starting in 2020, it became mandatory. Still, not all teaching faculty members showed engagement due to original resistance, lack of training and infrastructure, among other issues that have been dragging since then.

Program scope and limited OE support

Broad OE diversity in design, delivery, programs and formatting required intensive technical training and development of personal attitudes and adaptation to transit from the physical to the digital environment. Moreover, personality traits and privacy considerations, although less critical than health risks, in many instances prevented faculty and students from adopting and enjoying technological innovation.

The global surveys identified the most common causes of abandoning OE studies during lockdowns (Schleicher, 2020; United Nations, 2020; INEGI, 2021):

1 Inadequacy of instruction

- Deployment was considered an exploratory initiative, not a well-planned transition, but a jump.
- Teachers and staff were pressed to adapt traditional classes to online education format in record time with most not being trained.
- Lack of guidelines and syllabus on online learning pedagogics, didactics and expertise to measure performance and outcomes.
- Significant improvisation created obstacles exacerbated by Covid-19 pandemic's chaotic and terrifying environment.

2 Lack of supportive environments for learning

- Lack of empathy, abilities, cognitive knowledge and mastery of important Soft Skills aligned with HCM described by Lepeley et al. (2021a,b).

- Lack of teachers' and students' technical knowledge to manage educational technology.

3 Lack of access to the required technology.

- Lack of teachers' and students' technical and technological in-home infrastructure
- High cost of electricity and Internet connection.

These issues disturbed educators and institutions. There were multiple and limited solutions. Teachers were in charge of course implementation using succinct and insufficient instruction about available solutions and when training was available, it was late. There were major concerns that the problems had started before the pandemic and the pandemic had only dragged on and increased them.

In general, the transition was easier for young people as students using digital games and social networks. Adults and older people (many teachers are!) were hesitant to expose themselves to social and public networks and to use invasive educational technologies in confinement. It was confirmed that older people prefer to use social networks privately and exclusively for social purposes.

Thus, surveyed participants reported security issues and privacy threats, including abuses and criminal activities that nobody was prepared to handle. Neither OE instructors nor students received support to manage privacy violations in isolation. Nonetheless, during Covid-19, school and work exposed people to unprecedented risks that, for some, seemed like a private space invasion. Depressive emotions increased as online settings did not secure OE healing potential. These experiences and perceptions unveiled the need for solutions.

Technology acceptance

Davis' Technology Acceptance Model (1989) explains the relationships between technology acceptance, adoption and use (Marikyan & Papagiannidis, 2022). Further research confirms that frequent use of technology in daily practices helps people perceive it as easy and useful. Some studies found that perceived use correlates highly with personal proficiency contrasting with people who reject ICT when they consider it difficult and useless (Lai, 2017).

The pandemic's disruptive environment confirmed to this author that academia needs to transcend from the traditional resource-focused culture to the advanced principles that position the wellbeing of people at the center (Lepeley, 2017, 2021a,b). A study conducted by the author showed that to anticipate and increase their capacity to solve problems in periods of crisis, which are increasingly often, HEIs must learn and apply the principles of Disruption Resilience HCM's second Pillar, detailing along Human Centered Leadership. There is extensive evidence that rejecting technology, lack of interest and low preparation in ICT and OE competencies, in particular, will become a growing problem for educational achievement, economic growth and social and inclusive development. To a large extent, technology rejection, associated exclusively with pandemic disruptions, is misleading because there are multiple human dimensions involved that have not been properly addressed.

People's attitudes and environmental effects

Research in Environmental Psychology reports that people's behavior is influenced by environmental conditions (Hu, 2022). That was the case during the pandemic in 2020 and 2021. Health risks, uncertainty and vulnerability affected people's emotions, fear and worry increasing the incidence of depression and anxiety as leading causes of sleep deprivation and cognitive gaps affecting learning and decision-making.

Confinements affected people's reasoning and focus on engagement and performance – these effects stand out when people answered surveys and expressed lower than actual achievement perception. On the contrary, research comparing pandemic effects on students' achievement in OE before and during the pandemic showed an instructional modality positive moderate impact on learning regardless of subject and country (Ulum, 2022); motivation was the most relevant factor of perseverance and achievement (Giesbers et al., 2013; Castillo Merino & Serradell López, 2014; He et al., 2015) which confirms the perceptions during lockdowns were affected.

Therefore, my research confirms environmental effects on people's perceptions, including the use of strategies to humanize OE (Ulloa-Cazarez, 2021), the deployment of Soft Skills consistent with online learning, impacting success in education, in life and the workplace.

Pending solution: Disruption resilience and human centered leadership

Surmounting evidence shows that the Covid-19 pandemic and ongoing disruptions in the environment had and continue to have detrimental impact on people's life and work. And similar conditions replicate across countries, societies and organizations in all sectors and industries. The pandemic tested the strength of educational systems. Some did better than others, but all suffered deep and prolonged internal crises during the abrupt transition from the physical environments to digital platforms and OE.

Management had previously identified problems of technology rejection in academic scenarios impacted by institutional and personal strategies aimed to cope with confinement that required intensive use of technologies. Moreover, OE is now the norm rather than the exception. Therefore, ICT should no longer be a debatable issue but another approach to advance teaching and learning opportunities.

In this new environment, it is imperative to identify pending issues obstructing a smoother transition, taking advantage of improved infrastructures and advanced intellectual capital creating a human centered culture (Lepeley, 2021b), an organizational culture that provides meaning to individual contributions addressing head-on.

HEIs problems expose technology difficulties (Ribeiro et al., 2018) and impact the mental health of professors and students (Lister & McFarlane, 2021). Thus, there is pending work for HEIs to deploy continuous assessment and improvement of educational leadership (Majluf & Abarca, 2021) to solve the problems at hand. Moreover, increasing and strengthening the resilience capacity of people and institutions is an essential condition to identify disruptions that have long been dragging on, negatively impacting the wellbeing of people.

Majluf and Abarca (2022) present a framework to identify, improve and value sensible leaders to promote a resilient organizational culture. The model goes beyond personal characteristics on abilities to adapt and behave according to the context and situation. HEI leadership should advance in this direction and would benefit significantly from deploying HCM principles and practices focusing on the wellbeing of teachers, students and staff, recognizing feelings and perceptions and collecting information for improvement.

OE is a most effective tool when it is purposely implemented with reliable information. It enables consolidatation of institutional capacity to recognize the origins of disruptions and act with resilience, considering resilience as a precondition to improve wellbeing for HEIs to advance and excel in attaining sustainability in normal times, but overall in times of crises.

References

Azevedo, J. et al. (2021). *The State of the Global Education Crisis: A Path to Recovery (English)*, World Bank Group. United States of America. Retrieved from https://policycommons.net/artifacts/2004880/the-state-of-the-global-education-crisis/2757316/ on 24 Apr 2023. CID: 20.500.12592/cgmfm3

Bartik, A.W., Bertrand, M., Cullen, Z., & Stanton, C. (2020). The impact of Covid-19 on small business outcomes and expectations. *PNAS*, 117(30), 17656–17666. 10.1073/pnas.2006991117

Beutell, N.J., Kuschel, K., & Lepeley, M.T. (2021). Life-work continuum: The new organizational culture In Lepeley, M. T., Morales, O., Essens, P., Beutell, N. J., & Majluf, N.(Eds.). *Human centered organizational cultural: Global dimensions* (pp. 23–33). Routledge.

Bogdan, S. (2022, January 19). London Ont. small businesses closing, say Covid restrictions make it impossible to stay open. *Global News*. https://globalnews.ca/news/8524275/london-ont-small-business-omicron-struggle/

Castillo-Merino, D., & Serradell-López, E. (2014). An analysis of the determinants of students' performance in e-learning. *Computers in Human Behavior*, 30, 476–484. 10.1016/j.chb.2013.06.020

Davis, F.D. (1989). Perceived usefulness, perceived ease of use, and user acceptance of information technology. *MIS Quarterly*, 13(3), 319–340. 10.2307/249008

El Turk, S., & Cherney, I. D. (2016). Perceived online education barriers of administrators and faculty at a U.S. University in Lebanon. *Creighton Journal of Interdisciplinary Leadership*, 2(1), 15–31. 10.17062/CJIL.v2i1.30

Eurostat (2020, June 18). *Impact of Covid-19 crisis on short-term statistics*. Retrieved May 01, 2022, from https://ec.europa.eu/eurostat/statistics-explained/index.php?title=Impact_of_Covid-19_crisis_on_short-term_statistics

Fenton-O'Creevy, M., Soane, E., Nicholson, N., & Willman, P. (2011). Thinking, feeling and deciding: The influence of emotions on the decision making and performance of traders. *Journal of Organizational Behavior*, 32(8), 1044–1061. 10.1002/job.720

Ferran-Ferrer, N., Minguillón, J., & Pérez-Montoro, M. (2013). Key factors in the transfer of information-related competencies between academic, workplace, and daily life contexts. *Journal of the American Society for Information Science and Technology*, 64(6), 1112–1121. 10.1002/asi.22817

Ghallagher, S.R. (2016). *The future of university credentials: New developments at the interaction of higher education and hiring*. Cambridge: Harvard University Press.

Giesbers, B., Rienties, B., Tempelaar, D., & Gijselaers, W. (2013). Investigating the relations between motivation, tool use, participation, and performance in an e-learning course using web-videoconferencing. *Computers in Human Behavior*, 29(1), 285–292. 10.1016/j.chb.2012.09.005

He, W., Gajski, D., Farkas, G., & Warschauer, M. (2015). Implementing flexible hybrid instruction in an electrical engineering course: The best of three worlds? *Computers and Education*, 81, 59–68. 10.1016/j.compedu.2014.09.005

Hu, Y.-H. (2022). Effects of the Covid-19 pandemic on the online learning behaviors of university students in Taiwan. *Education and Information Technologies*, 27, 469–491. 10.1007/s10639-021-10677-y

Immordino-Yang, M.H. (2015). *Emotions, learning and the brain: Exploring the educational implications of affective neuroscience*. W. W. Norton & Company.

INEGI (2021, April 23). *Survey to measure the impact of Covid-19 on education (ECovid-ED) 2020*. Retrieved from https://en.www.inegi.org.mx/investigacion/eCovided/2020/

Kamal, T., & Illiyan, A. (2021). School teachers' perception and challenges towards online teaching during Covid-19 pandemic in India: An econometric analysis. *Asian Association of Open Universities Journal*, 16(3), 311–325. 10.1108/aaouj-10-2021-0122

Kukul, V. (2021). On becoming an online university in an emergency period: Voices from the students at a state university. *Open Praxis*, 13(2), 172–183. 10.5944/openpraxis.13.2.127

Lai, P. (2017). The literature review of Technology Adoption Models and Theories for the Novelty Technology. *Journal of Information Systems and Technology Management*, 14(1), 21–38. 10.4301/S1807-17752017000100002

Lepeley, M.T. (2017). *Human centered management. 5 pillars of organizational quality and global sustainability*. Routledge.

Lepeley, M. T. (2021a). Soft Skills. The Lingua Franca of Human Centered Management in the Global VUCA Environment. In Lepeley, M.T., Beutell, N.J., Abarca, N., & Majful, N. (Eds.). *Soft Skills for Human Centered Management and Global Sustainability*. Routledge, UK.

Lepeley, M. T. (2021b). Master Soft Skills. The Resilience – Agility Umbrella Model. InLepeley, M.T., Moralez, O., Essens, P., Beutell, N.J., & Majluf, N. (Eds.). *Soft Skills for Human Centered Management and Global Sustainability*. Routledge, UK.

Lister, K., & McFarlane, R. (2021). Designing for wellbeing: An inclusive learning design approach with student mental health vignettes. *Open Praxis*, 13(2), 184–200. 10.5944/openpraxis.13.2.126

Majluf, N., & Abarca, N. (2021). *Sensible leadership: Human centered, insightful and prudent*. Routledge.

Marikyan, D., & Papagiannidis, S. (2022). Technology acceptance model: A review. In Papagiannidis, S. (Ed.), *TheoryHub Book*. http://open.ncl.ac.uk

Moore, M. (1993). Theory of transactional distance. In Keegan., D. (Ed.). *Theoretical principles of distance education* (pp. 16–33). Routledge.

Paul, J., & Jefferson, F. (2019). A comparative analysis of student performance in an online vs. face-to-face environmental science course from 2009 to 2016. *Frontiers in Computer Science*, 1(7), 1–9. 10.3389/fcomp.2019.00007

Picciano, A.G., Seaman, J., & Allen, I. (2010). Educational transformation through online learning: To be or not to be. *Journal of Asynchronous Learning Networks*, 14(4), 17–35. 10.24059/olj.v14i4.147

Ribeiro, Í.J., Pereira, R., Freire, I.V., de Oliveira, B.G., Casotti, C.A., & Boery, E.N. (2018). Stress and quality of life among university students: A systematic literature review. *Health Professions Education*, 4(2), 70–77. 10.1016/j.hpe.2017.03.002

Romero, T. (2020, August 14). *Statista*. https://www.statista.com/statistics/1173472/adults-close-business-coronavirus-mexico/

Schleicher, A. (2020, June). The impact of Covid-19 on education. Insights from education at a glance 2020. *Organisation for Economic Cooperation and Development*. https://www.oecd.org/education/the-impact-of-Covid-19-on-education-insights-education-at-a-glance-2020.pdf

Seaman, J.E., Allen, I.E., & Seaman, J. (2018). *Grade increase. Tracking distance education in the United States*. Babson Survey Research Group. https://www.bayviewanalytics.com/reports/gradeincrease.pdf

Ubell, R. (2017, January 10). Why faculty still don't want to teach online. *The OLC Blog*: https://onlinelearningconsortium.org/faculty-still-dont-want-teach-online/

Ulloa-Cazarez, R.L. (2021). Soft skills and online higher education. In Lepeley, M. T., Beutell, N. J., Abarca, N., & Majluf, N. (Eds.). *Soft skills for human centered management and global sustainability* (pp. 77–92). Routledge.

Ulum, H. (2022). The effects of online education on academic success: A meta-analysis study. *Education and Information Technologies*, 27, 429–450. 10.1007/s10639-021-10740-8

UNICEF (2020, September s/d). *Education and Covid-19*. Retrieved from UNICEF: https://data.unicef.org/topic/education/Covid-19/

United Nations (2020, August 22). *Policy brief: Education during Covid-19 and beyond*. Department of Economic and Social Affairs. https://www.un.org/development/desa/dspd/wp-content/uploads/sites/22/2020/08/sg_policy_brief_covid-19_and_education_august_2020.pdf

Varela, O.E., Cater III, J.J., & Michel, N. (2012). Online learning in management education: An empirical study of the role personality traits. *Journal of Computing in Higher Education*, 24(3), 209–255. 10.1007/s12528-012-9059-x

Vlachopoulos, P., Jan, S.K., & Lockyer, L. (2019). A comparative study on the traditional and intensive delivery of an online course: Design and facilitation recommendations. *Research in Learning Technology*, 27. 10.25304/rlt.v27.2196

Part 4

Health Care: Disruptions and Solutions

13 Healthcare Professionals and Emerging Psychosocial Risks

Josep M. Blanch, Paola Ochoa, and David Coello-Montecel

Introduction

Since 2019, organizations and workplaces around the world are going through one of the most complex transitions in human history exacerbated by the pandemic crisis, deeply disrupting the workplace with abrupt changes and explosive expansion use of technology, digitization, virtualization and online connectivity. The new scenario presses to rethink in need to update old constructs of management models that hinder working conditions, quality of working life, sustainability in organizations demonstrating growing concerns in occupational health and emerging issues in the ongoing crises.

At practitioner's level, disruptions reveal intensifying harm of psychosocial risks threatening wellbeing in the workplace, harming performance and productivity and the quality of services provided to users and the community. There is a global concern to pay attention to improvement of working conditions and wellbeing of healthcare workers of the International Labor Organization (ILO, 2022, 2021, 2020, 2013), the World Health Organization (WHO, 2022, 2019, 2022), the WHO & ILO (2022), the United Nations Development Programme UNDP (2022a, 2022b, 2015) and the European Union (Eurofound, 2022; Eurofound and ILO, 2017; European Agency for Safety and Health at Work -EU OSHA-, 2015, 2014a, 2014b).

This chapter presents the key elements necessary to understand this complex process and suggests proposals for achieving improvement to diminish and prevent psychosocial risks that exploded during the pandemic. The discussion aimed to stimulate models to restore wellbeing in the workplace and focuses of convergence with Human Centered Management (HCM) principles and practices promoting job satisfaction, performance and productivity to secure institutional sustainability with resilience and agility to face disruptions and ongoing crises.

Changes in healthcare

Historically, healthcare professionals have been highly respected in communities and societies worldwide. In the last decades, they were at the top of

DOI: 10.4324/9781003330011-17

prestige and achievement in recognition for their work. By 2020, when unprecedented Covid-19 pandemic disruptions generated, explosive demand for healthcare services, largely pressed by life–death situations, an unending crisis thrusted healthcare professionals to work overloads, compassion fatigue, burnout, identity crisis, tampering work commitment, absenteeism and desertion. Critical situations have been attributed to growing asymmetry between increasing job demands (cognitive, emotional, social, communicative, digital and administrative) and scarcity of healthcare people (knowledge, skills) and resources (material, instrumental, organizational) required to managing unprecedented disruptions in work schedules. Overwork, time pressure and extra emotional involvement that emerged during the crisis are among many risk factors leading work burnout and other pathologies.

Covid-19 pandemic was a most disruptive development due to sudden, unforeseen and initially uncontrollable forces exposing vulnerability in people and organizations. The consequences were unparalleled in terms of high levels of uncertainty and insecurity interacting with work overload deteriorating performance and inducing remarkable harm in occupational wellbeing of healthcare workers.

The assessment of management approaches during the pandemic in healthcare and the wellbeing of health professionals covered in this chapter are an extension to pre-existing psychosocial risks of healthcare workers previously identified in the literature (Granero et al., 2018; Eurofound and the International Labour, 2017; Maslach & Leiter, 2017; 2016; Maslach et al., 2012, 2001; Ochoa & Blanch, 2016; EU-OSHA, 2015, 2014a, 2014b; Humphries et al., 2014; Blanch, 2014; Blanch et al., 2012a, 2012b; Duxbury et al., 2008).

It is important to note that although healthcare workers were more directly impacted by negative effects of the Covid pandemic and crisis than other service care industries, they serve as examples to assess effects in other sectors facing similar psychosocial problems, such as education, community services, family services, justice, banking, insurance, call centers and public administration confronting deep pandemic disruptions.

Magnitude of disruptions

Extreme disruptions caused by the pandemic pressed organizations in all sectors and worldwide to pay increased attention to surmounting evidence showing that external events have inevitable impact and have consequences on internal organizational management and dynamics (Lepeley, 2017). Sticking effects of the pandemic in healthcare institutions expose vulnerabilities of contemporary workplaces lacking resilience and agility strengthens essential to secure wellbeing in any workplace (Lepeley, 2017), and this was corroborated with evidence in healthcare institutions.

Among the most disruptive effects pressing change in healthcare systems were information digitalization and virtualization of technical resources. On the negative sideprocesses, impacting healthcare services and management, interfering in the shared responsibility of healthcare institutions with the state, the market and society.

Changes in the external environment impacted internal healthcare dynamics in different dimensions. On the constructive side, they help to improve rationality, supporting financial efficiency and accountability and availability of material and technical resources. On the negative side, exponential increases in healthcare services and demands resulted in unprecedented forms of work overload. These transformations affected workers' job engagement and performance detrimentally with work intensity and complexity led by emotional, digital, social, bureaucratic and communicational excesses increasing job disengagement, dissatisfaction with practice of the profession surmounting risks eroding performance and the quality of service provided to patients (Blanch, 2014; Blanch et al., 2012a, 2012b; Humphries et al., 2014).

Studies revealed inconsistent results among healthcare workers in reformed health systems. On one hand, some reports moderate increases in job satisfaction associated with improvements in the material workplace and technical conditions allowing to work more efficiently, in contrast with latent concern for work overloads and increasing levels of conflicts between managerial approaches and professional values (Granero et al., 2018; Ochoa & Blanch, 2016; Blanch, 2014). On the other hand, combination of work overload and time pressure became a concerning psychological experience, mixing overwork and overtime that has been summed up in the expression *too much to do, and not enough time* (Duxbury et al., 2008). When overload is the result of increasing demand for healthcare services, conflict and discomfort are more intense.

Observing the healthcare environment from the traditional Human Resource Management (HRM) perspective presents axes of tension that can be summarized low capacity to integrate two different cultural logics, not necessarily contradicting but based on different axiological priorities. On one side, the universal principles of professional ethics and identity, particularly relevant in healthcare to guaranteeing patients' wellbeing, human dignity, respect for their rights and embedded in best possible caring service. On the other side, a managerial approach intensely focused on profitability, efficiency, competitiveness and results evaluation misaligned with human imperatives inherent to healthcare. Conflicts exacerbate tension in the internal environment impacting practices of healthcare professionals and harming work and life balance resulting in a powerful source of psychosocial stress.

At this point, it is relevant to highlight that traditional resource-based management approaches unable to integrate organizational priorities with wellbeing of people in the workplace are inefficient and obsolete and cause more harm than help to healthcare institutions and the practice of the profession.

A pressing search for solutions points in the direction of HCM principles and practices (Lepeley, 2017) that in the last decade has served as an example to meet critical needs to solve problems. In HCM, the wellbeing of people is an imperative and a precondition to increase job satisfaction and engagement driving high performance, productivity and institutional sustainability. The interest in HCM deployment has grown fast supported by a series of books published by Routledge (Lepeley, 2017, Lepeley et al., 2021 Ochoa et al., 2019). In the 21st century and after the highly disruptive pandemic crisis affecting all organizations, positioning the wellbeing of human beings at the helm is not only an option, it is an imperative and the ongoing trend for sustainable development (Lepeley, 2019a,b).

Pandemic disruptions affecting healthcare practices

Throughout the world, the prolonged pandemic disruptions imposed on healthcare systems, and particularly on healthcare professionals, added new shocks to already chronic high levels of stress driven by an ongoing system transformation. At some specific times and places, pandemic disruptions generated such detrimental effects like stigmatization and even violence against healthcare workers. Therefore, the physical risk of contagion during initial outbreaks and successive Covid waves combined with psychosocial risks that the literature has described as the greatest threat to working life of health professionals. The environment was a breeding ground for burnout, compassion fatigue, emotional exhaustion, general psychosocial professional vulnerability with critical threats for the performance of healthcare systems.

Burnout

The set of disruptive effects on health professionals is summarized in the burnout syndrome as a combined result of work overload and compassion fatigue. Regarding work overload, the literature provides abundant evidence of close association of healthcare with work intensity, work pressure and attendance pressure (Blanch, 2020, 2021). These are characteristics of work overload, a psychologically unsatisfactory experience of excessive or "overwork" accompanied by perceptions of overflow, risk of collapse, inability to meet deadlines effectively and efficiently in quantitative and qualitative work responsibilities. According to Maslach & Leiter (2016), "burnout is a psychological syndrome emerging as a prolonged response to chronic interpersonal stressors on the job". The International Classification of Diseases (ICD-11), the World Health Organization (WHO, 2019) presented it as "a syndrome resulting from chronic workplace stress unsuccessfully managed", adding relevant nuance, the category burnout "should only be used in an occupational context" since this "disorder" is part of the "illnesses of occupational origin". This precision excludes burnout from the group of "mental disorders" or "diseases" circumscribed to the field of "occupational phenomena" related to "wellbeing in the workplace".

The burnout psychology tradition (Maslach & Leiter, 2017; Maslach et al., 1996, 2001, 2012), the ICD-11 distinguishes three categories of symptoms in the burnout syndrome: (a) feelings of energy depletion or exhaustion; (b) increased mental distance from one's job, or feelings of negativism or cynicism related to one's job; and (c) reduced professional efficacy (WHO, 2019).

Among explanatory models of the syndrome, the *job demands-resources* model (Bakker & Demerouti, 2017, 2018) stands out, presenting burnout as a state of psychological exhaustion determined by prolonged imbalance between demands and resources, characteristic of situations of chronic work overload. The *demands* are conceived as a set of quantitative and qualitative, cognitive and emotional, physical and social demands of work that entail psychological exhaustion. *Resources* refer to material, technical, organizational and social devices and personal and professional skills available to cope with labor demands. According to the JD-R theory, burnout is the result of chronic experience of high task demands, due to high volume, speed, intensity or complexity, that require excessive effort, physical, cognitive, emotional and social, to outweigh the resources (objective or perceived capacity) to deal with effectively with conflicts.

Emotional work

Healthcare professionals belong to the category of emotional workers, whose work involves daily dealings with people experiencing pain and suffering, illness and death. They are considered to integrate the "natural emotions", characteristic of these situations (Adams et al., 2008; Figley, 2002; Piragauta, 2021). In the study on "Helping the Helpers", Stamm (2012) draws attention to growing research on the psychosocial risks of emotional workers, such as healthcare professionals, and negative consequences of working in highly stressful environments and events. These experiences tend to mix the two dimensions of the experience of compassion: *satisfaction compassion* and *compassion fatigue*. The first is an emotion with a positive sign associated with commitment to care for people who suffer, empathy with their feelings, altruistic motivation for humane treatment of patients and sense of moral duty to provide help to those who needs it, aligned with the humanistic side of the profession. The second refers to the dark side of compassion fatigue and professional burnout reinforcing fatigue due to work in highly stressful and emotionally exhausting traumatic situations.

United Nations Development Programme (2022a) stated that "the Covid-19 pandemic far more than a health crisis is affecting societies and economies at their core" (UNDP, 2022a, b). International Labour Organization (2022) stated that the pandemic has had devastating impacts on the world of work and performed a *Global call to action for a human centered recovery from the Covid-19 crisis that is inclusive, sustainable and resilient* (International Labour Organization, 2022).

Healthy work environments

After an era characterized by the study of labor and organizational problems, dysfunctions, disorders, diseases and pathologies, the World Health Organization (WHO, 2022, 2010) proposal of *healthy workplaces* puts the focus – in line with Positive Psychology and the Constitutional Act itself (WHO, 1948) – in the optimal functioning of people and groups in labor organizations. This emphasis is based on the premise that the quality of work and organizational life is healthy, pleasant, productive and profitable for all the agents involved in the organization. The WHO (2010) provides three main reasons for planning *healthy work environments*: (a) economical rationality of considering healthy and safety work as something important for workers and for companies; (b) legal solidity of a safe and healthy work environment as a fundamental human right; (c) ethical foundation and moral imperative to prevent the deaths of millions of workers each year from work-related accidents, illnesses or injuries and non-fatal workplace accidents suffered by tens of millions of people, according to ILO periodic reports, and attributed to unsafe and unhealthy work environments.

For these reasons the WHO (2022; 2010) calls for urgency designing and implementing *healthy workplaces*. This construct evolved from focusing on occupational safety centered on physical, chemical, mechanical, biological, ecological and ergonomic factors to another approach centered on aspects such as work organization, workplace culture and other psychosocial factors related to health and work wellbeing. In this context, the World Health Organization (WHO, 2010) defined a *healthy workplace* as *"one in which workers and managers collaborate to use a continual improvement process to protect and promote the health, safety, and wellbeing of all workers and the sustainability of the workplace"*. More recently, the WHO (2022) promotes *"healthy, safe and resilient workplaces"* as those "where all people can perform their jobs (...) without getting sick or injured because of their work, with opportunities to enhance their physical and mental health and social wellbeing, while preserving harmony with nature and being protected in case of disaster in the community". In his original proposal, WHO (2010) presented as an "intelligent decision", the one that assumes that the wealth of companies depends on the health of workers and that occupational health is good business for companies: "Health, safety and wellbeing of workers are of fundamental importance for the workers themselves and their families, and for the productivity, competitiveness, and sustainability of companies and, therefore, for the economies of countries and the world".

Along the same lines, the European Union Agency for Occupational Safety and Health at Work launched its 2015–2020 campaign "*Make*

Europe a safer, healthier and more productive workplace" with the slogan *good-OSH-is-good-for-business*. In this way, it points to a paradigm shift, arguing that "in times of economic difficulty, it is important to remember that deficiencies in occupational safety and health cost money. In fact, there are case studies that show that good OSH management in a company is associated with improvements in performance and profitability" (EU-OSHA, 2014a).

HCM and wellbeing in the workplace

Yet pressures to develop healthy environments required management models that can successfully integrate the needs of people and their wellbeing with organizational sustainable mission, otherwise good intents remain theoretical but unpractical given the volume and diversity of disruptions affecting healthcare professionals during the Covid crisis and ongoing global conflicts of diverse nature.

In this challenging environment HCM and its five Pillars (Lepeley, 2017) become a most relevant guide to analyze the impact of psychosocial risks among healthcare professionals. In this sense, three of the five Pillars, namely human capital, talent management and resilience, are highly correlated with implications discussed in this chapter. Considering that human capital, Pillar 1, growth from education and training is required to support the careers and practices of healthcare professionals. Disruption resilience, Pillar 2, is an essential competence health workers must develop to face challenges unleashed by nonstop disruptions. And talent management, Pillar 3, represents the strategic vision to plan and program present and future operations optimizing peoples' creativity and contribution focusing on the quality of life of healthcare professionals. These three Pillars are necessary but are not sufficient to fulfill all HCM requirements. Given that Pillar 5: Sustainable Quality Management (SQM) provides the methodology for systematic assessment of progress required to attain quality standards. HCM highlights that systemic and systematic assessments of improvement in every division and across the organizations are essential to secure people's wellbeing in the workplace projecting in their lives (Lepeley, 2021; Lepeley et al., 2021a, 2021b; Beutell et al., 2021).

Concluding discussion

The HCM Model has high potential to provide realistic solutions to highly complex management problems affecting healthcare in general and the healthcare profession in particular, concerning quality of working life in the health sector. HCM is built on principles and practices that show new ways to face external threats, including those exacerbated by the pandemic in high alignment with institutional internal demands. This external–internal integration is critical to diminish and prevent risks promoting workplace wellbeing, occupational health and quality of working life as a necessary condition for sustainability of the human centered organizations discussed by Ochoa (Ochoa et al., 2019).

Lepeley (2017) stresses that one of the most important challenges to understand and deploy HCM in organizations is to acknowledge the unequivocal responsibility of every person in the organization – regardless of position or level – has to attain continuous improvement leading progress and success. And this responsibility can only be achieved with personal efforts and creativity to convert challenges in opportunities. This optimistic way of looking and operating applies equality to personal and professional dimensions. These processes deeply influence roles of the healthcare workers aiming to diminish and prevent psychosocial risks with positive impact on professionals' health, safety and wellbeing.

Using technology as a tool to expedite information and improve communications offers opportunity to optimize psychosocial benefits and minimize harmful effects on the professional practice in healthcare causing stress and harming wellbeing (Essens and Lepeley, 2019).

Seizing opportunity to turn challenges into opportunities to counterbalance psychosocial risks and promote workplace wellbeing is expedited with HCM and approaches leading innovation to organize and manage healthcare systems and services mobilizing and engaging managers and workers to cooperate in building healthier and safer work environments.

References

Adams, R. E., Figley, C. R., & Boscarino, J. A. (2008). The compassion fatigue scale, its use with social workers following urban disaster. *Research on Social Work Practice*, 18(3), 238–250. 10.1177/1049731507310190

Bakker, A. B., & Demerouti, E. (2017). Job demands–resources theory: Taking stock and looking forward. *Journal of Occupational Health Psychology*, 22(3), 273–285. 10.1037/ocp0000056

Bakker, A. B., & Demerouti, E. (2018). Multiple levels in job demands-resources theory: Implications for employee well-being and performance. In Diener, E., Oishi, S., & Tay, L. (Eds.), *Handbook of well-being* (pp. 1–13). DEF Publishers.

Beutell, N. J., Kuschel, K., & Lepeley, M. T. (2021). Life – Work continuum: The new organizational culture. In Lepeley, M. T., Morales, O., Essens, P., Beutell, N. J., & Majluf, N. (Eds.). (2021). *Human centered organizational culture: Global dimensions.* Routledge.

Blanch, J. M. (2014). Quality of working life in commoditized hospitals and universities (Original title: Calidad de vida laboral en hospitales y universidades mercantilizados). *Papeles del Psicólogo*, 35(1), 3–13. http://www.papelesdelpsicologo.es/pdf/2320.pdf

Blanch, J. M. (2020). Being business, una emergente maladie du siècle. In Ferreira, M. C. & Falcão, J. T. R. (Eds.). *Intensification, precariousness, emptying of work and margins of confrontation* (Original title: *Intensificação, Precarização, Esvaziamento do Trabalho e Margens de Enfrentamento)* (pp. 21–49). EDUFRN. https://repositorio.ufrn.br/handle/123456789/31580

Blanch, J. M. (2021). The new spacetime of telework: A challenge for the quality of worklife (Original title: El nuevo espaciotiempo de trabajo, un desafío para la calidad de vida laboral). *Praxis Psy*, 22(35), 65–78. 10.32995/praxispsy.v22i35.159

Blanch, J. M., Ochoa, P., & Sahagún, M. A. (2012a). Resignification of work and the medical profession under the new health management (Original title: Resignificación del trabajo y de la profesión médica bajo la nueva gestión sanitaria). In E. Ansoleaga, E., Artaza, O., & Suárez, J. (Eds.). *People who care people: Human dimension and work in health* (Original title: *Personas que cuidan personas: Dimensión humana y trabajo en salud)* (pp. 165–175). OPS/OMS.

Blanch, J. M., Crespo, F. J., & Sahagún, M. A. (2012b). Work overload, care time and psychosocial well-being in commercialized medicine (Originl title: Sobrecarga de trabajo, tiempo asistencial y bienestar psicosocial en la medicina mercantilizada). In Ansoleaga, E., Artaza, O., & Suárez, J. (Eds.). *People who care people: Human dimension and work in health* (Original title: *Personas que cuidan personas: Dimensión humana y trabajo en salud*) (pp. 176–182). OPS/OMS.

Duxbury, L., Lyons, S., & Higgins, C. (2008). Too much to do, and not enough time: An examination of role overload. In K. KorabicK, D. Lero, D. Whitehead (Eds.), *Handbook of work-family integration* (pp. 125–140). Academic Press.

Essens, P., & Lepeley, M. T. (2019). *Wellbeing@work*: Is buffering stress enough? In Ochoa, P., Lepeley, M. T., & Essens, P. (Eds.). *Wellbeing for sustainability in the workforce* (pp. 76–84). Routledge.

Eurofound (2022). *Social dialogue and collective bargaining in hospital sector during the Covid-19 pandemic.* Publications Office of the European Union. https://www.eurofound.europa.eu/publications/report/2022/social-dialogue-and-collective-bargaining-in-hospitals-during-the-Covid-19-pandemic

European Agency for Safety and Health at Work (EU-OSHA). (2014a). *Good OSH is Good for Business.* https://osha.europa.eu/es/topics/good-osh-is-good-for-business/index_html

European Agency for Safety and Health at Work (EU-OSHA). (2014b). *Psychosocial risks in Europe: Prevalence and strategies for prevention.* https://osha.europa.eu/es/publications/psychosocial-risks-europe-prevalence-and-strategies-prevention

European Agency for Safety and Health at Work (EU-OSHA) (2015). *First findings from the Second European Survey of Enterprises on New and Emerging Risks (ESENER-2).* https://osha.europa.eu/en/publications/reports/esener-ii-first-findings.pdf/view

Eurofound and the International Labour Office (2017). *Working anytime, anywhere: the effects on the world of work.* Office of the European Union & the International Labour Office. https://www.eurofound.europa.eu/publications/report/2017/working-anytime-anywhere-the-effects-on-the-world-of-work

Figley (Ed.) (2002). *Treating compassion fatigue.* Routledge.

Granero, A., Blanch, J. M., & Ochoa, P. (2018). Labor conditions and the meanings of nursing work in Barcelona. *Revista Latino-Americana de Enfermagem*, 26(e2947), 1–8. 10.1590/1518-8345.2342.2947

Humphries, N., Morgan, K., Conry, M. C., McGowan, Y., Montgomery, A., & McGee, H. (2014). Quality of care and health professional burnout: narrative literature review. *International Journal of Health Care Quality Assurance*, 27(4), 293–307. 10.1108/IJHCQA-08-2012-0087

International Labour Organization. (2013). *Decent Work Indicators. Concepts and Definitions. ILO Manual.* https://www.ens.org.co/wp-content/uploads/2016/11/Borrador-Manual-OIT-indicadores-de-Trabajo-Decente_opt.pdf

International Labour Organization (2022). *Lessons learned from employment diagnostics during the Covid-19 crisis.* ILO. https://www.ilo.org/wcmsp5/groups/public/---ed_emp/documents/publication/wcms_846775.pdf

International Labour Organization. (2020). *ILO Monitor: Covid-19 and the world of work* (3rd ed.). ILO. https://www.ilo.org/wcmsp5/groups/public/---dgreports/---dcomm/documents/briefingnote/wcms_743146.pdf

International Labour Organization (2021). *Global call to action for a human-centred recovery from the Covid-19 crisis that is inclusive, sustainable, and resilient.* ILO. https://www.ilo.org/infostories/en-GB/Campaigns/covid19/globalcall

Lepeley, M. T., Beutell, N. J., Abarca, N., Majluf, N. (Eds.). (2021). *Soft skills for human centered management and global sustainability.* Routledge.

Lepeley, M. T., Morales, O., Essens, P., Beutell, N. J., & Majluf, N. (Eds.). (2021). *Human centered organizational culture: global dimensions.* Routledge.

Lepeley, M. T. (2021). Soft skills: The lingua franca of human centered management. In Lepeley, M. T., Beutell, N. J., Abarca, N., Essens, P., & Majluf, N.(Eds.). *Soft skills in human centered management: Global dimensions* (pp. 3–22). Routledge.

Lepeley, M. T. (2019a). *EDUCONOMY: Unleashing wellbeing and human centered sustainable development.* Information Age Publishing.

Lepeley, M. T. (2019b). *EDUQUALITY: Human centered quality management in education: A model for deployment, assessment and sustainability.* Information Age Publishing.

Lepeley, M. T. (2017). *Human centered management: 5 Pillars of organizational quality and global sustainability.* Routledge.

Majluf, N., & Abarca, N. (2021). *Sensible leadership: Human centered, insightful and prudent.* Routledge, US.

Maslach, C. & Leiter, M. P. (2016). Understanding the burnout experience: recent research and its implications for psychiatry. *World Psychiatry*, 15(2), 103–111. 10.1002/wps.20311

Maslach, C. & Leiter, M. P. (2017). *Understanding burnout: New models.* Wiley Blackwell.

Maslach, C., Leiter, M. P., & Jackson, S. E. (2012). Making a significant difference with burnout interventions: researcher and practitioner collaboration. *Journal of Organisational Behavior*, 33(2), 296–300. 10.1002/job.784

Maslach, C., Schaufeli, W. B., & Leiter, M. P. (2001). Job burnout. *Annual Review of Psychology*, 52, 397–422. 10.1146/annurev.psych.52.1.397

Maslach, C., Jackson, S. E., Leiter, M. P., Schaufeli, W. B., & Schwab, R. L. (1996). *Maslach burnout inventory manual.* Consulting Psychologists Press.

Ochoa, P., Lepeley, M. T., Essens, P. (Eds.) (2019). *Well-being for sustainability in the global workplace.* Routledge.

Ochoa, P., & Blanch, J. M. (2016). Work, malaise, and well-being in Spanish and Latin-American doctors. *Revista de Saude Publica*, 50(21), 1–14. 10.1590/S1518-8787.2016050005600

Piragauta, C. (2021). *Neglecting Caregivers. Mental health and subjectivation of work in care services for trauma victims* (Original title: *Descuidando cuidadores: Salud mental y subjetivación del trabajo en servicios de atención a víctimas de trauma*) [Doctoral dissertation, University of San Buenaventura, Cali]

Stamm, B. H. (2012). Helping the helpers: Compassion satisfaction and compassion fatigue in self-care, management, and policy. In Kirkwood, A. D. & Stamm, B. H. (Eds.). *Resources for community suicide prevention* (pp. 1–4). Idaho State University. https://www.researchgate.net/publication/266284945

United Nations Development Programme UNDP (2022a). *Covid-19. Socio-economic impact.* https://www.undp.org/coronavirus/socio-economic-impact-Covid-19

United Nations Development Programme UNDP (2022b). *Uncertain times, unsettled lives: Shaping our future in a world in transformation.* Human Development Report (HDR 2021-22). https://hdr.undp.org/content/announcement-202122-human-development-report-set-be-released-8-september-2022

United Nations Development Programme. (2015). Work for Human Development. UN. https://www.undp.org/publications/human-development-report-2015

World Health Organization and International Labour Organization (WHO & ILO) (2022). *Healthy and safe telework*: Technical brief. https://www.who.int/publications/i/item/9789240040977

World Health Organization. (2022). *Promoting healthy, safe and resilient workplaces for all.* https://www.who.int/activities/promoting-healthy-safe-and-resilient-workplaces-for-all

World Health Organization. (2019). *International classification of diseases (ICD-11). 11th revision.* https://icdcdn.who.int/icd11referenceguide/en/html/index.html

World Health Organization (2010). *WHO healthy workplace framework and model: background and supporting literature and practices.* https://apps.who.int/iris/handle/10665/113144

World Health Organization. (1948). *Preamble to the Constitution of the World Health Organization.* https://apps.who.int/iris/handle/10665/268691

Part 5

Entrepreneurship: Disruptions and Solutions

14 Prosocial Entrepreneurship in Times of Crisis

Maureen O'Callaghan

Introduction

The purpose of this Human Centered Management book dealing with disruptions and crises affecting humanity since the beginning of this decade is aligned with this chapter on entrepreneurship offering innovative solutions to counterbalance unprecedented management problems caused by Covid-19 pandemic and ongoing global crisis. In this global VUCA (volatile, uncertain, complex, ambiguous) environment, traditional approaches are no longer effective to support management of business providing products and services to communities. The number of threats to the wellbeing of entrepreneurs has grown exponentially and solutions are needed to secure long-term business sustainability. Rapid world changes in general and in business in particular create surmounting need to assess standards and effectiveness of entrepreneurship and entrepreneurial education programs aiming to support prosocial values and behavior as a human centered solution to secure business sustainability of entrepreneurs facing disruptions (Lepeley et al., 2020, 2021).

The research in this chapter shows how entrepreneurs using prosocial approaches can improve management with higher potential to overcome workplace disruption. The study draws on literature from business management, psychology and sociology and the experience of entrepreneurs to demonstrate the important role entrepreneurs' wellbeing have in the success of their business addressing the needs of the communities they serve during turbulent periods of disruptions. The chapter includes an empirical study that explores the experience of entrepreneurs to assess the impact of disruptions, the Covid-19 pandemic and other ongoing crisis and the relationship between prosocial values and entrepreneurs' wellbeing leading to business sustainability aligned with societal contributions. Its assessment examines effects of resilience and agility, and Soft Skills supporting prosocial values and behaviors resulting in effective management during disruptions.

Entrepreneurship

Entrepreneurship is traditionally defined in the literature as the activity of setting up a business taking on financial risks to gain profits as necessary

DOI: 10.4324/9781003330011-19

condition to make it sustainable. Entrepreneurial activities are increasingly important because they play a role in the economy and society, spurring employment, growth and innovation. Entrepreneurs boost the economy introducing innovative technologies, new products and services and providing job opportunities (Liu, Lee, & Lee, 2020). Recently, the literature on entrepreneurship addresses subjects beyond business activities, but contribute to society. To such extent that promotion of entrepreneurship is today increasingly promoted by governments in nations worldwide as important development activity, consequently increasing need for research to advance the discussion (Global Entrepreneurship Monitor, 2019–2020).

Entrepreneurship disruptions and reactions

Recent studies of entrepreneurship are addressing causes and effects of entrepreneurial wellbeing and effects on business sustainability (Lepeley et al., 2020). Mackey (2000) correlated wellbeing with wellness, including mental, physical, social, financial, spiritual, environmental and vocational dimensions and each dimension being interdependent and influencing others. It is important to note that entrepreneurial responsibilities can improve or diminish wellbeing (Stephan, Rauch, & Hatak, 2022). The intrinsic nature is based on uncertainty requiring entrepreneurs to develop effective coping strategies to prevent stress and anxiety with potential to negatively impact personal performance and ability to run a business.

For example, Meahjohn and Persad (2020) found that entrepreneurs were facing the following disruptions and constraints on regular basis:

- Recurrent need to change entrepreneurial approaches
- Downturns in the global economy and business leading to declines in productivity and loss of employment
- Changes in government support and policies affecting business outcome
- Disruptions in supply change impacting most industries (electronics, automobiles, food, education, travel and tourism, sports, entertainment, IT, fitness industries)
- The global fallout in small-scale entrepreneurship impacting employment, wages, management of business operations

Consequently, increased understanding of what helps entrepreneurs cope with uncertainty and crisis safeguarding their wellbeing is increasingly needed. A global study of entrepreneurs' challenges, resilience and wellbeing conducted by Stephan, Rauch and Hatak (2022) argued to counterbalance effects of ongoing disruptions and crisis, entrepreneurs are seeking support in the following areas:

- Mechanisms to strengthen personal resilience, including increased awareness of mental support and holistic for entrepreneurs and staff

- Support to develop business resilience and agility capacity to identify effects of disruptions on emerging business opportunities
- Accelerated digitalization processes
- Renewed focus on community concerns and demands and the economy
- Support to develop inclusive efforts that contribute to support sustainable business models

Entrepreneurship *resilience, agility and wellbeing*

Our study of entrepreneurs' prosocial approaches showed that although effects of the Covid-19 threatened the survival of their business, entrepreneurs volunteered time and business products/services to help their clients, other business owners, charities and frontline workers, responding to emerging social disruptions and crisis in their communities.

There are theoretical models that help explain psychological wellbeing that allows assessing how entrepreneurs react to complex situations and disruptions affecting entrepreneurship. Ryff (2008) saw wellbeing as multi-dimensional attribute not narrowly focused on happiness or positive emotions. In the PERMA Model, Seligman (2011) outlined 5 dimensions of human flourishing that include positive emotions, engagement, relationships, meaning and accomplishments, all closely related to personal drive, physical health and life satisfaction that help to explain the complexity of entrepreneurship psychology. Ryan and Deci (2017) argued that human beings have a basic need for autonomy, competencies and relatedness that facilitate intrinsic motivation, personal growth and wellbeing. It is important to consider that autonomy is one of the strongest drivers of entrepreneurship. Additionally, Barrett Model (2010) adds values and culture that facilitate and assess framework that includes development of the following entrepreneurial needs:

- Building strong foundations to continuously assess sustainability aligned with stable relationships and effective performance
- Autonomy supportive of progress and growth
- Work toward achieving purpose through trust, ingenuity and collaborating with others to achieve a shared purpose contributing to a greater good of the community

Increasing number of psychological studies, like those mentioned above, converge with need to advance principles and practices of the Human Centered Management and Lepeley Wellbeing Model of the 7 dimensions that include life purpose, freedom and autonomy, physical fitness, love and affection, economic security, contribution to society, intellectual/spiritual growth and continuous learning (Lepeley et al., 2021). The study of prosocial approaches is built on Human Centered Management principles applied to entrepreneurship.

Prosocial behavior

Values are fundamental beliefs entrepreneurs pursue to determine priorities they aspire to including life purpose, interactions with others that impact how they conduct their business. The term "prosocial" refers to personal values and behaviors that benefit others and attribute enabling to interact harmoniously with others. Evolutionary psychologists link prosocial behavior to principles of natural selection arguing that helping members of the family strengthens family to survive obstacles passing genes to future generations. There is evidence that by their natural inclinations, people tend to help those close to them first (Hare, 2017). Similarly, Belottii et al. (2013) posit that helping others might lead to reciprocal kindness. Cognitive expressions of prosocial behavior include feelings of empathy toward persons who need help, also known as the empathy–altruism hypothesis (Batson, Lishner, & Stocks, 2015). Waugh et al. (2015) found that prosocial behaviors are developed in childhood and adolescence and encouraged by parents and teachers.

Predictors of prosocial behaviors include high levels of social support and psychological flexibility. Empathy, altruism, gratitude and reciprocity are linked to prosocial behaviors (Theilman et al., 2020). People with higher levels of intellectual humility tend to show more empathy and concern for the wellbeing of others, are more altruistic, more likely to value and protecting the welfare of other people and less interest in power (Krumrei-Mancuso (2017). Perlin and Li (2020) posited that prosocial behavior can elicit respect and feeling of protection in the presence of challenges. They went on to suggest that prosocial behaviors have the following results:

- Reduces attention on self-orientated concerns and increases attention on others
- Interacts with not only on self-interests but on multiple personal dimensions
- Is linked to more comprehensive models of self that value a holistic personal wellbeing

Studies show that prosocial behavior can be developed in several ways, including rewarding others, helping others and reciprocating beneficiaries of prosocial behavior and focusing on benefits and over effort involved (Lockwood et al., 2021). It is also developed accepting moral responsibility to help others improve (Cutler et al., 2021).

Prosocial actions benefit the recipient as much as the person acting in prosocial ways. Waugh et al. (2015) report that social support gained by prosocial behaviors has positive impact on wellbeing, reducing loneliness, alcohol use and depression. Rapossa et al. (2016) added that engaging in prosocial behavior mitigates negative effects of stress. Haller et al. (2021) found in an online survey conducted in multiple countries that during the

Covid-19 pandemic lockdowns in 2020 that prosocial behavior was frequently associated with better wellbeing conditions in the general population.

In terms of prosocial behavior associated with business contribution to philanthropy, Mickiewicz, Sauka and Stephan (2016) investigated business-size correlations and found that entrepreneurial-orientated small SMEs were more likely to be involved in philanthropic activities. Showing that philanthropy is not only a benevolent activity among large and powerful corporations but entrepreneurial SMEs participate actively to support their communities with altruistic values.

On this venue, Ramus and Kilmer (2007) identify four conditions of prosocial values and behaviors for effective social contribution:

- Consistency and alignment of prosocial values and behaviors across the organizations promoted unequivocally by organizational leaders.
- Alignment between organizational values, mission and culture fully reflected and supported by its structures, strategies, system processes, policies and incentives.
- Alignment between personal values of employers and employees to secure all feel prosocial behavior is important.
- Alignment between the motivation and purpose of employees.

These are conditions to establish a transformational process gaining commitment and ownership defining the organization's vision, mission, values and behaviors necessary to advance personal and organizational prosocial values.

Financial viability and prosocial approaches

Financial responsibility is a central concern for the sustainability in all businesses but it is critical for the survival of entrepreneurial firms. Entrepreneurs' finances are also a key contributor to their overall wellbeing. Financial security gives entrepreneurs peace of mind necessary to optimize work and efforts to earn profits and income to cover all business expenditures and also personal needs in addition to funding to advance future business and personal goals. Entrepreneurs carry by themselves all the financial risks of their businesses, in contrast to individuals employed who receive a secured salary in exchange. The human centered business model considers economic and financial sustainability aligned with social and environmental sustainability of equal importance, stressing responsibility building firms' purpose improving society, creating jobs and strengthening a financially sound human centered culture (Nahavandhi, 2019). These findings are significant because they demonstrate the breadth of factors impacting entrepreneurs expressing prosocial behaviors contextualized in prosocial approaches.

Entrepreneurs' experiences during Covid and prosocial approaches

The above concerns led to the following empirical study analyzing experiences of entrepreneurs and observing prosocial attitudes during the Covid pandemic. The study is based on a qualitative approach conducting semi-structured interviews with entrepreneurs. Sample selection was deliberate to get interviewees who could provide information relevance to the study objectives.

The sample

The sample included 19 demographically diverse entrepreneurs representing different industries in different stages of entrepreneurial progress. The intention was to ensure that sample size was large enough and diverse enough to demonstrate patterns across the data, yet small enough size to retain a focus and be manageable. The strategies to recruit participants included direct emailing to individuals who had expressed interest in participating and had responded to the researcher speaking at meetings, and also using social media platforms. No incentives or payments were made to participants.

Methodology

The semi-structured interviews took place online via Zoom using a flexible structure to gather information from participants. An interview script was used as a guide and the questions were open-ended to collect detailed and in-depth responses. Details were obtained through deeper exploration of participants' experiences.

This is a sample of questions the interviewees had to respond to:

- What has been your experience as entrepreneur?
- What impact has Covid had on your business?
- Give examples how you and others have coped with pressures and challenges of the Covid pandemic and Brexit.
- Give examples of situation when you used prosocial behaviors during the pandemic.
- What motivated you to act prosocial?
- What did you actually do?
- What impact did acting prosocial have on you, on other people, on your business and your community/society?

The next stage of data organization involved sorting data by category, merging or splitting categories and deciding on appropriate analysis that included descriptive accounts providing data summaries mapping range and diversity of responses. The next stage included identification of patterns presenting explanations, including contradictory statements.

Findings

Participants in the study became entrepreneurs because (a) leaving a paid employment, (b) activity alongside a paid employment or (c) seeking a main and only source of income. Their motivation included personal satisfaction, practical reasons and stronger links with personal values. The positive aspects of being an entrepreneur included: avoiding negative people and office politics, having greater autonomy, avoiding burnout, spending more time with family, making more money and making a difference.

Negative experiences described included loneliness, greater workload and intense challenges knowing the market and seeking and securing clients. Participants perceived entrepreneurs as being resilient and able to cope, recognizing importance of personal care, creating time for reflection and using adversity as a springboard to move forward.

They had all lived through the Covid-19 pandemic and observed changes in society and shared feeling that *everyone was in this together.* They expressed that some people focused on survival and hard times, for others it created a welcome breathing space and for others it created new opportunities. Participants noticed negative and positive effects during Covid-19 pandemic, including loss of income, increased use of information and communication technologies, more time working in the business when it was possible to open, delays in decision making leading to business disruption, and harder efforts to maintain a positive mindset.

Examples of prosocial behaviors among entrepreneurs included supporting local charity fundraising, offering services for free or at reduced rates, using it as an opportunity to request that others adhere to their values and beliefs. Motivations for acting in prosocial ways included business reasons and specifically linked to overall business purpose, marketing their business, PR opportunities to increased sales and personal reasons, feelings of gratitude, wanting to give something back to society, belief they would be rewarded for "being good", being part of the community and for political reasons. They coincided that the most positive outcome of acting prosocial translated in more work leading to more personal satisfaction, a sense of peace, contentment, community engagement and opportunity to work with like-minded people. Negative experiences mentioned included that their good ideas had been stolen and exploited, not being appreciated, high-time commitment, lack of interest and feeling overwhelmed. The main factor helping them to be prosocial was opening access to new sources of income. They reported that factors hindering their efforts include more effective management of their time and energy levels.

Concluding discussion

The chapter explored how prosocial values and behaviors translate into benefits and minimize negative effects of disruptions impacting entrepreneurs' health, wellbeing and performance during the Covid-19 pandemic. The study integrated theoretical constructs from the disciplines of psychology, sociology and business with empirical evidence to observe benefits of acting in prosocial ways with potential to improved entrepreneurial wellbeing, including mental health, relationships and gaining higher societal benefits.

The chapter described how entrepreneurship provided opportunities for people to contribute to society, beyond business interests and responsibilities, recognizing the importance of personal wellbeing to secure business sustainability during disruptions caused by Covid-19 deploying prosocial values and behavior to minimize negative impacts. The findings confirmed that entrepreneurs faced serious challenges during the two years of Covid-19 pandemic, highlighting needs to assess standards to secure improvement using prosocial values and behavior.

This study showed that prosocial behavior can help entrepreneurs manage disruption providing opportunities to reposition their business and increase demand for their products or services. It also creates opportunities to advance personal satisfaction contributing to enhance wellbeing, providing opportunities to connect and work with like-minded people. In spite of positive outcomes, the study needs to help entrepreneurs improve management to better protect their health to avoid feeling to be overwhelmed projects and their ideas and projects to avoid misuse and lack of personal appreciation.

It is recommended that entrepreneurial education need to help entrepreneurs understand the importance of ethics and moral values that informs business decisions integrated with feeling valued and empowered with a sense of purpose that goes beyond business success and includes societal benefits they communicate openly in order to motivate others and serve the needs and demands of their clienteles.

References

Barrett, R. (2010). The importance of values in building a high-performance culture. *Barrett Values Centre*. https://www.valuescentre.com/wp-content/uploads/PDF_Resources/Additional_Articles/Article_Importance_of_Values.pdf

Batson, C. D., Lishner, D. A., & Stocks, E. L. (2015). The empathy—altruism hypothesis. In Schroeder, D. A., & Graziano, W. G. (Eds.). *The Oxford handbook of prosocial behavior* (pp. 259–281). Oxford University Press. 10.1093/oxfordhb/9780195399813.013.023

Bellotti, V. , Carroll, J. M., & Han, K. (2013). Random acts of kindness: The intelligent and context-aware future of reciprocal altruism and community collaboration. In 2013 International Conference on Collaboration Technologies and Systems (CTS) . (pp. 1–12). IEEE.

Cutler, J., Nitschke, J. P., Lamm, C., & Lockwood, P. L. (2021). Older adults across the globe exhibit increased prosocial behavior but also greater in-group preferences. *Nature Aging*, 1(10), 880–888. 10.1038/s43587-021-00118-3

Global Entrepreneurship Monitor. (2019). *Diagnosing Covid-19 impacts on entrepreneurship: Exploring policy remedies for recovery*. London Business School. https://www.gemconsortium.org/file/open?fileId=50521

Haller, E., Lubenko, J., Presti, G., Squatrito, V., Constantinou, M., Nicolaou, C., Savvas, P., Aydin, G., Chong, Y. Y., Chien, W. T., Cheng, H. Y., Ruiz, F. J., Garcia-Martin, M. B., Obando-Pasada, D. P., Segura-Vargas, M. A.,Vasiliou, V. S., McHugh, L., Höfer, S., Baban, A., Gloster, A. et al. (2021). To help or not to help? Prosocial behavior, its association with well-being, and predictors of prosocial behavior during the coronavirus disease pandemic. *Frontiers in Psychology*, 12. 10.3389/fpsyg.2021.775032

Hare, B. (2017). Survival of the friendliest: Homo sapiens evolved via selection for prosociality. *Annual Review of Psychology*, 68, 155–186. 10.1146/annurev-psych-010416-044201

Krumrei-Mancuso, E. J. (2017). Intellectual humility and prosocial values: Direct and mediated effects. *The Journal of Positive Psychology*, 12(1), 13–28. 10.1080/17439760.2016.1167938

Lepeley, M. T., Beutell, N., Abarca, N., & Majful, N. (Eds.). (2021). *Soft skills for human centered management and global sustainability*. Routledge.

Lepeley, M. T., Kuschel, K., Beutell, N., Pouw, N., & Eijdenberg, E. (Eds). (2020). *Wellbeing of women in entrepreneurship: A global perspective*. Routledge.

Liu, Y., Lee, J. M., & Lee, C. (2020). The challenges and opportunities of a global health crisis: The management and business implications of Covid-19 from an Asian perspective. *Asian Business & Management*, 19(3), 277–297. 10.1057/s41291-020-00119-x

Lockwood, P. L., Abdurahman, A., Gabay, A. S., Drew, D., Tamm, M., Husain, M., & Apps, M. A. (2021). Aging increases prosocial motivation for effort. *Psychological Science*, 32(5), 668–681. 10.1177/0956797620975781

Mackey, S., (2000). Towards a definition of wellness. *Australian Journal of Holistic Nursing*, 7(2), 34–38.

Meahjohn, I., & Persad, P. (2020). The impact of Covid-19 on entrepreneurship globally. *Journal of Economics and Business*, 3(3). 10.31014/aior.1992.03.03.272

Mickiewicz, T., Sauka, A., & Stephan, U. (2016). On the compatibility of benevolence and self-interest: Philanthropy and entrepreneurial orientation. *International Small Business Journal*, 34(3), 303–328. 10.1177/0266242614555245

Nahavandi, S. (2019). Industry 5.0—a human-centric solution. *Sustainability*, 11(16), 4371. 10.3390/su11164371.

Perlin, J. D., & Li, L. (2020). Why does awe have prosocial effects? New perspectives on awe and the small self. *Perspectives on Psychological Science*, 15(2), 291–308. 10.1177/1745691619886006

Ramus, C. A., & Killmer, A. B. (2007). Corporate greening through prosocial extra-role behaviors—a conceptual framework for employee motivation. *Business Strategy and the Environment*, 16(8), 554–570. 10.1002/bse.504

Raposa, E. B., Laws, H. B., & Ansell, E. B. (2016). Prosocial behavior mitigates the negative effects of stress in everyday life. *Clinical Psychological Science*, 4(4), 691–698. 10.1177/2167702615611073

Ryan, R. M., & Deci, E. L. (2017). *Self-determination theory: Basic psychological needs in motivation, development, and wellness*. Guilford Press.

Ryff, C. D. (2008). Challenges and opportunities at the interface of aging, personality, and well-being. In O. P. John , R. W. Robins , & L. A. Pervin (Eds.), *Handbook of Personality: Theory and Research* (pp. 399–418). The Guilford Press.

Seligman, M.E. (2011). Building resilience. *Harvard Business Review, 89*(4), 100-106.

Stephan, U., Rauch, A., & Hatak, I. (2022). Happy entrepreneurs? Everywhere? A meta-analysis of entrepreneurship and wellbeing. *Entrepreneurship Theory and Practice*, 10422587211072799. 10.1177/10422587211072799

Thielmann, I., Spadaro, G., & Balliet, D. (2020). Personality and prosocial behavior: A theoretical framework and meta-analysis. *Psychological Bulletin*, 146, 30–90. 10.1037/bul0000217.

Waugh, W., Brownell, C., & Pollock, B. (2015). Early socialization of prosocial behavior: Patterns in parents' encouragement of toddlers' helping in an everyday household task. *Infant Behavior and Development*, 39, 1–1010.1016/j.infbeh.2014.12.010.

15 Emerging Human Centered Entrepreneurship

Katherina Kuschel and Fernando Merino

Introduction

For many years, businesses and economists have considered that the firm's main goal is profit maximization. In the words of 1976 Nobel laureate in Economics, Milton Friedman, a central business responsibility is "*to increase profits, so long as the firm stays within the rules of the game and engaging in open competition, without deception or fraud*" (Friedman, 1962). This profit-focused view is aligned with the traditional framework where a national dimension of the business sector is to generate profits and for governments to collect income levying taxes to finance social pursues. However, this business perspective has changed in the last half-century. Societies increasingly anticipate that businesses, besides generating profits, also support social aims overcoming the divide between business ventures and altruistic endeavors similar to non-profit organizations (NGOs) (Parrish, 2010) but with different tax codes.

The ongoing debate generated contrasting points of view (Mintzberg, 1983) but increased attention in favor of firms promoting corporate social responsibility (CSR). In fact, increasing numbers of firms now integrate CSR as part of key activities and a common strategy when measuring organizational performance. Up to now, there has been minimal attention on the incidence and outcome of CSR in small firms in general and entrepreneurial businesses in particular. Largely because CSR became an important issue for large corporations overlooking the importance to contribute to support the development of the communities where their clients came from in order to secure nosiness sustainability (Lepeley, 2017a).

Sustainability and the triple bottom line

The concept of sustainability has been used with many different meanings and in general remains as a fuzzy term (Cohen et al., 2008; Muñoz & Cohen, 2018). Over a decade ago, Wikstrom (2010) proposed a distinction between business for sustainability, sustainable organization and sustainable business. But this term is superseded by the broader concept of sustainable

DOI: 10.4324/9781003330011-20

development meaning "*meets needs of the present without compromising ability of future generations to meet their needs*" (Brundtland, 1987).

Associated with sustainability is the concept of the triple bottom line (TBL or 3BL). TBL was coined by the British author John Elkington in 1994 to integrate profits along with people and planet to describe the goal of sustainability. The first bottom line of a firm is to accomplish the "profits' account", the second bottom line is the "people's account", related to the social impact, and the third bottom line is the "planet's account", related to the environmental impact of the firm's activities. Elkington argued that the full cost of doing business and the results of a firm's operations could be measured with reports of these three dimensions and a series of indicators. Although indicators were intended to be industry-dependent, the work of the Global Reporting Initiative, establishing guidelines, periodically updated and improved, since 2000, harmonized a general framework to present "TBL" in a more homogenous and comparable manner. The reports based on standardized criteria across firms are a measure of the result aligning "people" and "planet" with the classical bottom line "profits" along the basis for risk evaluations and volatility. Evaluation of these three dimensions was intended to support management strategies, including innovation, minimizing environmental impact and people variable commonly overlooked when a firm only pays attention to the "profit" bottom line. It was assumed that the TBL would also play a more active contribution to the attainment of UN's SDGs[1] that to some extent academic research is hindering (Kolk et al., 2017). In 2018, Elkington published an article in the *Harvard Business Review* stating that after 25 years it was time to rethink the TBL formula (2018). The basic argument was that although TBL had helped businesses to stop focusing solely on profits and had expanded their focus to include people and planet, the "TBL" thinking had been reduced to a mere accounting tool and a way of balancing trade-offs instead of doing things differently.

Sustainability in entrepreneurial firms

It is important to note that TBL was a new perspective to assess comprehensive results mainly for large businesses and corporations whose owners are financial investors not closely attached to the company or decision making in a personal way. This level of business responsibility contrasts deeply with entrepreneurial firms where the involvement and responsibility of the owner is crucial and covers all aspects of the business to a significantly deeper extent than large firms and corporations owned by financial investors.

Considering that entrepreneurs assume all costs in their firm as personal liabilities, investing their personal reputation, social connections, family responsibilities, personal aspirations and dreams, not only financial resources. Similarly, their work involvement differs from pure shareholders and also from hired business managers, because they are liable to leverage all resources they have invested and in what direction they do it largely as personal expenses.

This leads to thinking that the results of entrepreneurial firms cannot be measured under the same assumptions or with the same instruments as other business and non-entrepreneurial firms. From the point of view of 3BL, profits are obviously a necessary pursuit. Yet research shows that the entrepreneurs' understanding of sustainability is far more complex than 3BL (Muñoz & Cohen, 2018). Furthermore, the consideration of personal wellbeing, for the most part, absent in large business corporations, is central to entrepreneurs and highly aligned with business sustainability, income and returns to investments. Entrepreneurial firms are nurtured by values and principles the owner incorporates when establishing, building up and managing the firm, including developing an organizational culture, or starting a family business as a legacy, aligned with ethical values and compensations that impact performance, results and long-term sustainability. Naturally, entrepreneurial firms assign different weights to each one of the 3BL than non-entrepreneurial firms. Moreover, larger firms led by managers who are less sensitive to the profit dimension have the potential to attain better performance on the other two dimensions and sustainable firms show better financial results (Soto-Acosta et al., 2016).

In entrepreneurial firms, an additional and unique element is present. In addition to business investment, entrepreneurs invest in personal dimensions including social connection, family time, personal time and care, getting results in different dimensions from social recognition to satisfaction of personal needs and dreams.

Overall, there is an additional important factor that must be considered when assessing the performance of entrepreneurial firms which is consistently overlooked. It is the level of impact of business performance and responsibility on the wellbeing of entrepreneurs. So, we pose that entrepreneurial firms not only integrate the three perspectives – the 3BL "profits", "people" and "planet" – but add an important perspective, that is, the personal wellbeing of the owner. This revised 3BL formula requires a change in the vision and assessment methodology of entrepreneurial firms that reformulate management function to incorporate dimensions driving the profits, people and "planet" bottoms lines, but adding the wellbeing of the entrepreneur, a "human/personal" dimension that is excluded in the people element of 3BL.

Unique pursuit of entrepreneurial firms

Academic literature has studied the differences between entrepreneurs and hired managers of firms. Broadly speaking, differences are found in two lines. On one hand, entrepreneurship provides the business owner additional satisfaction based on a greater degree of autonomy, more opportunity for personal growth allowing creativity to develop business plans and work strategies leading to more meaningful rewards to personal effort. On the other hand, entrepreneurs are exposed to significantly higher levels of stress achieving work demands on time with greater responsibility because their work is far more deeply integrated with life responsibilities. There is no concrete evidence of which dimension has a greater impact on business success.

We pose that in entrepreneurial firms the owner/manager's goal is not limited to traditional performance measured by economic profits, but we include personal dimensions influencing business performance related to the wellbeing of the entrepreneur. Wellbeing is important because it implies to rearrange business results including other dimensions. For example, an extra effort of an entrepreneur increasing number of hours working may result in additional economic benefits but also decisions to have higher levels of stress.

Entrepreneur's wellbeing tends to increase when social recognition is acknowledged along with other business performance dimensions. Moreover, it is observed that personal elements that increase the wellbeing of the entrepreneur are closely linked to social and environmental aims. Therefore, it is not surprising that agile entrepreneurial firms are leading change and transformation to a much larger extent than other business models related to the Solidarity Economy, Common Good Economy, Circular and Green Economy, Blue Economy (Pauli, 2010).

Our entrepreneurial wellbeing proposal has high convergence with principles and practices of Human Centered Management (HCM) (Lepeley, 2017a, 2017b) and follows its wellbeing analytical framework.

Some features of this business model are not exclusive of entrepreneurial firms because firms' management has played an important role in changing societies and the conglomerate of needs, values and means addressing business transformation (Arin Tapia, 2017), but in many cases, entrepreneurial firms play a significant role. Consequently, both at the practitioners' level as well as in academic literature, personal/internal elements of the entrepreneur have increased in importance becoming topics of high interest (Wiklund et al., 2019). These new approaches force to rethink firms' results in new dimensions, and also in new institutions (Turco & Leopizzi, 2020; Alwakid et al., 2021), laws (Ventura, 2020), certifications and audits (Chancé et al., 2018).

Wellbeing in entrepreneurship

Until now there are few instruments to assess the multiple dimensions affecting the holistic wellbeing of people and effects in the workplace in general and particularly in entrepreneurship. Features of happiness and wellbeing are addressed in psychology, but wellbeing related to entrepreneurship requires additional considerations. Until now entrepreneurial firms, like traditional business firms and corporations, follow 3BL as the main indicator to assess performance and sustainability. 3BL is supported by extensive literature anchored in the traditional Elkington's 1994 framework relating profits, people, planet or economics with social and environmental variables. But our proposal pays attention to Elkington (2018) call to re-evaluate 3BL because it has become an accounting tool that is hardly considered as fundamental features of the 3BL under ongoing global conditions. Consequently, we are not ignoring the need for 3BL but we add a fourth element to assess wellbeing of entrepreneurs. Our wellbeing assessment follows the wellbeing model aligned with HCM principles and practices developed by Lepeley (2021). The model is a comprehensive approach that includes the 7 complementary dimensions: life purpose, freedom and autonomy, physical fitness and good health, income to secure financial security, love, affection and meaningful relationships, continuous intellectual and spiritual growth (lifelong learning), all together are necessary to make contributions to improve the workplace and society. The 7 dimensions are illustrated in Figure 15.1.

This wellbeing model addresses the importance of interactive life dimensions relevant to personal wellbeing. Lepeley (2021) developed the model founded in Aristotelian eudaimonic principle where a person must assume responsibility for continuous self-care and improvement as a

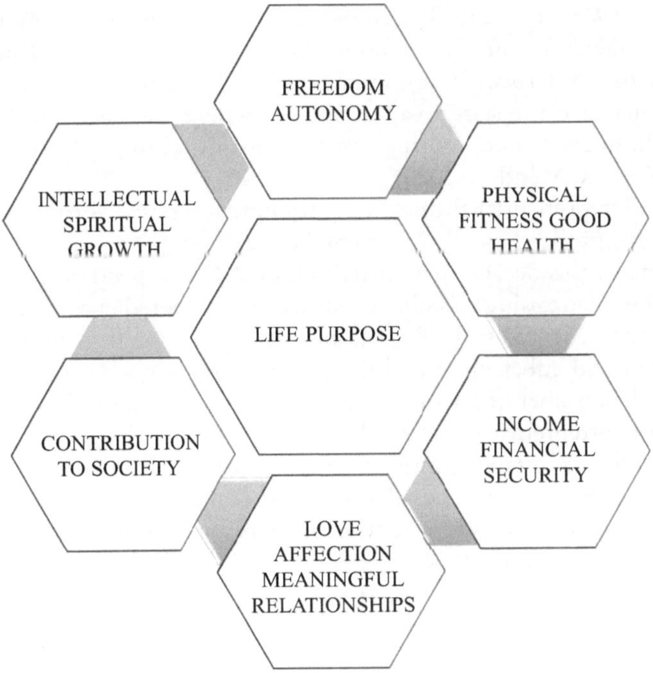

Figure 15.1 The 7 complementary dimensions of wellbeing.

Source: Lepeley (2021).

precondition to be apt and able to help others as precondition to help improve the organizations where they work and the communities and societies where they live. This new model of wellbeing opens a whole new research agenda to test relevant issues affecting entrepreneurs' wellbeing and success, thus creating a set of new key indicators as the "fourth" bottom line supporting the performance assessment of entrepreneurial firms.

The following psychological studies add consistency to the 7 wellbeing dimensions. Ryan et al. (2008) and Schultz and Ryan (2015) stated that autonomous motivation ("why"), intrinsic life-goals orientation ("what") and mindfulness ("how") lead to satisfaction of basic psychological needs. Psychologists have highlighted that "purpose" serves as a compass, gives sense of direction and motivation for everyday tasks, even in turbulent times. However, the wellbeing model we are adapting to entrepreneurship also includes social dimensions. Considering that prosocial and ecological-friendly behavior (Ryan et al., 2008) contribute to amplify the sense of community belonging. Note that these variables vary depending on context and cultural values (Bilsky & Schwartz, 1994; Sagiv & Schwartz, 2000).

Management entrepreneurial firms in turbulent times

Entrepreneurship characteristics depend on the historical, political and social contexts (Welter, 2011). The impact of an entrepreneurial firm in the environment depends on the context where the new firm emerges (Sengupta, Sahay, & Croce, 2018). Furthermore, the "purpose" of the firm is a motivational factor to start up a business (Kuschel & Méndez, 2021) and to keep the business running during smooth and also during difficult times (Kuschel, Vélez, & Méndez, 2020).

Although entrepreneurial firms are continuously exposed – to a significantly larger extent than large firms – to higher volatility in the environment, the disruptions of this decade that started with the Covid pandemic and are exacerbated by the ongoing crisis have harmed and hindered entrepreneurial firms in an unprecedented way. The ongoing financial crisis has surmounted risks with profound effects to curtail the normal flow of goods and services worldwide. The number of oncoming shocks is unpredictable and extremely concerning for entrepreneurs worldwide. Consequently, in the present global VUCA (volatile, uncertain, complex, ambiguous) environment, a firm's assessment must be evaluated based on the three traditional bottom lines adding special considerations for the fourth wellbeing bottom line to secure business sustainability. This imperative is consistent with the principle that entrepreneurial firms are continually re-inventing and changing their value proposition while keeping the organizational purpose as a keystone (Kuschel, Vélez, & Méndez, 2020).

Then in terms of performance assessment and vulnerability related to external shocks, effects cannot be evaluated how these impact the economic, social and environmental performance, but the wellbeing of the entrepreneur. Events that impact and challenge health issues, the life/family balance or "Life–Work Continuum" (Beutell et al., 2021), or contribution to society must be evaluated in the comprehensive strategy described.

In terms of the purpose of entrepreneurial firms, the need to develop strategies and actions aligned with wellbeing jump to the forefront of effective and reliable studies and assessment successfully implemented converging with disruptions in the global VUCA environment.

Concluding discussion

The traditional approach to assess the performance of business firms, based on profit maximizing in the production of goods or services, had overlooked employee's wellbeing and social aspects that impact effective Human Centered performance assessment, as required in HCM. Recent disruptions unleashed by the Covid pandemic and other ongoing global crisis exposed, not new, but the unattended shortcomings of objective Covid performance assessment that require broader perspectives of the firm including impact on society and protection of the environment.

After decades of behavior analysis of entrepreneurial firms, we realized that it cannot be solely explained in terms of profit maximization, neither on the TBL model supported by the global sustainability discourse that has dominated. The ongoing crises reveal that "personal" dimensions of wellbeing of entrepreneur are key to objective assessment of firm performance. Today, the need to consider these "personal" elements compels to search for values, aims and indicators for the successful entrepreneurship. It is in this challenging situation entrepreneurs face where HCM approaches are helpful in providing a solid framework supporting personal values aligned with economic activity essential for long-term sustainability.

HCM's personal wellbeing principles can be expressed as indicators that can be objectively measured. This study advances entrepreneurship by adding the wellbeing dimension to the traditional 3BL formula contributing to a more resilient path to secure the growth of entrepreneurial firms.

Note

1 In United Nations Global Compact (https://www.unglobalcompact.org), World Business Council for Sustainable Development (https://www.wbcsd.org)

References

Alberti, F.G., & Varon Garrido, M.A. (2017). Can profit and sustainability goals coexist? New business models for hybrid firms. *Journal of Business Strategy*, 38(1), 3–13.

Alwakid, W., Aparicio, S., & Urbano, D. (2021). The influence of green entrepreneurship on sustainable development in Saudi Arabia: The role of formal institutions. *International Journal of Environmental Research and Public Health*, 18(10), 5433.

Arin Tapia, A. (2017). Nuevas economías transformadoras. GIZAEKOA-Revista Vasca de Economía Social//GEZKI, (14).

Beutell, N., Kuschel, K., Lepeley, M.T. (2021). Life–work continuum. The new organizational culture. In Lepeley, M.T., Morales, O., Essens, P., Beutell, N., & Majluf, N. (Eds.) (2021). *Human centered organizational culture. Global dimensions*. Routledge, UK.

Bilsky, W., & Schwartz, S.H. (1994). Values and personality. *European Journal of Personality*, 8(3), 163–181. 10.1002/per.2410080303

Boons, F., & Lüdeke-Freund, F. (2013). Business models for sustainable innovation: State-of-the-art and steps towards a research agenda. *Journal of Cleaner Production*, 45, 9–19.

Brundtland, G.H. (1987). *Our common future: World commission on environment and development*. Oxford University Press, Oxford, UK.

Chancé, E., Derrible, S., & Ashton, W.S. (2018). The need to adapt sustainability audits to atypical business models. *Clean Technologies and Environmental Policy*, 20(5), 1113–1118.

Cohen, B., Smith, B.B., & Mitchell, R. (2008). Toward a sustainable conceptualization of dependent variables in entrepreneurship research. *Business Strategy and the Environment*, 17(2), 107–119.

Elkington, J. (2018). *25 years ago i coined the phrase "triple bottom line." here's why it's time to rethink it. Harvard Business Review*. June 25. https://hbr.org/2018/06/25-years-ago-i-coined-the-phrase-triple-bottom-line-heres-why-im-giving-up-on-it

Elkington, J., & Hartigan, P. (2008). *The power of unreasonable people: How social entrepreneurs create markets that change the world*. Harvard Business Press.

Friedman, M. (1962). *Capitalism and freedom*. The University of Chicago Press.

Kolk, A., Kourula, A., & Pissani, N. (2017). Multinational enterprises and the sustainable development goals: What do we know and how to proceed? *Transnational Corporations*, 24(3), 9–32.

Kuschel, K., & Méndez, M. (2021). Creating shared value and social innovation: Cases of success from South American entrepreneurial ventures. In Afacan Findikli, Mine M. & Erdur, Duygu Acar (Eds.). *Creating Social Value Through Social Entrepreneurship* (pp. 171–191). IGI Global. 10.4018/978-1-7998-4727-4.ch010

Kuschel, K., Vélez, A., & Méndez, M. (2020). Business models and shared value strategy during the crisis: South American social entrepreneurship. Communication presented at the G-Forum: 24th Annual Interdisciplinary Conference on Entrepreneurship, Innovation and SMEs. Virtual edition organized by Karlsruher Institut für Technologie. Karlsruhe, Germany, September 28th to October 2nd, 2020.

Lepeley, M.T. (2017a). *Human centered management. The five global pillars of organization quality and sustainability*. Routledge, UK.

Lepeley, M.T. (2017b). Bhutan's gross national happiness. An approach to human centered sustainable development. *South Asian Journal of Human Resource Management*, 4(2), 174–184.

Lepeley, M.T. (2021). Soft skills: The *lingua franca* of human centered management in the global VUCA environment. In Maria-Teresa Lepeley, Nicholas J. Beutell, Nureya Abarca, Nicolas Majluf (Eds.). *Soft skills for Human Centered Management and global sustainability*. Routledge, UK.

Lepeley, M.T., Kuschel, K., Beutell, N., Pouw, N., & Eijdenberg, E. (eds). (2019). *Wellbeing of women in entrepreneurship. A global perspective*. Routledge, UK.

Michelini, L., & Fiorentino, D. (2012). New business models for creating shared value. *Social Responsibility Journal*, 8(4), 561–577.

Mintzberg, H. (1983). The case for corporate social responsibility. *Journal of Business Strategy*, 4(2), 3–15.

Muñoz, P., & Cohen, B. (2018). Entrepreneurial narratives in sustainable venturing: Beyond people, profit, and planet. *Journal of Small Business Management*, 56(1), 154–176. 10.1111/jsbm.12395

Parrish, B.D. (2010). Sustainability-driven entrepreneurship: Principles of organization design. *Journal of Business Venturing*, 25(5), 510–523.

Pauli, G . (2010). *Blue Economy - 10 Years, 100 Innovations, 100 Million Jobs*. Paradigm Publisher.

Porter, M.E. & Kramer, M.R. (2011). Creating shared value. *Harvard Business Review*, 89(1/2), 62–77.

Porter, M.E., & Kramer, M.R. (2006). Strategy and society: The link between competitive advantage and corporate social responsibility. *Harvard Business Review*, 84, 84-90.

Ryan, R.M., Huta, V., & Deci, E.L. (2008). Living well: A self-determination theory perspective on eudaimonia. *Journal of Happiness Studies*, 9(1), 139–170. 10.1007/978-94-007-5702-8_7

Schultz, P.P., & Ryan, R.M. (2015). The "why", "what", and "how" of healthy self-regulation: Mindfulness and well-being from a self-determination theory perspective. In *Handbook of mindfulness and self-regulation* (pp. 81–94). Springer. 10.1007/978-1-4939-2263-5_7

Sengupta, S., Sahay, A., & Croce, F. (2018). Conceptualizing social entrepreneurship in the context of emerging economies: An integrative review of past research from BRIICS. *International Entrepreneurship and Management Journal*, 14(4), 771–803.

Sagiv, L., & Schwartz, S.H. (2000). Value priorities and subjective well-being: Direct relations and congruity effects. *European Journal of Social Psychology*, 30(2), 177–198. 10.1002/(SICI)1099-0992(200003/04)30:2<177::AID-EJSP982>3.0.CO;2-Z

Soto-Acosta, P., Cismaru, D.M., Vătămănescu, E.M., & Ciochină, R. (2016). Sustainable entrepreneurship in SMEs: A business performance perspective. *Sustainability*, 8(4), 342; 10.3390/su8040342

Stephan, U., Rauch, A., Hatak, I. (2022). Happy entrepreneurs? Everywhere? A meta-analysis of entrepreneurship and wellbeing. *Entrepreneurship Theory and Practice*, in press.

Terán-Yépez, E., María Marín-Carrillo, G., Casado-Belmonte, M.P., & Capobianco-Uriarte, M.M., Sustainable entrepreneurship: Review of its evolution and new trends. *Journal of Cleaner Production*, 252, 119742.

Turco, M., & Leopizzi, R. (2020). The role of public governance in the pursuit of sustainable development of the ILVA steel plant: An interpretative framework. *Sustainability*, 12(19), 8282.

United Nations (2017). APPENDIX: Transforming our world: The 2030 agenda for sustainable development. In William, R. (Ed.). *A new era in global health: Nursing and the United Nations 2030 agenda for sustainable development* (pp. 539–527). Springer. 10.1891/9780826190123.ap02

Upward, A., & Jones, P. (2016). An ontology for strongly sustainable business models: Defining an enterprise framework compatible with natural and social science. *Organization & Environment*, 29(1), 97–123.

Ventura, L. (2020). The essential role of enterprises for an inclusive and sustainable development: Towards a new uniform model law for the social enterprise? *European Company Law*, 17(1), 7–14.

Welter, F. (2011). Contextualizing entrepreneurship—Conceptual challenges and ways forward. *Entrepreneurship Theory and Practice*, 35(1), 165–184.
Wiklund, J., Nikolaev, J., Shir, N., Foo, N.-D., & Bradley, S. (2019). Entrepreneurship and well-being: Past, present, and future, *Journal of Business Venturing*, 34(4), 579–588.
Wikström, P. A. (2010). Sustainability and organizational activities – Three approaches. *Sustainable Development*, 18(2), 99–107. 10.1002/sd.449

16 Women Entrepreneurs and Time Management

Stacy Brecht and Séverine Le Loarne-Lemaire

Introduction

The entrepreneurship literature presents contradictory assumptions about work and life balance, especially about women entrepreneurs pursuing high growth and long-term sustainability of their firms. In general, studies relate work with the number of hours working to obtain desirable business results but to large extent ignoring fundamental aspect of the wellbeing of the entrepreneur (Hatak & Zhou, 2021). For example, women entrepreneurs who pursue wellbeing are assumed to be constrained to develop a satisfactory lifestyle compatible with high business growth (Jones et al., 2020). This contributes to shape the generalized perception that women entrepreneurs, and particularly mothers, tend to create low growth ventures (Cliff, 1998) and mainly seek to find work autonomy to meet a desirable work–life balance (De Clercq & Brieger, 2022). Nonetheless international studies about the wellbeing of women entrepreneurs show that some women succeed balancing personal and family responsibilities and managing business growth when conditions are supportive (Lepeley et al., 2020). Moreover, Lepeley (2020) elaborates on causes and effects when the wellbeing of women entrepreneurs results in a multiplier effect that not only benefits women and their business firms, but society at large. Important social effects of entrepreneurial business endeavors of women have been largely unexplored and overlooked.

The study and follow-up

This chapter aims to answer these questions. It is based on the results of an empirical study collecting systematic data to evaluate work and life patterns of women entrepreneurs involved in high business growth. The methodology consisted in analyzing detailed daily work diaries of 8 women entrepreneurs pursuing growth of their ventures along with their wellbeing to observe how they managed and distribute time between work, family and personal activities. Results show that women mix family and personal duties with business responsibilities thorough the week and eventually weekends

DOI: 10.4324/9781003330011-21

with an average work of 35 hours weekly. The chapter is structured as follows: the first part discusses the state of the art on time management (TM) of women entrepreneurs, identifying research gaps. Then, details of the research design are presented followed by results along 2 lines: possibility to generalize to other contexts and effects of TM building wellbeing in times of crisis.

Women entrepreneurship: business growth and wellbeing

The literature on women entrepreneurship tends to show that business growth and personal wellbeing are incompatible. Studies reveal that women often pursue entrepreneurship instead of paid employment to have more autonomy (De Clercq & Brieger, 2022). This perception of autonomy comes from theories of work in organizations, assuming that working women have to cope with what scholars call "women's life", implying family responsibilities, especially when they are mothers (Brush et al., 2009). But regardless of the work context (Welter et al., 2016), women must perform additional traditional roles spending significantly more time and efforts in household duties than men do (Eddleston & Powell 2012; Jennings & McDougald 2007; Wood & Eagly 2010).

According to the literature, this set of assumptions is interpreted as follows: First, women who own business firms are generally associated with small home-based ventures that have difficulty to access capital, limited business networks, operate part-time and consequently generate low volumes of sales, revenues and profits (Fraser, 2015; Harding, 2006). Research on high-growth women entrepreneurship firms is scarce (Hechavarria et al., 2018) but reveals a stereotyped vision of male-led companies more than feminine business companies (Gupta et al., 2018).

While criticizing stereotypes about "who and what" it means to be an entrepreneur (Marlow et al., 2017, p. 121), comparative research reveals that women who decide to pursue high-growth ventures perform at the same level as men do (Jennings & Brush, 2013). Second, the stereotyped perception is most likely created by scholars assuming, according to tradition, that women who pursue growth of their ventures are incapable of balancing work and life responsibilities (Le Loarne-Lemaire et al., 2021). In general, it is true that high-growth entrepreneurs usually give priority to "work" over "life" and work excessive number of hours (Adisa et al., 2019). To a large extent this happens because research rarely considers the private life of male entrepreneurs. Furthermore, assume that the personal and family lives of women entrepreneurs are highly interconnected with the business (Bruni et al., 2004). Consequently, women success to grow their business is generally associated with giving up their traditional role as mothers and family care givers or have spouses who accept to take active responsibility in family duties and children education

(Nikina et al., 2013). Adding to the definition of effective work–life balance "*satisfaction and good functioning at work and at home, with minimum role conflict*" (Clark, 2000).

A perception criticized by Beutell, Kuschel and Lepeley (2021) in their innovative publication the *Life–Work Continuum*, aligned with fundamental Human Centered Management (HCM) principles of human wellbeing built on 7 complementary life dimensions that include: life purpose, autonomy, physical fitness good health, income to secure economic and financial solvency, love, affection meaningful relationships and contribution to society (Lepeley, 2021). From the HCM approach, wellbeing is based on the capacity not only to balance life and work but also in the ability to consider life and work as a continuum seeking best possible integration of life and work duties and responsibilities.

Women entrepreneurship in practice: time management for wellbeing

Research in TM is limited (Ancona et al., 2001). In the field of entrepreneurship, TM often refers to the capacity of the entrepreneur to identify optimal conditions to enter a market resulting in significant increase in sale volumes (De Oliveira Mota et al., 2021). TM also refers to the optimal time for raising funding to develop and launch business solutions when market conditions are at best. Therefore, the TM concept in entrepreneurship may vary across contexts and industries (Lévesque & Stephan, 2019).

It is important to note that the crisis unleashed by the Covid-19 pandemic (Brown et al., 2020) significantly impacted the perception of TM, pressuring large numbers of entrepreneurs to cope with forced idle lockdowns followed by excessive increase in work hours causing surmounting distress in order to maintain their business active and avoiding bankruptcy.

Beyond the previous analysis, it is necessary to discuss how entrepreneurs, who by definition are free to work as much or as little as they want, organize their workdays to achieve desirable business results aligned with personal wellbeing. This double purpose is essential for entrepreneurs to have capacity to undertake overwhelming responsibilities as business owner. In this respect the amount of research is limited. Moreover, beyond stereotypes, research on women entrepreneurs pursuing high business growth and personal wellbeing, as necessary condition for business sustainability, is pending. Attention to these queries became more important in the context of the pandemic, exposing entrepreneurs, like most business, to transform their operations with explosive use of technology, digital devises and platforms and online connectivity substitution for face-to-face interactions inducing increasing conflicts between work and family responsibilities (Ferguson et al., 2016) with significant greater distress for women entrepreneurs pursuing high business grow (Mc Carrick and Keine, 2019).

Methodology

To identity TM practices of women entrepreneurs who declared to pursue personal wellbeing aligned with high growth of their venture, our study is focused on review and assessment of their established practices. Data were collected from activity calendars of the 8 women entrepreneurs who participated in the study, and had completed, as per researcher's instructions, for 3 months, from December 2020 to February 2021. Following Mintzberg's (1968) study that examined activities of managers in organizations, we observed the frequency of activities and commitments the participants had written and scheduled in their calendars. Additionally, to data collected to assess TM, participants responded to 2 interviews previously planned and announced to collect further details.

Sample description

The study was conducted in the State of California, a region recognized by fast-growing entrepreneurial ventures and in this case, seeking personal wellbeing as integral element of business performance. A total of 8 women entrepreneurs registered in the Stella Lab Accelerator program participated in the study. This organization was selected to enhance the high-growth drive of the participants. Table 16.1 describes sample characteristics.

Data collection and analysis

Data were collected from digital calendar schedules and from online video interviews recorded verbatim. Participants submitted digital calendar with detail activity schedules during the 3 months of the study. The activity calendars were collected as electronic screenshots of the participants' daily schedules. Participants received instructions to format their calendars and what labels to use. Daily calendar schedules served as the foundation for the study. After collecting calendar schedules, 2 separate in-depth online video interviews were conducted to get details about calendar labels and to understand the daily working practices of these women entrepreneurs. A total of 16 recorded interviews, from 1 up to 2.5 hours duration, were conducted twice for each participant. Data were collected during the pandemic and confinements, from December 2020, included traditional holidays like Christmas, Hanukkah and New Year. The rest was collected in January and February 2021 representing common activity throughout any calendar year. The time distribution of activities of women entrepreneurs is shown in Table 16.2.

Table 16.1 Characteristics of women entrepreneurs

Participants	*Years in business*	*Type of business/industry*	*Average hours work per week*	*Married*	*# of children*
Participant 1	5 years	Personal and professional coaching	20 hours	No	1 child living away
Participant 2	6 years	Business teacher and trainer	25 hours	No	1 grown child living away
Participant 3	1.5 years	Business operations consultant	20 hours	No	No
Participant 4	7 years	Compliance consultant for medical industry	21 hours	Yes	2 children, 10 and 7
Participant 5	10 years	Public relations	40 hours	Yes	1 child, 2 years old
Participant 6	1.5 years	Composting industry/waste management	98 hours	No	No
Participant 7	11 years	Web/tech company	35 hours	Yes	3 children, one 16 year old, living at home and 2 living away
Participant 8	5 years	Marketing	30 hours	Yes	No

Table 16.2 Frequency of specific activities of women entrepreneurs during the observation period

Activity description	*Frequency of activities*
Client meetings	274
Children's school activities	262
Business development meetings	173
Finances	160
Time with friends and family	151
Team meetings	102
Professional development	97
Client work	83
Marketing	82
Logistics/operations	78
Administrative work	72
Caring for children	72
Networking events	60
Physical exercises	53
Hobbies	52
Doctor's appointments	51
Errands	48

Findings

Findings show that the participant women entrepreneurs managing high-growth firms combine time at work with family, children's activities, friends, hobbies and health care. They reported to work on average 35 hours, with a range that fluctuates between 20 and 98 hours.

The TM choice and working hours were justified as follows:

> Participant 2:
> *I don't take only jobs I want to do and love to do ….. Last year I reached my maximum burnout do now, I am only committed to work on things I like and enjoy. I hired a business partner. She is completely different than me, so we complement well and I can delegate a great deal of work.*
>
> Participant 4:
> *My business is important to me, and my kids are also very important. I take my business seriously. It's not a hobby. It's not a side gig. It's my deal, it's what I do.*
>
> Participant 6 is the exception:
> "*My business is an expression of who I am. I work all the time. I had to cut back because I was getting exhausted*". She explained she was trying to set aside time from work on weekends.

The participants distributed work time in the mornings, afternoons, evenings during weekdays and participants 2 and 3 reported they also worked during weekends, with a significant focus on client meetings, business development meetings, finances, team meetings, professional development, client work and marketing.

Childcare responsibilities first, clients second, the rest comes after

Even though all 8 entrepreneurs have the ambition to make their business grow fast, they devoted a substantial amount of time on their schedules to personal activities including childcare and school activities, time spent with family and friends, physical exercises, hobbies and doctor's appointments. Additionally, 4 of the participants scheduled times on their calendars for prayer and meditation during the 3-month period. Children's school activities were the second time-consuming activity. The school activities were primarily part of Participant 4, and 2 other participants listed children's activities but their scheduled time for this activity was less in comparison with Participant 4. Table 16.2 shows the frequency of specific activities during the observation period; e.g., the women had 274 meetings with clients, 262 school activities, 173 meetings for business development.

The most frequent overall activity reported by the 8 participants was client meetings. 7 participants listed time for hobbies in their calendars. Only 1 participant consistently scheduled night activities with her husband. She stated:

> *In terms of work-life balance, I did not find much balance until I had the business for 7 years. My husband was my co-founder and at one point we started having work related conflicts. That was when we realized we needed to separate work and life time and duties. We tried renting separate offices, away from the house. But we finally found a good balance and are now back working at home where we have clearly designated office space. When we started the business it was necessary to devote much more time to networking and setting up connections than we do now (participant 7).*

Participant 8, who also operates a business with her husband, found a way to integrate her hobbies into her work:

> *We are on the road quite a bit because our client's lifestyle is in the outdoor industry. My husband and I are passionate about being outdoors and we use our network to try and get new clients through outdoor adventures. So, we can be traveling and still working.*

Aligning personal wellbeing with business growth

Our findings largely coincide with current research on women entrepreneurs showing high commitment to their role as mothers. Also confirm time distribution alternating family and personal activities with work, during the day, the week and in this case even during weekends.

Despite clear focus on entrepreneurial business activities, these women seem to have reached a desirable level of wellbeing considering the 7 complementary dimensions of life wellbeing (Lepeley, 2021, Lepeley et al., 2021) aligned with HCM principles (Lepeley, 2017). Moreover, for women with children living at home, motherhood is their main responsibility (Brush et al., 2009).

The results indicate that their TM to large extent fits expectations of this group of entrepreneurs. It confirms this perception when they state that their role as entrepreneurs does not impose excessive demands. They rather refer as an entrepreneurial lifestyle. In the literature, lifestyle entrepreneurship refers to an activity that follows a passion, in similar fashion as a sport or pleasure associated with traveling (Jones et al., 2020). And also to a lifestyle that allows mothers to be autonomous and independent from others (Foley et al., 2018). Our findings seem to go further because they convey the idea that growing their business gives them more time free from other activities they do not enjoy as much therefore increasing their sense of wellbeing. A result that seems new in entrepreneurship literature.

Wellbeing across contexts and crises

In previous sections, we briefly mentioned the relevance of the context where the entrepreneurial business takes place. It is important to reiterate because context has potential to enhance or curtail business growth and personal wellbeing. Lepeley et al. (2020) analyze multiple perspectives of the wellbeing of women entrepreneurs in different industries and counties in North and South America, Europe, South Asia, Austria and Africa. In contrast, this study collected data in California, United Stares close to Silicon Valley that has reputation as one of the most dynamic entrepreneurial ecosystems in the world for fast-growing companies but also aligned with a particular lifestyle of entrepreneurs. Some of the limitations of the study may be associated with a specific context that is unique worldwide.

On the other hand, the context offered optimal conditions to conduct a robust assessment of entrepreneurship associated with the wellbeing of women. It may be realistic to infer that the same objectives may not be as easily achieved in different contexts and condition that present obstacles instead of stimulus for entrepreneurial activities in general and particularly among women. Nonetheless we agree with Lepeley et al. (2020) that women everywhere can choose what they want to do with their lives and their work pursuit, regardless of the context where the endeavor takes place, recognizing that some ecosystems do provide more effective education programs and more fruitful role models (Yadav & Unni, 2016) and easier access markets, clients and subcontractors than other places considering entrepreneurial practices that are accepted in specific fields and rejected in other sector (Suchman, 1995). In this respect, it could be inferred that in relation of the few working hours among women entrepreneurs registered in a Californian Accelerator, might not be perceived as the usual contexts, contrasting deeply with male-dominated places or where the dominant entrepreneurship practice requires many more working hours per week.

Last, in the context of the Covid pandemic we noticed the participants did not mention Covid assuming that crisis did not have notable effects in the TM of their businesses or did not impact them until later on in 2021. We inferred that either the Californian context did not experience drastic effects and distress as the rest of the United States or since all the participants were exposed to the same disruptions, deterrent signs did not play a role to affect the business growth pursuit of Californian women entrepreneur, although they were concerned and experienced feelings of distress.

Concluding discussion

The study supports HCM principles observed in practice among women entrepreneurs seeking wellbeing at the global level. It differs in this case covering intentions explicitly seeking personal wellbeing aligned with business growth. These create restrictions to extrapolate findings to the population of women entrepreneurs across different contexts. Thus, there is a pending need to explore, contrast and compare other contexts where the lifestyle of women entrepreneurs is less diffused and strategically complex. This would imply use a similar analytical model to assess activity data daily and consistent with the 7 HCM principles of wellbeing. Last, the importance of the subject to increase opportunities for women to seek and attain wellbeing working independently along the Life–Work Continuum (Beutell et al, 2021) deserves serious attention.

To overcome limitations, the analysis calls for innovative research approaches to gather more evidence that making a business grow is not necessarily associated with increased numbers of working hours but personal wellbeing that confirms Lepeley's Multiplier Effect of women entrepreneurs (2020) and how can the dual benefit gain legitimacy regardless of context and even in times of crises opening business opportunities for women who seek independence and enticing work challenges.

Acknowledgement

The authors thank Stella Labs accelerator in San Diego, California for being a partner in this academic research study.

References

Adisa, T. A., Gbadamosi, G., Mordi, T., & Mordi, C. (2019). In search of perfect boundaries? Entrepreneurs' work-life balance. *Personnel Review*, 48, 1634–165110.1108/pr-06-2018-0197.

Ahl, H. (2006). Why research on women entrepreneurs needs new directions. *Entrepreneurship Theory and Practice*, 30(5), 595–621. 10.1111/j.1540-6520.2006.00138.x.

Ancona, D. G., Goodman, P. S., Lawrence, B. S., & Tushman, M. L. (2001). Time: A new research lens. *The Academy of Management Review*, 26(4), 645–663. 10.2307/3560246.

Beutell, N., Kuschel, K., Lepeley, M. T. (2021). Life–work continuum: The new organizational culture. In Lepeley, M. T., Morales, O., Essens, P., Beutell, N., & Majluf, N. (Eds.). *Human centered organizational culture: Global dimensions*. UK: Routledge.

Brown, R., Rocha, A., & Cowling, M. (2020). Financing entrepreneurship in times of crisis: exploring the impact of Covid-19 on the market for entrepreneurial finance in the United Kingdom. *International Small Business Journal*, 38(5), 380–390. 10.1177/0266242620937464

Brush, C. G., De Bruin, A., & Welter, F. (2009). A gender-aware framework for women's entrepreneurship. *International Journal of Gender and Entrepreneurship*, 1(1), 8–24. 10.1108/17566260910942318

Bruni, A., Gherardi, S., & Poggio, B. (2004). Entrepreneur-mentality, gender and the study of women entrepreneurs. *Journal of Organizational Change Management*, 17, 256–268. 10.1108/09534810410538315.

Clark, S. C. (2000). Work/family border theory: A new theory of work/family balance. *Human Relations*, 53(6), 747–770. 10.1177/0018726700536001.

Cliff, J. E. (1998). Does one size fit all? Exploring the relationship between attitudes towards growth, gender, and business size. *Journal of Business Venturing*, 13(6), 523–542. 10.1016/s0883-9026(97)00071-2

De Clercq, D., & Brieger, S. A. (2022). When discrimination is worse, autonomy is key: How women entrepreneurs leverage job autonomy resources to find work–life balance. *Journal of Business Ethics*, 177(3), 665–682. 10.1007/s10551-021-04735-1

De Oliveira Mota, R., Godinho Filho, M., Osiro, L., Ganga, G. M. D., & De Sousa Mendes, G. H. (2021). Unveiling the relationship between drivers and capabilities for reduced time-to-market in start-ups: A multi-method approach. *International Journal of Production Economics*, 233, 108018. 10.1016/j.ijpe.2020.108018

Eddleston, K. A., & Powell, G. N. (2012). Nurturing entrepreneurs' work–family balance: A gendered perspective. *Entrepreneurship Theory and Practice*, 36, 513–541. 10.1111/j.1540-6520.2012.00506.x.

Ferguson, M., Carlson, D., Boswell, W., Whitten, D., Butts, M. M., & Kacmar, K. M. (Micki) (2016). Tethered to work: A family systems approach linking mobile device use to turnover intentions. *Journal of Applied Psychology*, 101, 520–53410.1037/apl0000075.

Foley, M., Baird, M., Cooper, R., & Williamson, S. (2018). Is independence really an opportunity? The experience of entrepreneur-mothers. Journal of Small Business and Enterprise Development, 25, 313–329. 10.1108/jsbed-10-2017-0306.

Fraser, S. (2015). Finance for Small and Medium Sized Enterprises: A Report on the 2004 UK Survey of SME Finances. Coventry: SME Centre, University of Warwick.

Gupta, V. K., Wieland, A. M., & Turban, D. B. (2018). Gender characterizations in entrepreneurship: A multi-level investigation of sex-role stereotypes about high-growth, commercial, and social entrepreneurs. *Journal of Small Business Management*, 57(1), 131–153. 10.1111/jsbm.12495.

Hatak, I., & Zhou, H. (2021). Health as human capital in entrepreneurship: individual, extension, and substitution effects on entrepreneurial success. *Entrepreneurship Theory and Practice*, 45(1), 18–42. 10.1177/1042258719867559

Harding, R. (2006). *Global Entrepreneurship Monitor UK 2004*. London: GEM UK.

Hechavarria, D., Bullough, A., Brush, C., & Edelman, L. (2018). High-growth women's entrepreneurship: Fueling social and economic development. *Journal of Small Business Management*, 57, 5–13. 10.1111/jsbm.12503.

Jennings, J. E. & Brush, C. G. (2013). Research on women entrepreneurs: challenges to (and from) the broader entrepreneurship literature?. *Academy of Management Annals*, 7(1), 663–715.

Jennings, J. E., & McDougald, M. S. (2007). Work-family interface experiences and coping strategies: Implications for entrepreneurship research and practice. *Academy of Management Review*, 32, 747–760.10.5465/amr.2007.25275510.

Jones, P., Ratten, V., & Hayduk, T. (2020). Sport, fitness, and lifestyle entrepreneurship. *International Entrepreneurship and Management Journal*, 16(3), 783–793. 10.1007/s11365-020-00666-x

Lepeley, M. T. (2021). Soft skills: The lingua franca of human centered management in the global VUCA environment. In Lepeley, M. T., Beutell, N., Abarca, N., & Majful, N. (Eds.). *Soft skills for human centered management and global sustainability* (pp. 3–22). Routledge, UK.

Lepeley, M. T. (2020). The multiplier effect of wellbeing of women entrepreneurs: A practical approach and a personal account. In Lepeley, M. T., Kuschel, K., Beutell, N., Pouw, N., & Eijdenberg, E. (Eds). *Wellbeing of women in entrepreneurship: A global perspective*. Routledge.

Lepeley, M. T., Kuschel, K., Beutell, N., Pouw, N., & Eijdenberg, E. (Eds). (2020). *Wellbeing of women in entrepreneurship: A global perspective*. Routledge.

Lepeley, M.T. (2017). *Human Centered Management. The Five Global Pillars of Organization Quality and Sustainability*.Routledge.

Loarne-Lemaire, S. L., Bertrand, G., Razgallah, M., Maalaoui, A., & Kallmuenzer, A. (2021). Women in innovation processes as a solution to climate change: A systematic literature review and an agenda for future research. *Technological Forecasting and Social Change*, 164, 120440. 10.1016/j.techfore.2020.120440.

Lévesque, M., & Stephan, U. (2019). It's time we talk about time in entrepreneurship. *Entrepreneurship Theory and Practice*, 44, 163–184. 10.1177/1042258719839711.

Marlow, S., Greene, F. J., & Coad, A. (2017). Advancing gendered analyses of entrepreneurship: A critical exploration of entrepreneurial activity among Gay Men and Lesbian Women. *British Journal of Management*, 29(1), 118–135. 10.1111/1467-8551.12221.

McCarrick, H., & Kleine, D. (2019). Digital inclusion, female entrepreneurship, and the production of neoliberal subjects: Views from Chile and Tanzania. In Graham, M. (Ed.). *Digital economies at global margins* (pp. 103–127). MIT Press. www.idrc.ca/sites/default/files/sp/Images/idl-57429_2.pdf

Mintzberg, H. (1968). The manager at work; determining his activities, roles, and programs by structured observation(Doctoral dissertation, Massachusetts Institute of Technology).

Nikina, A ., Shelton, L.M., Le Loarne, S. (2013). Does he have her back? A look at how husbands support women entrepreneurs. *Entrepreneurial Practice Review*, *2*(4), 17–35.

Suchman, M. C. (1995). Managing legitimacy: Strategic and institutional approaches. *Academy of Management Review*, 20(3), 571–610. 10.5465/amr.1995.9508080331

Welter, F., Gartner, W. B., & Wright, M. (2016). The context of contextualizing contexts. In Welter, F., & Gartner, W. B. (Eds.). *A research agenda for entrepreneurship and context* (pp. 1–15). Edward Elgar Publishing.

Wood, W. , & Eagly, A. H. (2010). Gender. In S. T. Fiske, D. T. Gilbert, & G. Lindzey (Eds.), *Handbook of social psychology* (5th ed., Vol. 1, pp. 629–667). New York: Oxford University Press.

Yadav, V., & Unni, J. (2016). Women entrepreneurship: research review and future directions. *Journal of Global Entrepreneurship Research*, 6(1), 1-18. 10.1186/s40497-016-0055-x.

Index